"The fragile foundations of
institutions are being shake
reading for all serious stude,
Former Vice President of th, ~~~ Commission

"*Great Powers and World Order* provides an authoritative account of the
normative underpinnings of international security. The rules of the road
founded on the liberal world order are now under attack, and normative and
institutional restraints are crumbling. This book presents a cogent and instructive
interpretation of the prevailing problems darkening contemporary international
realities." —**Joel Rosenthal, President of the Carnegie Council for Ethics in
International Affairs**

"Combining history and theory, Kegley and Raymond have composed a clear
and insightful primer for understanding great-power politics and international
relations, past and present. Their lucid descriptions of the challenges
faced by officials after World War I, World War II, and the Cold War are
seamlessly linked to an illumination of the policy choices that lay ahead.
This is a terrific text for beginning students studying international relations."
—**Melvyn Leffler, Edward Stettinius Professor of History at the University
of Virginia**

"Citizens, and particularly future military officers, cannot begin to think about
and study big questions and strategic issues too early. *Great Powers and World
Order* is an excellent introduction to these questions and issues and should be
required reading for both civilian students and military officers in training."
—**Dan Caldwell, Chair, Committee on Student Veterans and Distinguished
Professor of Political Science at Pepperdine University**

"Informed and informative, *Great Powers and World Order* provides an engaging
introduction to international politics. This is the best available text addressing
what is arguably the most important set of issues on the global agenda."
—**M. Leann Brown, Professor of International Relations at the East China
Normal University in the People's Republic of China and Former Associate
Professor at the University of Florida**

"In this important book, Kegley and Raymond reexamine the pillars of world
order at a turbulent time when global conditions are nearing a turning point
of potentially epic proportions. *Great Powers and World Order* brings historical
perspective and theoretical analysis to bear on the impact of momentous
changes—for example, climate change, cyberwarfare, the weaponization
of outer space, and, critically, a global arena that is no longer dominated
by Western liberal values." —**William Bain, Associate Professor of
International Theory at the National University of Singapore and Coeditor
of *International Relations***

"A penetrating and timely analysis of the collision course on which the great powers are heading, which uncovers the basic tenets of international relations in the context of the eroding world order." —**Alpo Rusi, Professor of World Affairs at Vytautas Magnus University in Lithuania and Former Chief Foreign Policy Adviser to the President of Finland and Finnish Ambassador Emeritus**

"Prolific scholars and creative educators, Kegley and Raymond have published many innovative textbooks with original pedagogical features about American foreign policy and world affairs. *Great Powers and World Order* goes beyond provoking students to think for themselves about the important questions regarding contemporary threats to sustainable international security. It also advances important concepts that reframe theories about great-power relations in particular, and international politics generally." —**Llewellyn D. Howell, Professor of International Studies Emeritus, Thunderbird School of Global Management at Arizona State University**

"For an insightful interpretation of the threats to world order fomented by the great powers' return to cut-throat competition and rejection of multilateral cooperation, this evocative, compelling and accessible text provides pedagogical medicine. Highly recommended for all global citizens investigating international politics." —**Roger A. Coate, Chair, Academic Council on the United Nations System (ACUNS) and Paul D. Coverdell Professor of Public Policy at Georgia College**

"This book illuminates the timeless obstacles to world order whenever the great powers ruthlessly compete for hegemony, as they presently are doing as they head into perilous confrontations. Highly recommended reading for all policymakers and students of world affairs." —**Pierre Gehlen, President of the Complaints Commission of the Luxembourg Press Council, and Former President of the District Court of Luxembourg**

"Case studies of great-power rivalries since the twentieth century are deployed to exceptional pedagogical advantage to instruct students about enduring questions in today's turbulent times. The innovative format forces students to think for themselves. This textbook is highly recommended for university courses focusing on this troubling topic on the contemporary global agenda." —**Shannon Lindsey Blanton, Dean of the Honors College and Professor of Government at the University of Alabama at Birmingham**

"This is an outstanding book, covering critically important global issues which makes a significant and original contribution to the storehouse of available textbooks dealing with contemporary world affairs." —**Ole R. Holsti, George V. Allen Professor of Political Science Emeritus at Duke University, and President of the International Studies Association, 1979–1980**

"The global political transformation underway will impact everyone. Study this compelling text to understand the form and consequences of past power rivalries and the critical choices before us now." —**Charles F. Hermann, Professor and Brent Scowcroft Chair in International Policy Studies Emeritus, The Bush School of Government & Public Service at Texas A&M University**

Great Powers and World Order

To Debbie and Christine,
In loving appreciation for their encouragement and support

Sara Miller McCune founded SAGE Publishing in 1965 to support the dissemination of usable knowledge and educate a global community. SAGE publishes more than 1000 journals and over 800 new books each year, spanning a wide range of subject areas. Our growing selection of library products includes archives, data, case studies and video. SAGE remains majority owned by our founder and after her lifetime will become owned by a charitable trust that secures the company's continued independence.

Los Angeles | London | New Delhi | Singapore | Washington DC | Melbourne

Great Powers and World Order

Patterns and Prospects

Charles W. Kegley

and

Gregory A. Raymond

FOR INFORMATION:

CQ Press
An Imprint of SAGE Publications, Inc.
2455 Teller Road
Thousand Oaks, California 91320
E-mail: order@sagepub.com

SAGE Publications Ltd.
1 Oliver's Yard
55 City Road
London EC1Y 1SP
United Kingdom

SAGE Publications India Pvt. Ltd.
B 1/I 1 Mohan Cooperative
Industrial Area
Mathura Road, New Delhi 110 044
India

SAGE Publications Asia-Pacific
Pte. Ltd.
18 Cross Street #10-10/11/12
China Square Central
Singapore 048423

Library of Congress Cataloging-in-Publication Data

Names: Kegley, Charles W., author. | Raymond, Gregory A., author.

Title: Great Powers and World Order : Patterns and Prospects / Charles W. Kegley and Gregory A. Raymond.

Description: Los Angeles : SAGE, [2021] | Includes bibliographical references and index. |

Identifiers: LCCN 2019034637 | ISBN 9781544345833 (paperback) | ISBN 9781544358741 (epub) | ISBN 9781544358734 (epub)

Subjects: LCSH: International relations. | International relations–History. | World politics. | Globalization.

Classification: LCC JX1395 .K394 2021 | DDC 327–dc23

LC record available at https://lccn.loc.gov/2019034637

Acquisitions Editor: Anna Villarruel
Editorial Assistant: Lauren Younker
Production Editor: Andrew Olson
Copy Editor: Megan Markanich
Typesetter: Cenveo Publisher
        Services
Proofreader: Laura Webb
Indexer: Judy Hunt
Cover Designer: Scott Van Atta
Marketing Manager: Jennifer Jones

Brief Contents

Detailed Contents

The past is never dead.
It's not even past.

—William Faulkner

Preface

"Write about the big questions and the big issues," former U.S. Secretary of State Lawrence S. Eagleburger once advised us in a discussion of the academic study of international relations. It is in this spirit that we have written *Great Powers and World Order: Patterns and Prospects*. Few topics are bigger, timelier, or more consequential than the high-stakes competition among great powers over the challenge of fostering world order.

Whereas we believe that the challenges of managing great-power rivalry deserve to be made the starting point for exploring international relations, world affairs are often studied as a series of debates about which paradigm is best—realism, liberalism, or constructivism. Most textbooks devote more attention to scholars from each paradigm commenting on each other than on the ways in which relations among the great powers are shaping the prospects for world order. In these troubling times, a book that focuses on the difficulties in constructing ordering rules and institutions has never been more important.

Developed for use in courses on international relations, American foreign policy, and peace studies, we have written *Great Powers and World Order* with the needs of students uppermost in mind. Our aim is to encourage critical thinking about the nature of world order. By presenting the historical information and theoretical concepts needed to deepen the reader's understanding of the enduring patterns in great-power politics, we have tried to enhance her or his ability to investigate the upheavals of our day and make projections about the global future.

DESIGN OF THE BOOK

Great Powers and World Order is unlike most standard textbooks. Almost every introductory book attempts to cover the entire range of subjects within the academic study of international relations. They include not just salient topics on the global agenda but also the dense thicket of contending approaches to analysis and the methodological problems that bedevil researchers working in the field. All too often, more attention is paid to scholarly quarrels over approaches and methods than to examining real-world decisions and dilemmas. It's no wonder that many instructors who use these comprehensive textbooks pick and choose the most appealing chapters and skip the rest.

This book is different. It has a clearly defined focus—competition among the great powers to shape the future world order. As a perusal of broadcast, print, and digital news media would reveal, great-power politics is uppermost in people's minds when they think about foreign affairs. The summit of world power is where their attention is centered, for understandable reasons. Whether the United States, China, Russia, and other major powers clash or cooperate has enormous consequences for international peace and well-being. Without a framework of commonly accepted rules and institutions that define the permissible aims and practices of great-power politics, progress toward a more just and less violent world will be frustrated. Should today's leading states become locked in a divisive struggle over hegemony, everyone would be in jeopardy.

The design of *Great Powers and World Order* has been influenced by several pedagogical convictions. First, we believe that comparing retrospective cases is a powerful educational tool for generating propositions about the properties of a stable world order. Toward that end, we provide the reader with a series of chronologically sequenced case studies on great-power efforts to construct ordering rules and institutions during different historical periods. Although space limitations required us to condense these complex stories, we have tried to illuminate the dilemmas facing the individual leaders who made key decisions. Historical case studies open a window to see what strategies for constructing world order were tried before, why one course of action was chosen over another, and how those decisions shaped the future course of world affairs. They help readers sharpen their ideas about how we might proceed today to realize our hopes for tomorrow.

Second, while we consider theories to be vital for making the puzzling world around us intelligible, we are dismayed that theories of world politics are often taught without regard for their relevant historical context. By moving back and forth in each case study between history and theory, rather than treating them as separate topics, we hope to situate the assumptions, causal claims, and policy prescriptions of different schools of thought within the time periods in which they took root, thus giving the reader a better sense of why policymakers embraced a particular view of world order instead of an alternative vision.

Third, we believe that it is important for students to recognize that scholars, diplomats, and pundits have wrestled with proposals about world order since the birth of the modern state system in the seventeenth century. Although the roster of great powers has changed over time, certain perennial questions about ordering rules and institutions have been raised by every generation. They are worth pondering because they help clarify values and force consideration of possibilities that might otherwise be overlooked.

ORGANIZATIONAL STRUCTURE

The chapters in *Great Powers and World Order* are divided into three parts. Part I introduces different theoretical traditions for analyzing great-power competition over what rules and institutions should guide international politics.

After covering such basic concepts as anarchy, power transition, and hegemonic war, it describes the Westphalian notion of order, which laid the foundation for the modern nation-state system by accentuating the importance of sovereignty, legal equality, and nonintervention in the domestic affairs of foreign countries. To explain the rationale for the contemporary liberal order that was erected on these fragile footings, we compare the peace settlements of the First and Second World Wars, with primary attention devoted to what the victors presumed were the primary causes of those gruesome struggles and how the settlements ostensibly would prevent such tragedies from recurring.

The liberal international order shaped world politics throughout the last half of the twentieth century and the early decades of the twenty-first century. By *liberal*, we do not mean left-of-center politics, as the term is generally employed in the United States. Rather, we use it to describe an open, rule-based order that endorses free trade, democratic governance, and multilateral institutions— principles supported by both liberals and conservatives since the end of the Second World War. In contrast to agent-based orders, where the desires and demands of a haughty, domineering state govern international politics, rule-based orders are grounded in principles of statecraft that apply to all international actors, even the most powerful.

Part II of this book describes how the liberal order evolved throughout the Cold War, when Soviet-American bipolarity was the defining structural characteristic of the international system, and immediately afterward, when the Soviet Union collapsed and the United States stood at the apex of a unipolar system. Following two decades of ambitious plans to spread democracy and market capitalism, American efforts to augment the postwar liberal order stalled. With the rise of China, the resurrection of Russian military power, and American retrenchment from some of its overseas commitments, the rules and institutions of the liberal order began unraveling.

Whereas the previous two parts of the book focused on the genesis and growth of the liberal, American-led order, Part III looks at what might happen to it now that America's unipolar moment is fading. As military and economic power becomes more diffused, what problems might hinder attempts to construct a new world order? From climate change and environmental degradation to cyberattacks and lethal automated warfare, harrowing challenges face humanity today. Since none of these challenges can be addressed single-handedly, we conclude with some cautious observations about the prospects for multilateral cooperation among the great powers in the years ahead.

Given the sea changes now buffeting the world, we submit that a brief, accessible textbook designed to explore the possibilities of creating an international order that competitive great powers see as legitimate could not be timelier. It is our hope that *Great Powers and World Order* inspires readers to critically assess previous attempts to establish a framework of common rules and institutions and to draw upon the lessons of those experiences when weighing the relative value of alternative approaches to international security.

FEATURES AND PEDAGOGY

Great Powers and World Order contains a variety of study aids to help students understand the complexities of world politics.

- *"You Decide" box inserts.* Each chapter contains a decision-making dilemma that asks readers to imagine how, as a policymaker, they would have made hard choices in certain historical situations. We believe that examining world politics from this perspective will help students when they think about the global challenges that they will confront long after their formal education has concluded, when new actors, issues, and controversies populate the geostrategic landscape.

- *Maps and time lines.* This book provides a series of case studies on the evolution of great-power rivalries since the beginning of the twentieth century. We provide maps and chronologies of major events to assist students in grasping the nuances of each historical case.

- *Charts and figures.* Many students today are described as visual learners. This book contains numerous diagrams to illustrate the abstract concepts and theories presented in the text.

- *Key terms.* Like in other academic disciplines, people working the field of international relations use a specialized vocabulary to describe the phenomena that they observe. We boldface key terms upon their first reference in the text, and we list them at the end of each chapter in order to help students understand this vocabulary.

- *Suggested Readings.* We discuss recommended books and journal articles on a chapter-by-chapter basis in a set of bibliographic essays. Each essay highlights scholarly literature that pertains to the topics covered in a given chapter and thus provides students with readings if they wish to explore a particular issue in greater depth.

- *Glossary.* We define all of the key terms in a comprehensive glossary placed for easy reference at the end of the book.

Great Powers and World Order: Patterns and Prospects is inspired by fear and guided by hope. Our fear springs from the escalating tensions that unsettle the current relations among the great powers, which, if not allayed, could result in a tragic outcome. Our hope derives from the capacity that we have witnessed in today's students to learn from history and make contributions, in ways both big and small, that promote a more stable world order.

Acknowledgments

We have accumulated many debts in writing this book—far more than can be individually identified here. An appropriate place to begin is by acknowledging the professors who taught us about world politics and served as mentors at the beginning of our careers. We are especially grateful for the encouragement and guidance provided by Bill Coplin, Pat McGowan, Bob Gregg, Jerzy Hauptmann, Chester Bain, and Jim Holland.

Over the years, many people have shaped our thinking about how to teach international relations to the next generation's leaders. John Boehrer, who headed the Pew Faculty Fellowship in International Affairs program at Harvard University, deserves to be singled out. This book draws from our experience at Harvard, where he enthusiastically promoted active learning and finely honed our ability to use case study pedagogy.

We have also benefited from the insights of numerous colleagues, among them Shannon Blanton, Dan Caldwell, Roger Coaté, Chuck Hermann, Steve Hibbard, Jim Holderman, Lew Howell, Mel Leffler, Milan Ravic, Chuck Robinson, Joel Rosenthal, Alpo Rusi, Dragan Simić, John Vasquez, and Dragan Živojinović.

Kegley would particularly like to thank the U.S. Institute of Peace, the John D. and Catherine T. MacArthur Foundation, and the National Science Foundation for their generous support of his research that informed parts of this book.

Raymond thanks the staff at the Peace Palace Library in The Hague for their assistance with his research on topics for this book and is especially grateful to Constance Lawton and Jim Yoder for allowing him to use Terra Lodge in Sun Valley as a writer's retreat, where he spent countless hours reworking chapter drafts while being inspired by the raw, rugged beauty of Idaho's Boulder Mountains.

No book sees the light of day without the dedicated support from a team of publishing professionals. We have been exceedingly fortunate to work with CQ Press. Our acquisition editors, Scott Greenan and Anna Villarruel, had confidence in this project from the start and were unfailing in their support throughout the publishing process. In addition, we wish to express our appreciation for the invaluable help provided by our editorial assistant, Lauren Younker; our professional production editor, Andrew Olson; our dedicated copy editor, Megan Markanich; our proofreader Laura Webb; our graphic designer, Scott Van Atta, who worked on the book's cover and maps; the thorough compiler of our index, Judy Hunt; and those attending to the many other tasks necessary to prepare this book for marketing and distribution, including Jennifer Jones.

A number of scholars provided blind peer reviews of earlier versions of our manuscript. Valuable suggestions were provided by:

Christopher J. Saladino, Virginia Commonwealth University
Nicholas P. Giordano, Suffolk County Community College
Geoff Allen, University of California Santa Barbara
Andrew Kirkpatrick, Christopher Newport University
Kyeonghi Baek, SUNY Buffalo State
Charles J. Fagan, Western Carolina University
Adrien M. Ratsimbaharison, Benedict College
Richard Arnold, Muskingum University
Benn L. Bongang, Savannah State University
Brian Crothers, United States Naval Academy
Charles M. Swinford, Southern New Hampshire University

Last but without a doubt not least, we wish to acknowledge our wives—Debbie and Christine—who provided daily encouragement. We deeply appreciate their wisdom and patience.

Charles W. Kegley
Gregory A. Raymond

About the Authors

Charles W. Kegley (PhD, Syracuse University; BA, American University) is a past president of the International Studies Association, who has served on the Board of Trustees of the Carnegie Council for Ethics in International Affairs for the past two decades. He holds the title of Pearce Distinguished Professor of International Relations Emeritus at the University of South Carolina, where he chaired the Department of Government and International Studies and cochaired, with former U.S. Secretary of State Lawrence S. Eagleburger, the Byrnes International Center. A former Pew Faculty Fellow at Harvard University, Kegley previously served on the faculty at Georgetown University and has held visiting professorships at the University of Texas, Rutgers University, the People's University of China, and the Graduate Institute of International Studies and Development in Geneva, Switzerland. He has served as the editor of *The SAGE International Yearbook of Foreign Policy Studies* and has authored or edited over five dozen books on foreign policy and world politics, including eighteen editions of *World Politics: Trend and Transformation*, which has been translated into Arabic, Chinese, Hebrew, Korean, Serbian, Spanish, and Turkish. His research has been published in most leading foreign policy journals, and he has presented keynote addresses at many international conferences and universities.

Gregory A. Raymond (PhD, University of South Carolina; BA Park College) is University Distinguished Professor Emeritus at Boise State University, where he was the inaugural holder of the Frank and Bethine Church Chair of Public Affairs and served as the founding director of the Honors College, chair of the Department of Political Science, and director of the Survey Research Center. A veteran of the U.S. Army and former Pew Faculty Fellow at Harvard University, Raymond has received Boise State's outstanding researcher and outstanding teacher awards, served on the Idaho State Board of Education's Higher Education Research Council, and was selected as the Idaho Professor of the Year in 1994 by the Carnegie Foundation for the Advancement of Teaching. He has published over 100 articles, reviews, and op-ed essays, and has lectured on international issues at universities and research institutes in 22 countries. His work has been supported by grants from the American Political Science Association, the United States Institute of Peace, the U.S. Department of State, and other government agencies.

Together, Kegley and Raymond have coauthored *The Global Future* (2014), *The Multipolar Challenge* (2008), *After Iraq: The Imperiled American Imperium* (2007), *From War to Peace: Fateful Decisions in International Politics* (2002), *Exorcising the Ghost of Westphalia: Building World Order in the New Millennium*

(2002), *How Nations Make Peace* (1999), *A Multipolar Peace: Great-Power Politics in the Twenty-First Century* (1994), and *When Trust Breaks Down: Alliance Norms and World Politics* (1990). They have coedited *International Events and the Comparative Analysis of Foreign Policy* (1975) and coauthored over three dozen articles in such scholarly journals as the *International Studies Quarterly, International Organization,* the *Journal of Conflict Resolution,* the *Journal of Politics,* the *Journal of Peace Research, International Interactions, International Politics, Conflict Management and Peace Science, Korea and World Affairs,* and the *Harvard International Review.*

PART I

The Violent Origins of the Contemporary World Order

1 Great-Power Struggles for Primacy in the Modern Era

The story of international politics is written in terms of the great powers of an era.

—KENNETH N. WALTZ,

INTERNATIONAL RELATIONS THEORIST

During a speech delivered on January 19, 2018, to unveil the publication of a new *National Security Strategy of the United States of America*, then U.S. Secretary of Defense James N. Mattis declared that great-power competition was now the primary focus of American foreign policy. The United States, he asserted, faced a serious threat from revisionist states that were attempting to reshape world affairs to promote their values and interests. In his estimation, the ambitions of these authoritarian regimes imperiled the principles and practices that had underpinned global stability for decades.

Mattis's remarks highlighted an enduring feature of politics among nations. Rather than being a momentary problem, great-power competition is a deeply rooted continuity.[1] Because there is no central arbiter in world affairs with the ability to regulate how states interact, powerful countries use their military and economic muscle to impose their will on others, pushing for contentious issues to be handled in a manner to their satisfaction. As the ancient Athenians told representatives from the city-state of Melos over 2,000 years ago, in international politics "the strong do what they can and the weak suffer what they must."[2]

When trying to understand international politics, it is fitting to begin where most of the action is located—the competition among the largest, wealthiest, and most well-endowed military powers.[3] Controlling an enormous share of the planet's resources and possessing highly developed industrial and technological capabilities, the moves that these players make on the global chessboard affect almost everyone. Nowhere is this more evident than in their efforts to promote rules and institutions that set the parameters for acceptable conduct in international relations.

Every great power has its own ideas about what is acceptable. Sometimes their ideas differ, fueling bitter disagreements and diplomatic deadlock; occasionally they intersect, prompting hard bargaining to reach a consensus on the nature of legitimate political arrangements; and at other times they converge, laying the foundation for a commonly accepted framework that specifies the permissible goals and instruments of foreign policy. The aim of this book is to examine great-power competition over how to construct and maintain world order. We begin our analysis in this chapter by defining what constitutes a great power and describing patterns of great-power rivalry in modern history. This opens the way for the other chapters in Part I to make a comparison of the designs for world order that arose after the First and Second World Wars. Part II focuses on the evolution of world order during the Cold War and immediate post–Cold War period. Finally, Part III explores the problems and prospects of forging a new world order in the twenty-first century.

....

THE WESTPHALIAN FOUNDATIONS OF THE MODERN STATE SYSTEM

The landscape of contemporary world politics traces its origins to far-reaching changes that swept across Europe during the sixteenth and seventeenth centuries. Prior to the Protestant Reformation, most Europeans lived in a welter of fiefdoms, duchies, and principalities but thought of themselves as belonging to a larger Christian commonwealth led by the pope. As a result of the Thirty Years' War (1618–1648), this vertical conception of international order was superseded by a horizontal conception that recognized no higher authority (see Figure 1.1). Ever since, neither the pope nor a secular emperor would supervise international affairs.

The Thirty Years' War was a complex, multifaceted conflict. One dimension of the war was religious, involving a clash between Catholics and Protestants. Another dimension was governmental, consisting of a civil war over the issue of imperial authority within the Holy Roman Empire (a territory stretching from France to Poland, made up of various lands united through marriages to the Catholic Habsburg dynasty). A third dimension was geostrategic, pitting the Austrian and Spanish branches of the House of Habsburg against the Danish, Swedish, Dutch, and French thrones.

The war was devastating. Much of central Europe lay desolate in its aftermath, stripped of resources and drained of population by massacre, famine, and disease. When the belligerents finally reached a peace agreement, they replaced the old hierarchical medieval order with a decentralized system composed of autonomous **nation-states**. Under the terms of the Peace of Westphalia (so named because it was negotiated at concurrent conferences in the German cities of Münster and Osnabrück in Westphalia), all states possessed **sovereignty**, which gave them sole jurisdiction over their territory, the exclusive right to make, interpret, and enforce laws within that territory, and the freedom to negotiate

FIGURE 1.1 ALTERNATIVE TYPES OF STATE SYSTEMS

World politics can be organized in different ways. One form is hierarchical, where the constituent units of the state system are linked together in a vertical structure of superior-subordinate relationships. Another form is anarchical, where legally equal units of differential stature have no higher authority standing above them.

VERTICAL HIERARCHICAL STATE SYSTEM

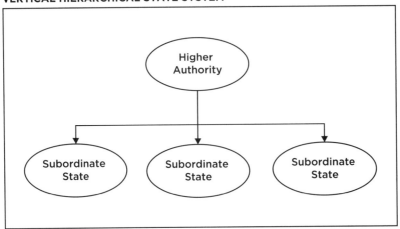

HORIZONTAL ANARCHIC STATE SYSTEM

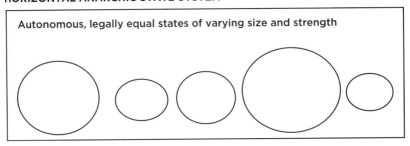

commercial treaties, form military alliances, and enter into other types of inter-state agreements without foreign interference.

The Peace of Westphalia colored nearly every aspect of world politics over the ensuing centuries. In the absence of a higher authority to resolve disputes and provide protection, each state became responsible for its own security, with retaliatory force functioning as the court of last resort. National leaders judged whether a wrong had been committed against their countries, and they were responsible for punishing wrongdoers. By accepting **anarchy** rather than **hierarchy** as a core tenet, the Peace of Westphalia encouraged the development of international laws that were anchored in custom, adjudicated under voluntary consent, and enforced through **self-help**. Despite the fact that these rules were not commands backed by the threat of punishment from a higher authority, states generally complied with them because their long-term interests were served by the predictability that came through shared expectations about appropriate behavior. Those who consistently played by the rules earned reputations for dependability, which made them valuable partners in collaborative undertakings. Those who broke them earned rebuke, which led them to be distrusted.

Under the canons of Westphalian diplomacy, all nation-states were equal before the law. They possessed the same rights and duties, they could appeal to the same legal rules when defending their actions, and they could expect to have those rules applied impartially whenever they consented to have an intermediary resolve their disputes. Even though nation-states were legal equals, they varied widely in size and strength. As Figure 1.2 illustrates, the Westphalian system

FIGURE 1.2 STRATIFICATION WITHIN THE STATE SYSTEM
Although there is no higher authority in world politics, the state system is stratified. Great (or major) powers enjoy the largest share of human and material resources, middle powers possess substantial but proportionally fewer resources, and minor powers have the least resources relative to everyone else. Occasionally, one or two great powers may achieve a position of dominance over the other great powers.[4]

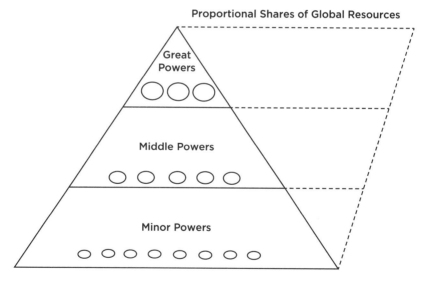

Proportional Shares of Global Resources

Great Powers

Middle Powers

Minor Powers

Source: Based on Richard Rosecrance, *International Relations: Peace or War?* (New York: McGraw-Hill, 1973), 108–109.

was anarchic but also stratified. Large wealthy states existed alongside small poverty-stricken ones, with the former populating the upper strata of the international pecking order and the latter occupying the lower tier. These rankings were not static. States rose and fell over time, experiencing uneven growth rates that increased the prominence of some while diminishing the standing of others. Because those with high stature had disproportionate influence over world affairs, routinely crafting the rules of the game under which everyone played, Westphalia's legacy was a recurring struggle for position. In the anarchic nation-state system that arose after the Thirty Years' War, all countries understood that the great powers were the chief architects of world order.

WHAT ARE GREAT POWERS?

Although the notion that some states were economically and militarily more significant than others informed the Westphalian peace settlement, the term *great power* did not appear until a few decades later, and only entered into regular diplomatic discourse in the early nineteenth century. Presumably, the lack of an agreed upon definition contributed to its slow adoption. People had an intuitive sense of the concept but used different criteria when they classified certain states as great powers.

Beneath these intuitive conceptions were impressions about the putative or potential **power** of different states. In political vernacular, power refers to the capacity to control the behavior of others, making the leaders of another country continue a course of action, change what they are doing, or refrain from taking certain steps. A powerful state can significantly raise the odds that others will behave in ways that it favors and lower the odds of behavior it opposes. Power, in other words, is a performance trait. We rate a state's power based on the amount of influence that it can exert under certain specified conditions.

Power is frequently described as the currency of politics. It is a means by which one party can influence the behavior of another. Measuring political power is difficult, akin to measuring purchasing power in a barter economy. In an economy without money, purchasing power cannot be calculated exactly, though it can be estimated based on the resources that someone has available to trade.[5] Similarly, without consensus on a standard unit of account for gauging political power, scholars and policymakers have problems quantifying a state's power, but it can be estimated by itemizing a state's capabilities—under the assumption that power is a function of certain aptitudes and endowments.

If the wellsprings of national power lie deep within the bedrock of capabilities, from which specific resources does power flow? People who agree that national power derives from a country's resource base often disagree over which components are most important. Normally some combination of geographic, demographic, economic, and other tangible factors are mixed with intangible factors like leadership, morale, and the cultural attractiveness known as **soft power**.[6] Though the formulas may differ, the end results are usually the same: Power is equated with those capabilities that enhance a country's war-fighting ability.

The importance routinely accorded to martial prowess arises from the tendency to regard force as the *ultima ratio* in anarchical systems. However, military strength may be effective for influencing behavior in some contexts, but it is ineffective in others. The capabilities that allow a state to influence one country under certain circumstances may have little value when trying to win over another country in a different situation. Indeed, they may be counterproductive. For example, threatening nuclear retaliation against an adversary might deter it from attacking, but brandishing these weapons would hardly persuade it to open its domestic market to the threatening country's exports. Military capabilities obviously contribute to a state's potential power, but we must be careful not to presume that arms are the only source of influence. The power to destroy is not the power to control.

In summary, a few titans stand out in any historical era owing to their extensive interests, superior capabilities, and willingness to project power abroad to influence the course of international events. Their relative power can be gauged in terms of the kinds of targets and behaviors that they can affect and the types of inducements and sanctions that they can employ when attempting to exert influence. A great power is a state that is able to exercise control over a *wide domain of targets* and an *extensive scope of behaviors* by virtue of having the economic and military capabilities that put a *broad range of rewards and punishments* at its disposal. While it has the inclination and assets to exert substantial clout in world affairs, such a state is not necessarily "great" in the sense of exhibiting exemplary behavior deserving of moral respect and social esteem.

Despite scholarly quibbling over which capabilities, singularly or collectively, determine national ranking in world affairs, there is broad agreement on the roster of modern great powers. Table 1.1 lists those states that have generally been seen as great powers since the Peace of Westphalia ended the Thirty Years' War. It shows that their numbers have fluctuated over time as membership expanded from a largely European core to encompass countries from North America and Asia. During this period, some states (France, the United Kingdom) have remained at the top of the global pyramid of power; others (Austria, the Netherlands, the Ottoman Empire, Spain, Sweden) have fallen away; a few (Russia/Soviet Union, Germany, Japan) have declined and then regained great-power status; and still others have emerged from an illustrious past (China) or relative obscurity (United States) to reach the pinnacle of global power.

Compared to other states from this period, the great powers listed in Table 1.1 were more likely to forge alliances, initiate militarized disputes, intervene into ongoing conflicts, and cause wars to expand.[7] Although they did not always get their way, as the French and American experiences in Vietnam illustrate,[8] these states were doggedly active in the international arena, wielding their power whenever opportunities arose to gain an advantage at an acceptable cost.

TABLE 1.1 GREAT POWERS SINCE THE PEACE OF WESTPHALIA

Scholars disagree over how to identify great powers. Although they use different criteria, diplomatic historians and social scientists generally agree on the list of great powers since the Peace of Westphalia. Although the hereditary and religious monarchs of the seventeenth century have been described as ruling entities more like dynasties than modern nation-states, most analysts have nonetheless described them as great powers.[9]

State	Qualifying Years
Austrian Habsburgs/Austria/Austria-Hungary	1648–1918
England/Great Britain/United Kingdom	1648–
France	1648–
Ottoman Empire	1648–1699
Spain	1648–1808
Sweden	1648–1721
The Netherlands	1648–1713
Russia/Soviet Union/Russian Federation	1721–1917, 1922–
Prussia/Germany/Federal Republic of Germany	1740–1918, 1925–1945, 1991–
Italy	1860–1943
Japan	1895–1945, 1991–
United States	1898–
China	1950–

REGULARITIES IN GREAT-POWER BEHAVIOR

Thus far we have emphasized how great powers differ from other members of the state system. These differences are important, but considerable variation can also exist among the great powers. One way to think about these power differentials is to look at the **polarity** of the state system. As depicted in Figure 1.3, polarity refers to the *distribution* of power among the system's leading states. **Unipolar** configurations have one dominant power center, **bipolar** configurations contain two centers of power, and **multipolar** configurations possess more than two such centers. Movement back and forth among unipolarity, bipolarity, and multipolarity is a manifestation of the more general process of capability concentration and diffusion. When the distribution of military and economic capabilities is extremely concentrated, a single preponderant power stands over its contemporaries like a colossus.

FIGURE 1.3 POLARITY AND THE DISTRIBUTION OF NATIONAL CAPABILITIES
Power can be distributed in different ways. It can be highly concentrated or widely dispersed. When it is dispersed in a multipolar configuration, the size of the system refers to the number of nearly equal great powers. Thus, multipolar systems may include three, four, or even more great powers that are on a par with one another.

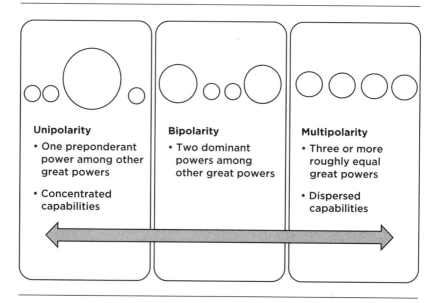

Unipolarity
- One preponderant power among other great powers
- Concentrated capabilities

Bipolarity
- Two dominant powers among other great powers

Multipolarity
- Three or more roughly equal great powers
- Dispersed capabilities

Conversely, when capabilities are highly diffused, several peer states occupy the summit of international power.

Although the political leaders of great powers prefer to stand alone at the apex of world power, most lack the means to do so. Unipolar periods are rare. Two standard examples from the early history of the Westphalian state system are France from 1659 to 1713 and again from 1797 to 1815. During the first period, King Louis XIV possessed a large, well-equipped, and professionally trained military. Unlike many previous European armies, which were a hodgepodge of mercenary units loyal primarily to the officers that recruited them, the French army was an efficient, disciplined instrument of national policy. No other great power could defeat it in battle. Only a large coalition of states was ultimately able to prevent France from solidifying its dominant position. Likewise, in the second period, Napoleon Bonaparte directed a formidable military that combined firepower and rapid flanking maneuvers to mass devastating force against the weakest point in an opponent's lines. Once again, France could best any state in combat and was stopped only by a grand coalition of other great powers. Despite having impressive capabilities at their command, neither Louis XIV nor Napoleon were able to achieve **hegemony**.

Whereas unipolarity entails a high concentration of capabilities in the hands of a single state, hegemony implies something more. In addition to being inordinately strong relative to other great powers, a hegemon aims to exercise international leadership and its mastery is largely accepted.[10] France under both Louis XIV and Napoleon not only surpassed the other great powers in military capability but also sought a position of leadership that would allow officials in Paris to overhaul the prevailing international order. Although the French failed in both cases, their unrelenting efforts highlight a persistent pattern in world politics.

Throughout the annals of modern world politics, the ascendency of one great power relative to the others prompted resistance. Sheer strength did not always command deference; often it bred defiant opposition. Great powers historically have tried to block any of their contemporaries from becoming hegemons that could single-handedly control everyone else. Whenever this struggle for primacy escalated to war, the victors normally designed rules and institutions that they believed would prevent a recurrence of hostilities and preserve their supremacy. However, staving off future challenges to the postwar settlement always proved costly, even for the leading member of the winning coalition. **Imperial overstretch**—the gap between external commitments and internal resources—can saddle a freshly minted global leader with expenses that retard long-term economic growth as its resources are increasingly devoted to military purposes rather than creating wealth.[11] Every dollar spent to counter a possible threat is a dollar not available for domestic needs. The dilemma, as U.S. president Dwight Eisenhower explained, is to "figure out how far you should go without destroying from within what you are trying to defend from without."[12]

Apart from the heavy toll extracted by global engagement, a new leader's position can also erode because national economies expand and contract at different rates. Competitors who chafe under the rules and institutions implemented by the leading state but are unencumbered by extensive foreign commitments can focus their efforts on the home front, developing national industries and innovative technologies that may ultimately yield productive, commercial, and financial advantages. According to what has been dubbed **power transition theory**, conflict between great powers that are satisfied with the status quo and those that question its legitimacy can turn violent when the distribution of power begins tilting toward the disgruntled (see Figure 1.4). War often involves a "rear-end" collision between a rising dissatisfied state and a once-preeminent state that is striving to arrest its decline. When the relative strength of the revisionist challenger and the former top dog begin converging, the odds of the two sides squaring off increase. Either the declining leader initiates a preventive war so as not to be overtaken by the challenger, or the

FIGURE 1.4   POWER TRANSITIONS AND WAR

According to power transition theory, war is unlikely when a satisfied defender of the prevailing world order holds a dominant position over any potential challenger. The danger of war mounts when the defender's preponderance erodes and a dissatisfied challenger increases in strength, eventually overtaking the defender in relative power.[13]

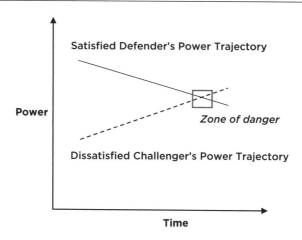

Source: Based on Ronald L. Tammer, et al., Power Transitions: Strategies for the 21st Century (New York: Chatham House, 2000), 21–22.

challenger strikes first, confident that it can accelerate its climb to the zenith of international power.[14] Another hegemonic war is not preordained, however. Shifts in relative power create discontinuities between the expectations of national leaders and the realities they face, but the more gradual the changes in the power trajectories of each side, the greater the likelihood that they can adapt and avert armed conflict.[15]

Table 1.2 displays the major, system-transforming wars that have been fought between aspiring hegemons and their principal rivals since the beginning of the seventeenth century. Research on these wars suggests that volatility in the great-power pecking order is destabilizing.[16] If a clear, coherent rank order exists among the great powers, with the leading state holding an obvious advantage over its nearest rival, then the probability that some other great power will underestimate the leader's strength and try to alter the system by force are diminished because the price for challengers is prohibitive. On the other hand, if the great-power ranking is nebulous, with the advantage of the leading state eroding, the chances of a confrontation increase. Stark inconsistencies between a challenger's potency and prestige tend to foster complaints of undeserved treatment, perceptions of strategic opportunity, and bids for primacy.

TABLE 1.2 HEGEMONIC WARS IN THE MODERN ERA

Over the past four centuries, states desiring to achieve hegemonic status have fought against coalitions of other great powers that have blocked their aspirations. Each of these major, system-transforming wars has been followed by a period of international rule-making and institution-building.

War	Aspiring Hegemon	Great-Power Opposition	Foundation for New World Order
Thirty Years' War (1618–1648)	Austrian Habsburgs (aligned with Spain)	England, France, the Netherlands, Sweden	Peace of Westphalia: Treaties of Münster and Osnabrück (1648)
Wars of Louis XIV (1688–1713)	France	Austrian Habsburgs, England, the Netherlands, Spain, Sweden	Treaties of Utrecht (1713) and Rastatt (1714)
Napoleonic Wars (1803–1815)	France	Austria, Great Britain, Prussia, Russia	Congress of Vienna (1815) and Concert of Europe
World War I (1914–1918)	Germany (aligned with Austria-Hungary)	France, Great Britain, Italy, Russia, United States	Treaty of Versailles (1919) and League of Nations
World War II (1939–1945)	Germany (aligned with Japan and Italy)	France, Great Britain, Soviet Union, United States	Bretton Woods system (1944), United Nations (1945)

CONTENDING APPROACHES TO WORLD ORDER

Given the relentless competition among great powers, what prevents world politics from being in a constant state of upheaval? The international system is anarchic; no higher authority governs state behavior. Surely, one might suppose that international life would resemble the "war of all against all" described by the sixteen-century English philosopher Thomas Hobbes. In his image of the state of nature—a hypothetical condition that preceded government—conflict is incessant as egoistic actors struggle with one another to acquire scarce resources. Yet even in the ruthless self-help arena of world politics, the competitors recognize that their interests are served by having a rudimentary set of ground rules. Just as the participants in a pickup game of basketball follow rules that regulate play, states expect that certain conventions will be observed when they interact. World politics is tempestuous, but it is not total bedlam. Instead of taking place in an utterly chaotic environment, politics among nations transpires within what has aptly been called an *anarchical society*, because a generally accepted framework of world order moderates state behavior.[17]

The framework of world order rests on two pillars, one anchored in international norms and the other in institutional mechanisms devised to prevent any one great power from subduing all others. The former spells out a set of prescriptions and proscriptions that define the limits of permissible action; the latter physically reinforces normative restraints on the aims and methods of foreign policy. Neither pillar eliminates great-power competition, but together they moderate it by helping ensure that conflicts are over adjustments to the political framework for coordinating international interactions rather than being challenges to the legitimacy of the framework itself.[18] Let us briefly examine each of these pillars more closely.

International norms are shared understandings about appropriate state conduct in specific situations. They convey a collective evaluation of what ought to be done and a collective expectation about what will be done. The injunctions they communicate vary over time, ranging from permissive to restrictive. *Permissive* norms give states wide latitude on using force as an instrument of statecraft and on repudiating agreements whenever they wish to free themselves from treaty obligations. *Restrictive* norms limit the use of force and uphold the sanctity of treaties.

Compliance with international norms elicits approval from other states; noncompliance, disapproval. Norms are particularly influential among states with leadership that is sensitive to their reputations because approval and disapproval, and the concomitant prospects of social inclusion or exclusion, reflect on one's identity as an upstanding member of the society of states. States that fail to abide by international norms tend to be seen in a negative light, which prejudices others against future collaboration. Concerned that the loss of prospective gains might outweigh any short-term benefits from noncompliance, national leaders generally observe the rules of the game even if they do not advance their immediate interests.

The institutional mechanisms in a framework of world order are organizational arrangements devised to induce restraint when and where normative rules break down. The structure and scope of these arrangements has also varied throughout modern history, ranging from tacit agreements among the great powers to block the rise of an aspiring hegemon to explicit covenants pledging concerted action against a wider array of security threats.

The rules and institutions of world order do not appear automatically. Foreign policy makers design them. In addition to deciding how to treat defeated powers after a hegemonic war (see Box 1.1), heads of state choose whether the framework should be based on permissive or restrictive norms as well what types of institutions will fortify the new code of statecraft. Forging a stable world order is difficult. No blueprint exists. The two most prominent theories of world politics—realism and liberalism—offer contradictory advice to policymakers. Of course, these are not the only theories that suggest how to build world order, but because they have had the greatest impact on policymakers, it is fitting that we briefly describe the worldviews that they espouse.

Box 1.1 You Decide

Picture yourself as the chief national security adviser to the political leader of your country. A long, devastating war has just ended. Over 2.5 million combatants have perished. When measured by battle deaths per population, the toll exceeds all previous wars fought during the preceding three centuries.

Your country was part of a broad coalition that triumphed over a brilliant military commander from a nearby state that seized power through a coup d'état. After ousting the old regime, he unleashed his powerful army on surrounding nations, implanting a revolutionary ideology throughout the lands he conquered as a preliminary step toward establishing hegemonic control over the entire state system. Following his defeat and incarceration, an international congress was convened to craft a set of rules and institutions to build a stable postwar international order. Your task is to recommend how the vanquished state should be treated now that the fighting is over.

There is no simple answer to the question of how victors should deal with the vanquished. No stock formula exists for constructing a durable postwar order. Policymakers confronting this question often find themselves pulled in opposite directions by two contending schools of thought. One school counsels leniency: Victors should be magnanimous to extinguish any desire for revenge by the loser. The other school calls for sterner measures: Victors should be harsh to ensure that the losing side's defeat is irreversible. The first approach seeks stability by building trust between former belligerents; the second is by eliminating a defeated foe's capacity to mount a future military challenge.

The conventional wisdom says you should act in terms of national interest. And why not? Why should anyone pass up an opportunity to make his or her country's situation better? That said, a fundamental problem remains: What defines how your interests are served?

Ascertaining whether a lenient or a punitive peace settlement is in a country's national interest is difficult because of the complex trade-offs between short-term security and long-term reconciliation. Victors face both demands for immediate revenge from domestic constituencies as well as the real possibility that they may need to seek the cooperation of the defeated state at some point later in time. What constitutes the national interest is not self-evident. Some victors do not enough to protect their security, humiliating the defeated without weakening their capacity to retaliate; others go too far, plundering the defeated only to create an archrival who dreams of getting even.

Determining how to treat defeated great powers is a crucial preliminary to constructing a durable postwar world order. What is your advice? Would you advocate a lenient or a punitive peace settlement in this case? Why?

Realism

Political realism has a distinguished pedigree, with intellectual roots in the seminal works of Thucydides, Kautilya, and Han Fei in ancient Greece, India, and China, respectively. As might be expected given its long history, several versions of realist thought have evolved over time, including a power politics (or *realpolitik*) version inspired by the sixteenth-century Italian philosopher Niccolò Machiavelli, a prudential version exemplified by the twentieth-century theologian Reinhold Niebuhr, and several recent structural versions that emphasize how state behavior is influenced more by the anarchic environment of world politics than the passions and material appetites of human nature.

Realists of all stripes see world politics as a ceaseless struggle for power among territorially organized states of unequal strength. Relations among states wax and wane according to the changes in the distribution of their military might. Without a higher authority to govern the state system, the powerful can take advantage of the powerless. Uncertain about the intentions of neighboring states, national leaders rely upon arms and alliances for security rather than count on the goodwill of potential adversaries.

Realists are pessimists on politics and consequentialists on ethics. They deny that there can be a perennial harmony of interests among competitive political actors and insist that decisions about world order can only be judged in terms of their consequences in particular situations. Whatever actions that are in the interest of state security must be carried out, no matter how discordant they may seem in the light of one's personal beliefs. Whereas moral values about right and wrong may guide the behavior of ordinary people in their daily lives, reason of state (*raison d'état*) must govern the conduct of leaders responsible for their nation's survival. Foreign policy emanates from strategic imperatives, not from the noble ideals.

Liberalism

Like realism, liberal theory has a long, distinguished history, dating back to the political writings of John Locke, Immanuel Kant, and Adam Smith. As in the case of realism, there are several variants of liberal thought. Drawing broad conclusions from a diverse body of theory risks misrepresenting any particular thinker on the topic of world order. Still, there are enough similarities to identify some common themes.

For liberals, foreign policy should be formulated by decision makers who recognize the costs of conflict and share significant interests. Rather than a struggle for relative gains, politics among nations is seen as a search for consensus and mutual benefits in an interdependent world. Believing in reason and progress, liberals profess faith in the capacity of humanity to adopt reforms, implementing practices that reduce the likelihood of armed conflict. One such reform entails facilitating economic exchanges among countries. Open markets and free trade, liberal theorists contend, create material incentives to resolve disputes peacefully.

Whereas war interrupts commerce, shrinks profits, and reduces prosperity, the unfettered flow of goods and services among nations increases communication, erodes parochialism, and encourages states to avoid ruinous clashes.

A second reform encourages democratization. Grounded in due process and the rule of law, democratic governments are touted by liberals as polities that rely on peaceful modes of conflict resolution. Instead of resolving disputes by brute force, they employ judicial methods. When democracies clash with one another in international affairs, they are more likely than autocratic regimes to use courts rather than combat to settle their quarrel.[19] Thus, according to liberals, if more countries had democratic governance, less warfare would occur.

Finally, a third reform typically found in liberal theories calls for building a network of **intergovernmental organizations**. Besides offering a forum where states can debate pressing issues and mediate lingering disagreements, these bodies provide a venue for sharing information and working together on problems that crisscross borders. Regular consultation and collaboration promote strategic restraint and help build a sense of common identity, which liberals view as the foundation for world order.

As summarized in Table 1.3, realists and liberals have different interpretations of world politics and hold divergent views on how to construct world order. Besides an empirical component that purportedly describes how states behave, both theories contain a normative component that prescribes how states allegedly should behave.

TABLE 1.3 THE PREMISES AND WORLD-ORDER PREFERENCES OF REALIST AND LIBERAL THEORIES

	Realism	Liberalism
Premises:		
View of human nature	Competitive, egoistic	Cooperative, altruistic
Core concern(s)	National interests	National and global interests
Policy orientation	Maintaining independence	Maintaining interdependence
Conception of politics	A struggle for relative gains	A search for mutual gains
Guiding principle	Strategic necessity	Moral duty
Philosophical outlook	Pessimistic	Optimistic
Preferences:		
Normative order	Permissive	Restrictive
Reinforcing mechanism	Countervailing power	Community of power

Realists are inclined to support permissive international norms—elastic standards that authorize leaders to do whatever it takes to enhance national security whenever foreign threats arise. As they see it, flexible rules allow heads of state to wield power robustly, suppressing challengers that may be dissatisfied by the international status quo. To realists, world order means finding a workable consensus and a durable balance of power that constrain clashing ambitions. In an environment where cordiality and graciousness at diplomatic ceremonies mask the self-regarding intentions of fierce competitors, it pays to have rules of the game so long as they do not compromise national security. Establishing and sustaining rules that everyone accepts as effective and legitimate is difficult, however. Great powers are self-regarding. Primarily interested in their own security and always attuned to opportunities that might increase their relative power, the danger of defection constantly looms over any framework of world order.

Liberal theorizing strikes a more optimistic tone. All states have an interest in peace, and most are led by reasonable people. With the right reforms—open markets, democratic governance, and common organizational memberships—great-power competition can be tamed, international comity promoted, and the world made safer. To advance these reforms, liberals advocate restrictive international norms and a web of quasi-legislative and judicial institutions. Unlike in permissive world orders, where considerations of expediency give immense discretion to foreign policy decision makers, liberal thinkers believe that restrictive orders, which obligate states to abide by their commitments, limit the scale of interstate competition, prompting the great powers to calibrate their behavior with an eye on the common good.

Proponents of realism and liberalism have long debated one another about the paths to peace, as the foregoing synopsis of their philosophies of statecraft suggests. When hegemonic wars end, their debate becomes intense because battlefield success, no matter how overwhelming, does not inevitably yield a durable postwar order. National leaders must decide how to design and implement a new world order. Should they be guided by realism? Should they heed the recommendations of liberalism? Or should they follow some other theory of world politics? The choices they face are among the most momentous they ever make.

BUILDING WORLD ORDER IN THE AFTERMATH OF HEGEMONIC WAR

Ever since the dawn of the modern international system, sovereign territorial states have varied in size, wealth, population, and military capabilities. Without a higher authority to call on for protection, they have relied on self-help to defend their interests. Small states with few resources posed little threat to their neighbors, but larger, brawnier countries have always been wary of their peers. Unsure of one another's intentions, great powers understandably regard each other with suspicion. Feeling vulnerable in an anarchic environment, the most ambitious among them have often sought to guarantee their security by achieving hegemony over the rest.[20] Any great power considers itself exposed "as long as there are others which are stronger," observed the eighteenth-century philosopher Jean-Jacques Rousseau. "Its security and its preservation demand that it becomes more powerful than all its neighbors."[21]

Efforts to attain absolute security by one great power tend to be perceived as creating absolute insecurity for the others, with the result that they all become locked into an upward spiral of countermeasures that diminishes each rival's safety. Scholars refer to this as the **security dilemma**, a condition that results when each great power's increase in military capabilities is matched by another's and all wind up being no better off than when they began arming.[22] Attempts to achieve "peace through strength" are understandable in a world where states alone are responsible for their security, but they can create an atmosphere that leads each side to arm, seek allies, and resort to coercive bargaining tactics. Individually, none of these factors may be sufficient to spark hostilities, but together they can lead to repeated military confrontations. Studies of crisis bargaining find that rivals tend to escalate the level of threats and demonstrations of force in each successive encounter, which elevates the probability of war as crises mount.[23]

Predicting exactly when a great-power war will occur is problematic due to the role of chance in world politics. Additionally, we have no way of knowing in what ways the future might resemble what has happened before. "All efforts to discern patterns of recurrence," Reinhold Niebuhr cautions, "must do violence to the infinite variety in the strange configurations of history."[24] Strictly speaking, the world situation is always unprecedented, yet it is never entirely unlike situations in the past. Even if history cannot provide us with perfect analogies, it is helpful to look for patterns that may provide insight into how world politics might develop. When used carefully, history can prevent premature cognitive closure, helping us frame sharper questions, suggesting alternatives that might otherwise have been overlooked, and encouraging us to search for additional information to inform us about the prospects for humanity to chart a safe path toward world order.

The next two chapters begin our investigation of historical patterns. They focus on the efforts of great powers to build world order after World Wars I and II. Juxtaposing these two hegemonic brawls helps provide a basis for assessing how past wars—and the way in which they were settled—may sow the seeds of either an enduring peace or a new confrontation. Moreover, comparing these epic struggles highlights the different policy prescriptions emanating from the realist and liberal theoretical traditions. In presenting these two wars and their peace settlements, Chapters 2 and 3 tell the story of a series of fateful decisions made during the first half of the twentieth century that ultimately shaped the second half of the century and the beginning of the new millennium.

KEY TERMS

anarchy   4

bipolar   8

hegemony   10

hierarchy   4

imperial overstretch   10

intergovernmental organizations   16

multipolar   8

nation-states   3

polarity   8

power   6

power transition theory   10

security dilemma   18

self-help   5

soft power   7

sovereignty   3

unipolar   8

2 World War I and the Versailles Settlement

*How fortunate we are to be living on this first day of the
20th century! Let us make a wish that as the 19th century
vanishes into the abyss of time, it takes away all the idiotic
hatreds and recriminations that have saddened our days.*

—LE FIGARO,

FRENCH NEWSPAPER, JANUARY 1, 1900

A spirit of optimism pervaded Europe at the dawn of the twentieth century. The marriage of science and industry produced one technological marvel after another; medical advances promised longer, healthier lives; and the exponential growth of international commerce generated extraordinary wealth, particularly for those in high society. The *Exposition Universelle* (Paris Exposition) of 1900 exemplified this buoyant mood, displaying moving walkways, diesel engines, and other dazzling inventions to the wonder and delight of over 50 million visitors. Hopes about politics among nations also ran high. Not only had the great powers avoided war for three decades but at The Hague Conference of 1899, they crafted rules to control the use of military force. Almost everyone assumed that the threat of armed conflict had receded. Peace and prosperity would grace the new century.

To be sure, a few skeptics doubted that the scourge of great-power war would fade away; however, most people expected to enjoy a more peaceful future. Persuaded by a six-volume work on advances in armaments and military tactics written by the Polish banker and railroad financier Ivan Bloch,[1] some individuals imagined that the destructiveness of modern weaponry made fighting on open terrain suicidal, which they assumed would reduce the probability of one great power attacking another. Others, influenced by the economic arguments of the British writer Norman Angell,[2] thought that the staggering costs of an all-out military clash in an increasingly interdependent world would make great-power war unlikely. Confidence in the prospects for peace was further supported by faith in progress: Humanity seemed to be making significant headway toward realizing the ancient aspiration of beating swords into plowshares. Andrew Carnegie, a wealthy industrialist and philanthropist who had emigrated in his youth from Scotland to the United States, was sure that the dream of perpetual peace was now within reach. To seize the moment, he provided funds to build a "Peace Palace" at The Hague in the Netherlands that would house a permanent court for the settlement of international disputes. Judicial decisions, he reckoned, would replace trial by combat. On August 28, 1913, following the opening ceremony for the new building, he wrote in his diary that establishing a world court would be "the greatest one step forward ever taken by man, in his long and checkered march upward from barbarism."[3]

Less than a year after Carnegie penned these words, war engulfed Europe. By the time it ended, several empires collapsed, over 16 million people were dead, and a generation of Europeans had become disillusioned with traditional foreign policy practices. It was not the bright future that so many envisioned for the twentieth century. Why did such an unanticipated, catastrophic war happen? What impact did it have on the way that foreign policy makers thought about rebuilding world order? Could a new design for international security eliminate the conditions that might spark another great-power war?

THE ORIGINS OF THE FIRST WORLD WAR

On June 28, 1914, a nineteen-year-old Bosnian Serb seeking to undermine Austro-Hungarian rule in Bosnia and Herzegovina assassinated Archduke Franz Ferdinand, heir apparent to the Habsburg throne. Convinced that the assassin was colluding with officials from the kingdom of Serbia, who policymakers in Vienna saw as the source of separatist agitation within their empire's Slavic population, Austria secured German support and issued an **ultimatum** on July 23 that was deliberately framed so Serbia would reject its terms, thus providing a pretext for punishing the kingdom militarily. Five days later, after Serbia refused to accept all of the ultimatum's demands, Austria declared war and bombarded Belgrade, setting in motion a series of impulsive moves and countermoves by other states that transformed what had been a local dispute into a wider war.

A relatively small state, Serbia stood little chance against Austria-Hungary, one of the great powers of the day. When it turned to Russia for help, political leaders in St. Petersburg recognized that their country's reputation among the South Slavs was at stake. Russia had yielded to Austrian and German pressure at the expense of Slav interests in 1878 during negotiations over territorial adjustments following war with the Ottoman Empire, again in 1908 during negotiations that preceded Austria's annexation of Bosnia and Herzegovina, and once more in 1913 during negotiations over the boundaries of Albania. To acquiesce again would destroy Russian credibility in the Balkans. After initially hesitating, Tsar Nicholas II issued an order late in the afternoon of July 30 to mobilize his forces along the Austrian and German frontiers. In turn, Germany declared war on Russia and its ally, France. When German troops swept into Luxembourg and Belgium in order to outflank French defenses, Britain declared war on Germany. Within the next week, Austria declared war on Russia, France and Britain declared war on Austria, and Serbia declared war on Germany. Eventually, thirty-two countries on six continents became embroiled in the conflict.

As shown in Table 2.1, a complex series of events preceded the outbreak of war. Scholars typically point to a combination of variables from three different **levels of analysis** (see Figure 2.1) when categorizing the determinants of foreign policy decisions. Influences on each level—individual, domestic, and systemic—help explain how the dispute between Austria-Hungary and Serbia escalated to what was called the Great War (known today as World War I).

TABLE 2.1 MAJOR TWENTIETH-CENTURY EVENTS PRECEDING WORLD WAR I

Date	Event
1900	*Exposition Universelle* opens in Paris
1902	Triple Alliance of Germany, Austria-Hungary, and Italy renewed
	Italy and France agree that each would remain neutral in the event of an attack on the other
	Great Britain and Japan form naval alliance in the Pacific region
1904	Russo-Japanese War; hostilities ended with 1905 Treaty of Portsmouth
	Great Britain and France sign "Entente Cordiale," settling colonial disputes and ending the long-standing antagonism between the two countries
1905	First Moroccan Crisis: Germany supports the Moroccans in their demand for independence from France; settlement in 1906 Algeciras Conference allows France to retain possession of Morocco
	Kaiser Wilhelm II of Germany and Tsar Nicholas II of Russia sign secret Treaty of Björkö pledging mutual security
	Alfred von Schlieffen, the German army chief of staff, designs a plan for defeating France and Russia in the event of war
	Anglo-Japanese naval alliance renewed
1906	Great Britain launches the HMS *Dreadnought*; the Germans begin building similar battleships
1907	Anglo-Russian Convention: Great Britain and Russia settle territorial disputes in Persia, Afghanistan, and Tibet
	Triple Alliance renewed

(Continued)

TABLE 2.1

Date	Event
1908	Germany launches the SMS *Nassau*, its first dreadnought-class battleship
	Annexation Crisis: Germany pressures Russia to accept Austro-Hungarian annexation of Bosnia and Herzegovina
1910	Germany surpasses Great Britain as Europe's leading manufacturing nation
1911	Second Moroccan Crisis: Germany sends the gunboat *Panther* to Moroccan port of Agadir to protest French growing military presence in Morocco; Great Britain backs France
	War between Italy and Ottoman Empire; hostilities ended with 1912 Treaty of Ouchy that cedes control of Tripoli to Italy
	Anglo-Japanese naval alliance renewed
1912	First Balkan War: Ottoman Empire cedes much of its European territory to the Balkan League, an alliance composed of Greece, Bulgaria, Serbia, and Montenegro; Albanian independence granted; hostilities ended with 1913 Treaty of London
	Triple Alliance renewed
1913	Liman von Sanders Affair: Russians object to the German general heading a mission to oversee the garrison at Constantinople
	Alliance of Germany, Austria-Hungary, and Rumania (now spelled Romania) renewed
	Second Balkan War: Unhappy with the Treaty of London, Bulgaria attacks Serbia and Greece but is defeated; hostilities ended with 1913 Treaty of Bucharest
1914	June 28: Archduke Franz Ferdinand and his wife are assassinated in Sarajevo
	July 5: Germany promises support to Austria-Hungary against Serbia
	July 23: Austria-Hungary sends an ultimatum to Serbia
	July 28: Austria declares war on Serbia
	July 30: Tsar Nicholas II of Russia orders general mobilization
	August 1: Germany declares war on Russia; France mobilizes
	August 2: Germany occupies Luxembourg; Italy announces its neutrality; Ottoman Empire aligns with Germany
	August 3: Germany declares war on France and invades Belgium; Rumania announces neutrality
	August 4: Great Britain declares war on Germany; the United States announces its neutrality
	August 5: Austria-Hungary declares war on Russia
	August 12: Great Britain and France declare war on Austria-Hungary

FIGURE 2.1 EXPLAINING INTERNATIONAL EVENTS: A FUNNEL OF CAUSALITY

The factors that influence the foreign policy choices leaders make can be classified according to different levels of analysis: Systemic influences emphasize the impact of changes in international circumstances and processes; domestic influences focus on the internal social, economic, and political characteristics of states; and individual influences pertain to the psychological factors motivating people who make decisions on behalf of states. Potentially all three types influences can affect international events.

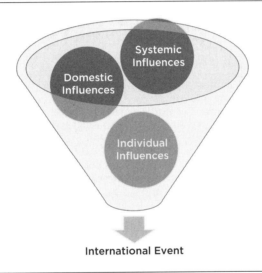

International Event

Many historians pinpoint psychological factors at the individual level of analysis as a leading source of the rivalries that ignited the First World War. Political leaders in Vienna, Berlin, and St. Petersburg generally held virtuous images of themselves, diabolical images of their adversaries, and fears that they were becoming increasingly vulnerable. Although the historical evidence suggests that no great-power head of state sought a major-power war, all felt compelled to act on what they saw as strategic necessities—circumstances that demanded they be willing to resort to war in defense of vital security interests which could not be compromised and must be upheld at any cost. Whereas each leader saw no alternative for his country, they all imagined that their adversaries had multiple options. Moreover, as they finalized their plans to do whatever they felt was necessary, they overestimated their capabilities, envisioning a military showdown as a way to settle the score with their rivals once and for all.

These misperceptions were compounded by a climate of virulent **nationalism,** which made it difficult for mistrustful leaders to see things from another country's point of view and anticipate how it would interpret and respond to their defense preparations. For example, believing that they were upholding their national honor, the Austrians could not comprehend why Russians labeled them aggressors. Similarly, the Russians did not appreciate how Austria, worried about slipping from the rank of a great power, viewed Serbian aspirations in the Balkans as a serious challenge to its fragile, multiethnic empire. Nor did the Germans understand Russia's concern about being humiliated if it allowed Austria to subdue fellow Slavs in Serbia. Ethnic prejudices flourished in this environment. Austrian foreign minister Leopold Berchtold, for example, complained that the Russians were conniving, Russian foreign minister Sergei Sazonov asserted that he despised Austria, and Kaiser Wilhelm II of Germany professed to hate Slavs.[4] With political leaders denigrating the each other's national character, diplomatic efforts to avert hostilities came to naught.

In addition to identifying various psychological factors at the individual level of analysis that influenced the decisions of political leaders during the summer of 1914, scholars also draw attention to how internal conditions at the domestic (or state) level of analysis contributed to the onset of World War I. Looking first at the characteristics of the belligerent great powers in Central and Eastern Europe, pressures were building for change in the authoritarian institutions of the Habsburg, Hohenzollern, and Romanov dynasties of Austria, Germany, and Russia, respectively. Each autocratic dynasty faced mounting public insistence for democratic reforms prior to the war, which prompted some political and military leaders in these countries to see militant diplomacy as a way to distract attention from internal problems and inspire political solidarity. France and Britain, the democratic great powers in the West, faced domestic pressures as well, especially over fiscal policy and military expenditures.

The rise of German power on land and at sea created anxieties in Paris and London over what moves Berlin might make on the geostrategic chessboard and what was required to counter German aspirations for global status. During the first half of the nineteenth century, Germans resided in a loose-knit confederation of more than three dozen small kingdoms and duchies that lacked the natural protection of formidable mountains or vast oceans. Apprehensive that their political separation and geographical vulnerability put them at the mercy of their larger neighbors, many German nationalists believed unification would provide security against external attack. Following a series of wars that culminated with a stunning victory by the northern German state of Prussia over France, the other German states joined together under King William I of Prussia (later proclaimed kaiser, or emperor) to create the German Empire on January 18, 1871. With over 40 million inhabitants, an excellent educational system; skilled labor; and unparalleled electrical, chemical, and steel industries, newly unified Germany prospered and used its growing wealth to create an awesome military machine. However, the manner in which unification occurred produced both enemies bent on revenge and bystanders wary of the empire's ambitions. France, humiliated by its recent defeat at the hands of Prussia and embittered by the loss of Alsace and Lorraine under the Peace of Frankfurt, chose to bide time for an opportunity to reverse its fortunes on the battlefield. Russia, suspicious of Berlin's territorial aims, worried about possible German expansion to the east. Although Otto von Bismarck, the empire's chancellor, devised an intricate set of alliances to keep France and Russia from making common cause against Germany, his successors lacked the vision and skills to prevent Paris and St. Petersburg from joining forces.

Germany's rise also alarmed policymakers in London. A power transition was underway, and there appeared no way to hold Germany back. At the turn of the century, Great Britain could proudly sing "Britannia rules the waves" and rightly could boast that it possessed an empire on which the sun never set. But by 1914, that era was ending. Besides fielding the world's foremost army, Germany now possessed formidable naval capabilities, which struck at the heart of British security. Command of the seas had long been deemed necessary to import food and raw materials, protect manufactured goods that British merchants exported, and safeguard the country's numerous far-flung colonies. When Kaiser Wilhelm II boldly proclaimed at the end of the nineteenth century that Germany would no longer be confined to the narrow boundaries of Europe and began a vigorous program of maritime construction, Britain responded by raising naval expenditures nearly 70 percent between 1907 and 1914,[5] which funded increases in the size and quality of its battle fleet. Germany responded in kind. Despite several attempts to control the ensuing **arms race**, Anglo-German relations deteriorated, which prompted Britain to strengthen political ties with France and Russia. London could not fathom that the Germans saw naval strength as symbolic of great-power status, while Berlin failed to grasp that rather than earning respect, rapidly expanding its navy aroused fear in an island nation that depended on sea power for security.

Finally, turning from the domestic conditions within the belligerent states to the third level of analysis—the features of the international system—scholars accentuate the impact that the tightening web of alliances had in bringing about the war. By the time Franz Ferdinand was assassinated, European military alignments had become polarized, pitting the Triple Entente of France, Russia, and Britain against the Central powers of Germany and Austria-Hungary, a counter-coalition that the Ottoman Empire subsequently joined. Once Russia mobilized in response to Austria's attack on Serbia, these ties pulled one European great power after another into the war. An atmosphere of urgency, created by the widespread belief that modern technology favored offensive military action, propelled great-power leaders to respond aggressively to the changing balance of power without pausing to reflect on the consequences of their actions. Only the United States stood aloof, seeking to isolate itself from involvement through a policy of neutrality.

Having promised Austria-Hungary unconditional support, Germany felt that it must act quickly to avoid being mired in a ruinous two-front war. According to a plan developed by General Alfred von Schlieffen, Germany could sidestep fighting France and Russia simultaneously by hurling the bulk of its army through neutral Luxembourg and Belgium in a complex flanking attack designed to overwhelm French positions on its lightly defended northern frontier. After routing the French, German combat units would pivot eastward and unleash the full weight of their military might against the slower-moving Russians. However, when a modified version of the plan was implemented by Schlieffen's successor, who had ill-advisedly reduced the strength of the right flank of his attacking force, several problems emerged. Not only did the invasion of the low countries bring Britain into the war against Germany but because the Russians moved faster than expected, troops needed to encircle the French were diverted to the eastern front. Furthermore, under the revised plan of attack, the Germans had to break through the fortified area of Liège in Belgium, which took longer than anticipated, therein providing the French with time to stop German momentum at the Marne River.

Fighting on the western front now shifted from a war of movement to one of position, with each side digging a series of defensive trenches that extended from the Belgian coast to the Swiss border. In contrast to the stalemate in the west, the Germans enjoyed greater success on the eastern front, arresting the Russian advance in the Battles of Tannenberg and the Masurian Lakes. On both fronts, science and technology made the conflict a war of machinery: Old weapons were improved and produced in great quantities; new and far more deadly weapons were rapidly developed and deployed. Widespread universal military conscription drew soldiers from nearly every family and touched the lives of every citizen. Huge armies had to be fed and equipped; consequently, entire national populations participated in the war effort, with mass communication rallying public opinion against the enemy. Demonizing the adversary would prove instrumental in the conduct of the war as well as in its conclusion. Nationalist passions might rationalize the sacrifice of life and property, but by vilifying the entire population of enemy nations, a peace settlement grounded in compromise and reconciliation would remain elusive. In short, the war became total: doing anything to achieve victory was permissible; surrender was unthinkable.

THE ARMISTICE AND ARRANGEMENTS FOR A PEACE CONFERENCE

Rather than being the short, decisive clash that the great powers envisaged, the fighting degenerated into a gruesome war of attrition. By the third year of the war, soldiers were dying by the thousands on the western front without a hope of breaching enemy lines. Mutinies erupted in the French army—to such an extent that at one point only two French divisions between Soissons and Paris were considered reliable enough to continue the struggle. But the Germans, outnumbered to begin with, were also in dire straits. Huge battlefield losses undermined the confidence of military commanders at the very time that the British naval blockade was sapping civilian morale. Despite careful planning and strict rationing, supplies of raw materials were running low, and long lines of people waited for dwindling stocks of food. Desperate German leaders saw no alternative but to resume unrestricted submarine warfare, which had been curtailed after the sinking of the passenger liners RMS *Lusitania* on May 7, 1915, and SS *Arabic* three months later. The toll that Germany's submarines would take on American shipping led Woodrow Wilson to reverse his neutrality policy. On April 6, 1917, the United States declared war on Germany.

On the eastern front, Russia had been ripped apart by the Bolshevik revolution, which toppled the Romanov dynasty and eventually forced Russia to withdraw from the war. In the Treaty of Brest-Litovsk (March 3, 1918), Germany annexed one-third of Russia's European territory and established a protectorate over the Ukraine. Having defeated its foe in the east, Germany was free to turn all of its forces westward. In the spring of 1918, Germany launched a massive offensive aimed at defeating French and British forces before American reinforcements could join the fight. Despite initial success, the offensive eventually stalled as the Germans suffered heavy casualties and were unable to keep their forward units supplied with food and ammunition. Allied counterattacks that summer on the overextended German lines began shifting the tide of battle. By fall, the German army was retreating. Germany lacked military reserves, its allies were on the verge of collapse, and political unrest was sweeping the country, which resulted in Kaiser Wilhelm II abdicating and a provisional government being formed.

With the military situation rapidly deteriorating and the country facing starvation, fuel shortages, and an influenza epidemic, Germany's leading military figure, Field Marshal Paul von Hindenburg, contacted the Supreme Allied Commander, Marshal Ferdinand Foch, to seek an armistice. His thinking was shaped by prevailing conditions on the battlefield and the home front as well as by the expectation of fair and equitable treatment. Months before, President Woodrow Wilson had preached from Washington that only a peace between equals could endure and urged that a spirit of evenhandedness underpin peace negotiations. Those principles, sketched in an address to the U.S. Senate on January 22, 1917, and elaborated upon in his widely proclaimed Fourteen Points speech delivered to a joint session of Congress on January 8, 1918, outlined a framework for ending what he trusted would be "the culminating and final war for human liberty."

As events unfolded, German hopes of negotiations among equals would be dashed by the angry emotions built up over years of bitter fighting. With nightmarish visions of trenches, barbed wire, poison gas, and mechanized slaughter fresh in their minds, the victors approached the task of making peace with vengeance in mind. The French government, in particular, sought retribution for the suffering its people had endured.

Aboard Marshal Foch's private train in the forest of Compiégne, early in the morning of November 11, 1918, a German mission led by Matthias Erzberger, a leader of the Center Party who favored a negotiated end to the war, reluctantly consented to the terms of a cease-fire agreement. There had been no bargaining. A few days earlier, Germany was given 72 hours to meet a series of demands or the war would continue. The conditions included a cessation of hostilities; the evacuation of all territory in Luxembourg, Belgium, and France (including Alsace-Lorraine) seized by Germany; the allied occupation of Germany west of the Rhine River; German renunciation of the Treaty of Brest-Litovsk and withdrawal of its troops from Austria-Hungary, Rumania, and the lands of the former Ottoman and Russian empires; and the surrender of Germany's capital ships, submarines, aircraft, railway locomotives, rolling stock, heavy artillery, and machine guns. Meanwhile, the crushing allied naval blockade of German territorial waters would continue until a peace treaty was signed.

To craft the final peace terms, in January 1919 a conference was convened at Versailles, outside of Paris, with representatives from 27 allied states, accompanied by hundreds of advisers and clerks. Before substantive issues could be debated, it was necessary to settle various procedural matters. Because no formal agenda had been established prior to the conference, on January 12, 1919, the delegates began to hammer out organizational issues. Ultimately it was decided that the key decision-making body would be a Council of Ten, composed of the foreign ministers and heads of state from France, Great Britain, the United States, Italy, and Japan. Not long thereafter, participation by the foreign ministers ended, thus leaving a Council of Five. Since Japan only was engaged when the council dealt with a topic pertaining to the Pacific region, most of the decisions were made by a Council of Four (which became a council of France, Great Britain, and the United States when Italy withdrew at the end of April). Because council members lacked detailed information about most substantive issues they addressed, 58 commissions of experts were established to study specific problems and make recommendations. Council deliberations over these recommendations were held in secret, and only eight plenary sessions involving all delegates to the peace conference were held.

BALANCE-OF-POWER THEORY AND WORLD ORDER

Once the procedural preliminaries were finished, the members of the council took up the question of how to construct a new world order. The choices that the leaders of great powers wrestle with when major wars end are among the most consequential they ever make because winning is not an end in itself. The geopolitical landscape is littered with military victories that never translated into stable world orders.

From the Peace of Westphalia (1648), which concluded the Thirty Years' War and marked the beginning of the modern state system, through the Congress of Vienna (1814–1815), which ended Napoleon Bonaparte's attempt to replace the Westphalian system of sovereign equals with an international hierarchy headed by France, envoys attending the major peace conferences that followed in the wake of large destructive wars tended to rely on **balance-of-power theory** as a blueprint for building world order. They believed that countervailing military capabilities restrained hegemonic threats to the system of independent nation-states. As expressed in Article II of the Treaty of Utrecht (1713), which spelled out the terms of the peace settlement after a coalition of European countries defeated King Louis XIV's bid for French dominance over the continent, a balance of power is "the best and most solid foundation of a mutual friendship, and of a concord which will be lasting on all sides."

During the period ranging from the seventeenth through the nineteenth centuries, advocates of power balancing claimed that it promoted world order by offsetting the military might of revisionist states—those which sought significant changes in the international status quo. If a pugnacious revisionist gained too much strength, so the reasoning went, it was likely to bully vulnerable countries within its reach; consequently, other states had an incentive to join forces in order to deter (or, if need be, defeat) dissatisfied states harboring aggressive aims. Although diplomats from that time occasionally described balancing as an automatic, self-adjusting process, most of them saw it as the result of deliberate actions undertaken by national leaders. Some actions, like augmenting military capabilities through armaments, alliances, or territorial compensation, try to add weight to the lighter side of the international balance; others, such as negotiating **spheres of influence**, **neutralization** agreements, and limits on weaponry, attempt to decrease the weight of the heavier side. By judiciously tipping the scales one way or the other, participants in postwar peace conferences allegedly could calibrate the relative distribution of power to establish an equilibrium of forces.

Once stability was achieved, balance-of-power theory advised that states follow certain rules of the game for the equilibrating process to function effectively. Foremost among them was the admonition to be vigilant. Because international anarchy makes each state responsible for its own security, and states can never be sure of one another's intentions, self-interest requires them to constantly monitor international developments and be ready to eradicate growing threats and seize emerging opportunities.

A second informal rule advised states to acquire allies whenever they could not match the armaments of their adversaries. As depicted in Figure 2.2, these alliances should be flexible, formed and dissolved according to the strategic needs of the moment, and not made with regard to cultural or ideological affinities.

The third rule of balance-of-power politics was to oppose states that sought hegemony. If some state achieved absolute mastery over others, it would be able to act with impunity, jeopardizing the autonomy and independence of all other countries. Prudence, therefore, counseled joining forces with one's peers to prevent any single great power from achieving military preponderance.

FIGURE 2.2 ALLIANCE DYNAMICS OF BALANCE-OF-POWER SYSTEMS
Alliances play an important role in the balancing process. They
provide a means for rapidly restoring the equilibrium between
contending states or groups of states. As illustrated here, State C
can help preserve the great-power balance by aligning itself with
the coalition of States A and B, which is weaker than the rival
coalition of States D, E, and F. This can occur two ways. First, a state
can switch alliances, as exemplified in the "Diplomatic Revolution
of 1756" engineered by Chancellor Wenzel Anton von Kaunitz of
Austria, which broke Vienna's bonds with England and replaced
them with ties to France, England's long-standing foe. Second, as in
the case of sixteenth-century Venice, a prominent state belonging to
neither countervailing alliance can temporarily support the weaker
side in order to bring the balance back into equilibrium.

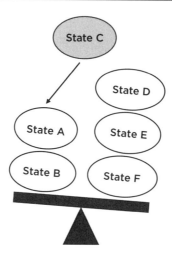

Finally, another rule of the game urged restraint. Recognizing that yesterday's
adversary may be needed as tomorrow's ally, national leaders were advised to
pursue moderate ends with measured means, exercising power with forbearance, and coupling firmness regarding their aims with fair-mindedness toward
the concerns of others. In the event of hostilities, the winning side should not
humiliate the defeated. Instead of being erased from the map, the vanquished
should be reintegrated into the postwar order.

A century earlier, the notions vigilance, flexibility, counterpoise, and moderation had influenced Austrian chancellor Prince Klemens von Metternich
and British foreign secretary Viscount Castlereagh as they worked assidu-
ously to craft a lenient peace settlement that would allow France to rejoin

the great-power club. If France became a responsible stakeholder in the post-Napoleonic world, both leaders assumed that it would play a meaningful role in balancing against aggressive great powers striving for universal hegemony. By acting in accordance with their understanding of the policy prescriptions of balance-of-power theory, Metternich and Castlereagh joined the ranks of those statesmen who had crafted the settlements that ended earlier hegemonic wars.

Throughout the history of the modern state system, maintaining an equilibrium among the great powers to preserve a stable balance of power has been regarded as a cardinal principle in international diplomacy. Presumably, similar thinking would also guide the delegates to the peace conference in 1919. However, the war's destructiveness prompted many people to question the wisdom of a philosophy that had rationalized watchful suspicion, weapons acquisition, and competitive alignments. A different approach to building world order seemed warranted. Rather than establishing a new balance of power, the American president Woodrow Wilson preached the need for a peace plan rooted in **collective security**.

WOODROW WILSON AND THE LIBERAL TRADITION IN WORLD POLITICS

President Woodrow Wilson personally led the American delegation to the peace conference. A rigid, tenacious individual, he arrived with strong opinions about how to construct a just and durable structure of world order. Much of his ire was directed at conventional power politics. "The center and characteristic of the old order," Wilson complained, "was an unstable thing which we used to call the 'balance of power'—a thing in which the balance was determined by the sword."[6] In his eyes, balance-of-power systems were immoral; they bred jealousy and intrigue, converting conflicts of interest between contending two parties into larger multiparty wars. What was needed was not another balance of power, but what he called a "community of power."

Liberal political thought shaped Wilson's outlook on world order. At the core of liberalism is a belief in reason and the possibility of progress. As discussed in the previous chapter, liberals view world politics as more of a search for compromises to maximize **absolute gains** than a competition for dominance and **relative gains**. Instead of blaming international conflict on a drive for power that is inherent in human nature, liberals fault the conditions under which most people live. Reforming those conditions would enhance the prospects for peace. Free trade, democratic governance, and intergovernmental organizations were at the forefront of the reforms they sought. As Wilson repeatedly insisted, unfettered commerce reduced the odds of war by enhancing the welfare of trading states; democracies made wars less likely because they shunned lethal force as a way to settle disagreements; and membership in a global organization lowered the probability of war by providing a judicial mechanism for resolving international disputes wherever misconceptions, wounded sensibilities, or aroused national passions threatened world peace.

Liberal Criticisms of Balance-of-Power Theory

Woodrow Wilson was hardly the first person to critique balance-of-power systems. Critics had long grumbled that "power" was an ambiguous concept. Tangible factors, such as the performance capabilities of different weapons, are hard to compare. Intangible factors, such as leadership and morale, are even more difficult to gauge. Without a precise measure of relative strength, how can policymakers know when power is becoming unbalanced? Furthermore, in an environment of secrecy and deception, how can they be sure who is really aligned with whom? A partner who is being counted on to balance the power of a rival may have covertly agreed to remain neutral in the event of a dispute. As a result, the actual distribution of power may not resemble the distribution that one imagines.

Problems in determining the strength of adversaries and the reliability of allies highlight another objection to balance-of-power theory: the uncertainty of power balances causes defense planners to engage in worst-case analysis, which can incite arms races. The intense, reciprocal anxiety that shrouds balance-of-power politics often fuels exaggerated estimates of an opponent's strength, which prompts one side, and then the other, to expand the quantity and enhance the quality of their arsenals. Relentless arms competition can transform the anarchical, self-help structure of world politics into a tinderbox that any haphazard spark might ignite.

Still another objection to balance-of-power theory was its assumption that decision makers were *risk averse*: When facing countervailing power, they refrain from fighting because the dangers of taking on an equal are too great. Yet national leaders assess risk differently. While some may hesitate to engage in dicey behavior, others are *risk acceptant* and believe that with a little luck they can prevail. Thus, rather than being deterred by the equivalent power of an adversary, they prefer to gamble on the chance of winning, even if the odds are long. Organizing comparable power against adversaries with a high tolerance for risk will not have the same effect as it would on those who avoid risks.

The upshot of these shortcomings was the repetitive failure of balance-of-power systems to foster peace. As Wilson put it in a speech delivered on January 3, 1919, power balancing "has been tried and found wanting."[7] Something else would be needed if this was to be the war to end all wars.

Liberal Aspirations for Collective Security

Embedded within Wilson's plan for a new world order was the conviction that a League of Nations—a multilateral institution for managing international politics—should supplant unbridled great-power competition and antagonistic alliances. In the list of fourteen points that he declared in

January 1918 as necessary for making the world safe for peace-loving countries, Wilson called for a "general association of nations" to provide "mutual guarantees of political independence and territorial integrity to great and small nations alike." His proposed League of Nations would be based on collective security, a **regime** containing different rules of the game than the balance of power.

Collective security theory views peace as indivisible. If aggression anywhere is ignored, it will eventually spread like a contagious disease to other countries and become more difficult to stop. Second, this theory assumes that all states would voluntarily join the collective security organization, whose universal membership would give it the legitimacy and the military strength to maintain peace. The third rule requires participants in such a collective organization to settle their disputes through pacific means. Finally, if a breach of the peace occurs, the last rule stipulates that the organization will apply timely, robust sanctions to punish the aggressor. Depending on the severity of the infraction, sanctions might range from public condemnation to an economic boycott or military retaliation.

As Figure 2.3 shows, collective security theory is anchored in the creed voiced by Alexandre Dumas's musketeers: "One for all and all for one!" It proceeds from the premise that threats are a common international concern and postulates that all members of the collective security organization would be willing and able to assist any state suffering an attack. By presenting predatory states with the united opposition of the entire international community, Wilson and like-minded statesmen insisted that collective security would have greater success inhibiting armed conflict than the balance of power. Exuding self-assurance, Wilson noted in a January 25, 1919, speech to a plenary session of the peace conference that establishing a League of Nations to implement the theory of collective security was the keystone in the architecture of a new world order.

NATIONAL SELF-INTEREST CONFRONTS WILSONIAN IDEALISM

As the delegates to the peace conference approached their historic mission, they were influenced by several additional principles in Wilson's Fourteen Points speech. Beyond promoting collective security, Wilson championed free trade, democratic governance, arms reductions, transparent negotiations, and settling territorial claims based on the right of nationalities to govern themselves through **self-determination**. However, once the delegates began their work, the knives of parochial self-interest began to whittle away at the policy prescriptions emanating from Wilson's liberal internationalist philosophy. Many European politicians believed that his recommendations were utopian dreams built on illusions about the willingness of egoistic states to sacrifice for

FIGURE 2.3 THE OPERATION OF COLLECTIVE SECURITY

Long before Woodrow Wilson championed the League of Nations, the idea of collective security was discussed by ecclesiastical councils held in Poitiers (1000), Limoges (1031), and Toulouse (1210) as well as in the writings of Pierre Dubois (1306), King George Podebrad of Bohemia (1462), and Maximilien de Béthune, Duke of Sully (1638). By the twentieth century, those working to establish a collective security organization had concluded that the prerequisites for its successful operation were universal participation, consensus on the existence of what constitutes a threat to peace, and a commitment to take concerted action against aggressors. The illustration below depicts how collective security is envisioned to function. The circular line connecting States A through F symbolizes common membership in a collective security organization. The block arrow represents aggression by State E against State C, and the dashed arrows depict the sanctions undertaken by the other members of the organization to punish State E for its wrongdoing.

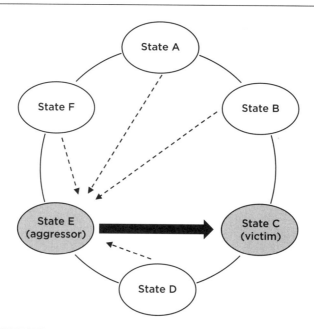

the larger collective good. They remembered that during the war Britain and France had made many secret (and occasionally conflicting) agreements concerning territories they hoped to obtain. Bargaining was driven not by shared ideals but by the national self-interested quest for defensible frontiers, ports and waterways, and supplies of raw materials. Statesmen reared on the ways of power politics were offended by the pontificating American president. "God was content with Ten Commandments," growled Georges Clemenceau, the French prime minister. "Wilson must have Fourteen."[8]

Clemenceau, a disciple of the **realpolitik** school of thought, contended that France needed security guarantees to ward off future German attacks and evaluated all recommendations for the peace settlement according to how much they strengthened France and weakened Germany. German military might, in his mind, was an existential problem for France, and he was committed to tilting the distribution of power in France's favor. Contrary to the American president's naïve faith in a League of Nations, Clemenceau averred that international politics entailed a relentless struggle for power among self-interested states that could not be tamed by collective security. "There is an old system of alliances, called the Balance of Power," he told the French Chamber of Deputies. "This system of alliances, which I do not renounce, will be my guiding thought at the Peace Conference."[9]

Great Britain's policy was managed by Prime Minister David Lloyd George, who, like Woodrow Wilson, was himself something of a reformer; nonetheless, Lloyd George had his ear attuned to the public's cry for a punitive treaty that would prioritize British national interests. Although campaigning in the 1918 election with the slogan "We will squeeze the orange till the pips squeak,"[10] he attempted to maneuver between the hardline approach urged by Clemenceau and the temperate approach offered by Wilson. For Lloyd George, establishing a League of Nations was neither an act of folly nor a panacea; it was simply a forum for great-power consultation, where the representatives of national governments could negotiate pragmatic adjustments to the peace settlement as evolving conditions merited.

As the discussions at the conference proceeded, Clemenceau's stark realpolitik thinking prevailed. His outlook was shaped by a desire for revenge, although he reluctantly gave his consent to Wilson's call for a League of Nations to preserve amity among the victors. Clemenceau believed that the league might serve as a supplementary guarantee of French security, bringing the armies of other nations to France's defense in the event of another war with Germany. While also willing to support a League of Nations, the British were concerned that targeting Germany would make the organization provocative, undermining its potential to serve as an instrument for consultation and conciliation. Wilson tirelessly prodded the delegates in Paris to adopt his vision of the league. If established, he vouched that it would allow the victors to rectify any flaws that might tarnish the final peace settlement, help future disputants avoid accidental wars, and uphold the postwar peace by providing the machinery for dealing with bellicose states.

Designing the league's structure proved highly contentious, sparking vigorous debates among the delegates. How should decisions be made? Would the league have a permanent staff and an international army? What roles and responsibilities should the great powers have in comparison to small- and medium-sized countries?

Although Wilson had asked his trusted adviser Colonel Edward House to devise a prototype for the new organization, other countries advanced their own ideas. Lord Phillimore of Great Britain, Léon Bourgeois of France, Vittorio Orlando of Italy, and Jan Christiaan Smuts of South Africa all offered different proposals. The assertive American president may have focused attention on the topic of a League of Nations, but the organization would only emerge through a patchwork of compromises with allies striving to protect their competing national interests. After considerable wrangling, a combined Anglo-American draft was issued by Cecil Hurst and David Hunter Miller, which then served as the basis for the Covenant of the League of Nations, the organization's charter.

THE VERSAILLES SETTLEMENT

The settlement finally reached is known as the Treaty of Versailles because it was signed in the glittering Hall of Mirrors in the Palace of Versailles— the same place in which a united Germany was proclaimed in 1871 after the Franco-Prussian War. The treaty ratified the end of the Kaiser's rule in Germany, and the newly created republican government submitted to the agreement on June 28, 1919. The League of Nations that had been promoted so vigorously by Woodrow Wilson was written into the peace treaty with Germany as the first of 440 articles. The rest of the settlement became largely a compromise among the ambitious, self-interested demands of the other victors. Important decisions were made behind closed doors, where the vanquished were excluded from full representation. With its extremely harsh terms, the treaty departed from the spirit of "peace without victory" that Wilson had espoused earlier when explaining his decision for the United States to cease its **isolationist policy** and enter the war. Whereas Wilson's Fourteen Points had proposed open diplomacy, arms reductions, free trade, and self-determination, the final treaty's stipulations were far more punitive toward Germany and distant from the principles for world order that Wilson had championed.

In thinking about the ways that the Germans should be treated in defeat, the victorious Allied powers could not help but to take into consideration how, had Germany won the war, it probably would have treated the countries it subjugated. They shuddered over the earlier Treaty of Brest-Litovsk between Germany and Russia. The document was so exploitative that the Russian negotiator, Leon Trotsky, at first refused to sign, in reaction to terms that would deprive Russia of 26 percent of its population, 27 percent of its arable land, and 33 percent of its manufacturing industries. Trotsky was overruled by his comrade, Vladimir Lenin, who was willing to accept these enormous losses in order to allow the Bolsheviks the opportunity to consolidate communist control over Russia. The Allies concluded that, if victorious, the Germans would have imposed equally severe terms on them.

The Terms of the Peace Settlement

Bitter over the hardships their countries endured and convinced that Germany would have treated them callously had the fortunes of war been reversed, the delegates to the peace conference forced the new government in Berlin to relinquish sovereign control over vast stretches of its former territory. Specifically, the Versailles settlement required Germany to give Alsace-Lorraine to France; Eupen and Malmédy to Belgium; North Schleswig to Denmark; the Memel district to Lithuania; and West Prussia, Posen, portions of East Prussia, Outer Pomerania, and Upper Silesia to Poland. Furthermore, the peace treaty mandated the Saar region to the administrative control of the League of Nations and made Danzig a "free city" in which Germany had no jurisdiction. Germany was also prohibited from uniting with Austria.

In addition to boundary revisions, the Versailles treaty called for eliminating German fortifications, **demilitarizing** the Rhineland, and restricting Berlin's war-making capability. The army was limited to 100,000 volunteers and was barred from possessing tanks, military aircraft, and large caliber guns. The treaty also severely limited the navy, prohibiting Germany from building submarines and controlling the number and displacement of battleships, cruisers, destroyers, and torpedo boats. According to Article 231 of the treaty—also known as the "war guilt" clause—Germany was obliged to accept responsibility "for causing all the loss and damage to which the Allied and Associated Governments and their nationals have been subjected as a consequence of the war imposed upon them by the aggression of Germany and her allies." Moreover, as spelled out in Article 232, Germany was held responsible for paying huge monetary **reparations** "for all damage done to the civilian population of the Allied and Associated Powers and to their property." Although war indemnities had been imposed on defeated states in the past, they normally specified how much was owed and outlined a schedule for payments, so debtors knew their obligations. Contrary to this practice, the Versailles treaty did not establish a fixed sum or an installment plan; instead, a Reparation Commission handled these matters, arriving in May 1921 at a total liability of 132 billion gold marks (worth over $400 billion in today's dollars). Since Germany lacked the wherewithal to pay this astronomical amount, and France needed funds from Germany for reconstruction, the reparations issue soon became a major impediment to creating a stable postwar order, undermining Germany's fledgling democracy (see Box 2.1).

Box 2.1   You Decide

Imagine that you are French prime minister Raymond Poincaré in early January 1923. You are frustrated with repeated German defaults on reparations payments, which France needs in order to rebuild its battle-scarred economy and repay loans that were used to help finance the war. Furthermore, you are alarmed at the Treaty of Rapallo signed nine months earlier by Germany and the Russian Soviet Federative Socialist Republic, which reestablished economic relations between the two countries and, you suspect, provided the groundwork for military cooperation. With a growing population, industries intact, and hints that its postwar isolation may be ending, you worry that Germany could once again threaten your country.

France, you reckon, has two options. First, it could agree to a two-year moratorium on reparations payments in order to stabilize the German economy, a plan supported by the British government. While selecting this option would ease tensions with London, whose support is important for French security, you worry that it would undermine the Versailles settlement and reward Berlin for defaulting. A second option would be to militarily occupy the Ruhr valley, the heart of Germany's metallurgical industry and a valuable source of coal and iron ore. Military occupation would guarantee reparation payments by giving France control over Germany's mines and steel industry but at the cost of straining relations with Britain and inflaming German nationalism. If the Germans responded to the occupation by organizing strikes and other forms of passive resistance, the ensuing chaos could paralyze the German economy, jeopardize the flow of reparations, and weaken France's position in the postwar order.

You face a dilemma. Agreeing to a moratorium in reparations could improve relations with Britain, but if German payments stopped, they might never resume. On the other hand, occupying the Ruhr would allow France to extract restitution from Germany, but relations with Britain would sour if Germany resisted and its economy collapsed.

Which option would you choose?

Harsh terms were also included in the treaties imposed on Austria-Hungary, the Ottoman Empire, and Bulgaria. As Maps 2.1 and 2.2 display, the Austro-Hungarian Empire was dissolved. According to the Treaty of Saint-Germain (September 10, 1919), Austria was allowed to retain only 27 percent of its former territory, its army was limited to thirty thousand soldiers, and it was saddled with a large indemnity. Likewise, the Treaty of Trianon (June 4, 1920)

MAP 2.1 EUROPE ON THE EVE OF WORLD WAR I

When the First World War began, the Triple Entente of Britain, France, and Russia confronted the Central powers of Germany and Austria-Hungary, who were soon joined by the Ottoman Empire. Italy had been in a formal alliance with Germany and Austria-Hungary since 1882 but aligned with the Triple Entente in 1915 and opened a front against Austria-Hungary.

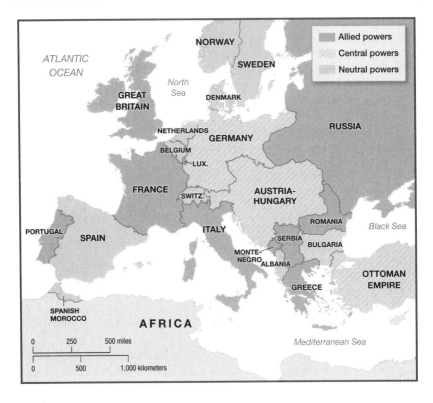

Source: Department of History, United States Military Academy.

required Hungary to surrender 71 percent of its territory, pay reparations to the Allies, and reduce its armed forces to thirty-five thousand soldiers. The Treaty of Neuilly (November 27, 1919) forced Bulgaria to cede four strategically important areas to Yugoslavia and its Aegean coastline to Greece. Similarly, the Treaty of Sèvres (August 10, 1920) dismantled the Ottoman Empire, with Greece gaining ground in Thrace and Asia Minor, and Arab provinces placed under League of Nations mandates.

MAP 2.2 EUROPE AFTER THE TREATY OF VERSAILLES

When the First World War ended, the winners redistributed territory at the expense of the defeated. Under the principle of self-determination, new states were carved out of the old German, Russian, and Austro-Hungarian empires.

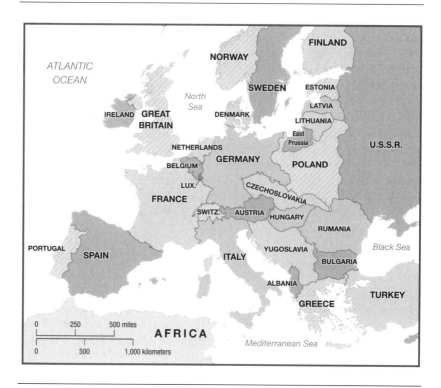

Problems With the Peace Settlement

The difficulty with the peace settlement was that it was neither harsh enough to remove Germany from the roster of great powers nor lenient enough to reintegrate it as an acceptable member of the great-power club. Although Germany was not subdivided into a kaleidoscope of smaller countries, it had been humiliated by the "war guilt" clause in the Versailles treaty, burdened with onerous reparations payments, and eventually lost control over the industrial area of the Ruhr Valley to occupying French and Belgian troops. On learning of the provisions in the treaty, the exiled Kaiser was said to have mused that the "war to end wars" had yielded a "peace to end peace."

By signing the treaty, Germany's new democratic government, the so-called Weimar Republic (named after the town where the first constitutional assembly occurred), was immediately discredited in the minds of many Germans. Successive German politicians and policymakers denounced the settlement and demanded revisions in its terms. It was not until late 1925, when a series of agreements were negotiated in the lakeside resort of Locarno, Switzerland, that the groundwork was prepared for Germany's return to great-power status and membership in the League of Nations.

In addition to crafting various **arbitration** agreements between Germany and its neighbors, the negotiators at the Locarno Conference assembled a Rhineland Security Pact in which Germany, France, and Belgium agreed to respect the borders outlined in the Versailles treaty, and Britain and Italy pledged to help repel any unprovoked attack that crossed these lines. The cooperative spirit at Locarno was then hailed as the dawn of a new era. However, the euphoria masked a serious problem: Germany had accepted its truncated frontiers in the west but not in the east. Even more troubling, while Britain was willing to guarantee territorial boundaries between Germany, France, and Belgium, it refused to make similar assurances to uphold the boundaries between Germany, Poland, Lithuania, Czechoslovakia, and other states chiseled out of the Russian and Austro-Hungarian empires. Thus, while Germany faced established great powers in the west, it bordered new, relatively weak powers in the east.

For those intoxicated by the heady atmosphere of Locarno, the League of Nations seemed to offer a path to safeguard vulnerable states. Under Article 10 of the Covenant, countries belonging to the league were obliged to respect and preserve "the territorial integrity and existing political independence of all Members of the League." Article 16 (1) called for isolating and economically punishing an aggressor, and Article 16 (2) sketched how military force would be brought to bear if these nonlethal sanctions proved insufficient. However, decisions to use force required unanimity, and diverging interests and inconsistent cooperation among the Allies made securing a unanimous vote difficult. Without a clear definition of "aggression" or a consensus on how to share the costs and risks of mounting an organized response to aggressors, league members failed to act as if any threat of war was "a matter of concern to the whole League," as proclaimed in Article 11 (1) of the Covenant. Just as the British at Locarno had been unwilling to guarantee the borders of the fragile new states in Central and Eastern Europe, league members felt no compulsion to take military action in places where they did not see compelling national interests.

Other difficulties for the league arose over membership. To the disappointment of its supporters, the league did not include all of the great powers. Ironically, the United States, which had pushed for collective security under Woodrow Wilson, refused to join the League of Nations. Taking an isolationist stance that portrayed the league as an entangling alliance, the U.S. Senate chose not to ratify the Treaty of Versailles. Whereas the United States refrained from becoming a member, Germany was excluded from the league until 1926 and the Soviet Union (the successor state to Tsarist Russia) until 1934. Without the full participation and complete collaboration of the great powers, Britain, France, Italy, and the small and middle-ranked members of the league lacked sufficient means for effective military action.

Skeptical of the capacity of the league to provide the framework for a new world order, France sought to buttress its security through more traditional means. On the one hand, it began constructing the Maginot Line, a chain of fortifications along its border with Germany. On the other hand, it forged alliances with Belgium, Poland, and the so-called Little Entente of Czechoslovakia, Rumania, and Yugoslavia. Recognizing that these military partnerships would not provide adequate assistance in the event of a showdown with Germany, France also searched for ways to establish defense ties with the United States. In a speech given on the tenth anniversary of the American entry into World War I, French foreign minister Aristide Briand raised the possibility of a bilateral treaty with the United States that disavowed the use of war in relations between the two countries. U.S. secretary of state Frank Kellogg saw Briand's offer as an attempt to lure the United States into an alliance with France. To avoid becoming ensnared in European affairs, he submitted a counterproposal: *All* nations should be invited to join France and the United States in a multilateral treaty repudiating war as an instrument of national policy. Because such an agreement would undermine the commitment of France's allies to take up arms on her behalf, he expected that Briand would let the matter drop. But having received the Nobel Peace Prize for his role in concluding the Locarno Treaties, Briand could hardly dismiss Kellogg's response, though he would suggest modifications that better supported France's security interests. After months of parrying French proposals to rework the draft treaty, an agreement was reached. On August 27, 1928, representatives from 15 states met in Paris to sign the General Treaty for the Renunciation of War, which became popularly known as the Kellogg-Briand Pact. Eventually 63 states became signatories to the treaty, which did not contain provisions for termination and thus was considered by many legal scholars of the day to be binding in perpetuity.

In summary, three elements of a new post–World War I order were now in place. Peace would be sustained not through traditional balance-of-power diplomacy but through collective security, pacific modes of redress, and the outlawry of war. As the 1920s drew to a close, a feeling of guarded optimism permeated many world capitals. In 1926, the League of Nations helped resolve a border dispute between Turkey and Iraq, which had been under British control after the defeat of the Ottoman Empire; the following year, the league resolved an armed clash between Greece and Bulgaria; and a year later, it defused a quarrel between Poland and Lithuania. The Permanent Court of International Justice, which had been established in The Hague under Article 14 of the League Covenant, also enjoyed modest success, rendering 15 advisory opinions and litigating 22 contentious cases by the end of the decade. During his Armistice Day address on November 11, 1929, U.S. president Herbert Hoover declared that the "outlook for a peaceable future is more bright than for half a century past." The great powers, in his estimation, were "becoming more genuinely inclined to peace."[11]

A WORLD IN DISARRAY

Believing that they had crossed what British foreign secretary Austen Chamberlain described as the dividing line between the years of war and peace, diplomats from the great powers turned their attention to the pressing issue of arms reductions. According to Article 8 of the League Covenant, "the maintenance of peace required the reduction of national armaments to the lowest point consistent with national safety." At the Washington Naval Conference of 1921–1922, the leaders of the United States, Britain, Japan, France, and Italy agreed to adjust the relative number and tonnage of capital ships in their fleets.

The time seemed ripe to negotiate reductions in land and air forces. How that might be accomplished divided the league's members: Some states asserted that disarmament would engender greater security; others argued that security must precede disarmament. Disagreement also existed over what types of armaments and military personnel should be limited. In December 1925, the League Council appointed a commission to work through these preliminary matters in preparation for a World Disarmament Conference.

After years of diplomatic squabbling, representatives from 61 states arrived in Geneva during February 1932 to open the conference. Two intertwined developments complicated the negotiations. First, the world economic depression, which began with the October 1929 crash on the New York Stock Exchange, reached its nadir as the conference commenced. Highly dependent on foreign capital, the German economy unraveled as investment funds dissipated and creditors called in their short-term loans. Unemployment spiked and public confidence in the fledgling Weimar Republic plummeted, furnishing an opportunity for demagogues and armed militias to disrupt national politics.

The second development arose when Adolf Hitler, the leader of the National Socialist German Workers' (or Nazi) Party, which had become the largest party in the German parliament with 37.3 percent of the vote in the July 1932 election, was named to the chancellorship in January 1933. Germany, with its military limited by the Treaty of Versailles, had consistently argued for parity. Unless other great powers reduced their armaments to its level, Germany claimed it would be justified in upgrading to their level. Wary of Hitler's intentions, France balked at any proposals that might reduce its strength or license German rearmament. With negotiations deadlocked, Germany withdrew from the conference, announced its resignation from the League of Nations, and soon repudiated the military clauses of the Versailles treaty.

Roughly a decade after the Treaty of Versailles had been signed, war clouds began gathering over Europe. Signs of the approaching storm appeared in the failure of the World Disarmament Conference and the inability of the League of Nations to respond effectively to the 1931 Japanese invasion of Manchuria, the 1932 Chaco War between Bolivia and Paraguay, and Italy's 1935 attack on Ethiopia. Operating on a miniscule budget and without members who were inclined to forsake their individual interests for the common good, the League of Nations proved unable to forestall another hegemonic war.

Whereas collective security was based on the expectation of great-power collaboration, the immediate postwar world was marked by disarray. In addition to a defeated great power yearning to revise the structure of the global system (Germany), it contained victorious great powers that differed over how to preserve the status quo (Britain and France), other victors that were dissatisfied with their circumstances (Italy and Japan), and still others that were either excluded (Soviet Union) or abstained from participating in multilateral action (United States). Given these rifts, collective security's vision of great powers acting in unison seemed far-fetched. As Marshal Ferdinand Foch presciently observed, rather than delivering peace, the postwar world order would only yield a twenty-year armistice.

The Great War of 1914–1918 marked the end of an era. War was considered permissible in the balance-of-power system of the previous two and a half centuries so long as it was fought for narrow objectives and did not threaten the standing of any great powers. Cultural connections, technological limitations on firepower and mobility, and the crisscrossing of marriages among the royal and aristocratic families of Europe had further tempered the scope and intensity of warfare. Europeans believed that their countries belonged to a wider commonwealth. Rather than being a "confused heap of detached pieces," explained the eighteenth-century Swiss jurist and philosopher Emer de Vattel, European states formed "a kind of Republic of which members—each independent, but all linked together by the ties of common interest—unite for the maintenance of order and liberty."[12]

Unfortunately, things had changed by the end of the Great War. World politics came to be seen as a **zero-sum game** played by diabolical enemies. Whereas earlier diplomats would have interpreted the war as a tragic but inherent property of international life, the authors of the Versailles treaty framed it in moral terms, not just blaming the leaders of the defeated nations but their entire populations, holding them collectively responsible for the evil that had occurred. When work on the draft of a peace treaty began, Wilson himself shifted from magnanimity toward the Germans to the opinion that they had acted dishonorably and therefore would not be allowed to participate in the peace conference. Nor would they be welcomed into the League of Nations until they had redeemed themselves.

In retrospect, the vindictive nature of the Versailles settlement diluted the treaty's legitimacy in London and Washington, weakening its ability to underpin a new world order. Secretary of State Robert Lansing, a member of the U.S. delegation to the peace conference, reflected the opinions of many of the younger British and American delegates when he described his response to the treaty as "one of disappointment, of regret, and of depression."[13] Demeaning an adversary's national character, while useful for mobilizing the home front during a war, is a daunting obstacle to building workable arrangements for conducting great-power politics after the guns fall silent. To muzzle the losing side in armistice and peace treaty negotiations is to deny it a stake in the future world order; to deny it a stake is to ignore the possibility that yesterday's enemy may be needed as tomorrow's friend. So long as a country is not dealing with an utterly ruthless, sinister opponent, restraint and a readiness for reconciliation can encourage a positive spiral of tension-reducing reciprocation. Shared interests may not be immediately apparent, but ordinarily there are aspects of any peace settlement whereby the victors can satisfy some concerns of the vanquished without damaging significant interests of their own. Victors who couple firmness regarding their own interests with fairness toward the interests of the losing side encourage defeated powers to work within the postwar order.

Owing to the failure of the victorious great powers to construct a durable peace settlement after World War I, renewed emphasis was placed on building a framework of world order following World War II. In Chapter 3 we will examine what the victors did differently and whether they were any more successful than the delegates to the Versailles peace conference.

KEY TERMS

absolute gains 32

arbitration 42

arms race 26

balance-of-power theory 30

collective security 32

demilitarizing 38

isolationist policy 37

levels of analysis 22

nationalism 24

neutralization 30

realpolitik 36

regime 34

relative gains 32

reparations 38

self-determination 34

spheres of influence 30

ultimatum 21

zero-sum game 45

World War II and the Birth of the Liberal Order

3

The settlement of the Czechoslovak problem which has now been achieved is, in my view, only the prelude to a larger settlement in which all Europe may find peace.

—NEVILLE CHAMBERLAIN,

BRITISH PRIME MINISTER

On September 30, 1938, a British Airways Lockheed 14 carrying Prime Minister Neville Chamberlain landed at Heston airfield west of London. After disembarking, Chamberlain proudly showed a document to journalists and well-wishers gathered near the plane. Earlier that morning, the prime minister informed the group that he had reached an agreement with German chancellor Adolf Hitler to resolve all outstanding disputes through diplomacy. In Chamberlain's recounting of what had happened, the two leaders signed a pledge to disavow the use of military force because they ardently believed that their countries should never again take up arms against one another. Speaking to a crowd outside 10 Downing Street later that day, the prime minister declared, "I believe it is peace for our time."

Chamberlain had met with Hitler, French prime minister Édouard Daladier, and Italian prime minister Benito Mussolini in Munich to defuse a crisis over Czechoslovakia, one of the successor states carved out of the Austro-Hungarian Empire after the Great War of 1914–1918. Roughly 30 percent of its people were ethnic Germans, living primarily among the Sudeten Mountains, which are adjacent to Germany's eastern frontier. According to Hitler, the Sudeten Germans were being oppressed by the government in Prague. Invoking the Wilsonian principle of self-determination, he demanded that the Sudetenland be ceded to Germany and threatened to annex the territory by force if necessary.

Although Czechoslovakia had a well-trained and suitably equipped army, it still needed help to fend off a German attack. France had promised to defend Czechoslovakia but was unwilling to act without British support, and Great Britain did not wish to risk war over what Prime Minister Chamberlain characterized as "a quarrel in a far-away country between people of whom we know nothing."[1] Pointing to what he touted as the success of the 1935 Anglo-German Naval Agreement, which limited German maritime forces to 35 percent of those possessed by Britain, Chamberlain assumed that it was also possible to reach an accommodation with Hitler over the Sudetenland. If Britain acknowledged Germany's grievances with the Versailles settlement and helped alleviate those that were legitimate, he expected Hitler would henceforth behave reasonably. "If only we could find some peaceful solution of this Czechoslovakian question," Chamberlain mused, "I should myself feel that the way was open again for a further effort for a general appeasement."[2]

At the Munich conference—which representatives from Czechoslovakia were not invited to attend—the participants ceded the Sudetenland to Germany and pressured the Czechs into acquiescing. Altering Czechoslovakia's borders, Chamberlain reasoned, was an acceptable price for maintaining peace on the continent, so long as the process unfolded without violence. Although Hitler had sworn that he had no other territorial ambitions beyond assimilating the Sudeten Germans into the fatherland, less than six months later his army occupied the rest of Czechoslovakia and he began making demands on Lithuania and Poland. Soon a conflict even more horrific than the Great War of 1914–1919 erupted, resulting in the deaths of 60 million people worldwide. According to Winston Churchill, who succeeded Neville Chamberlain as prime minister, the conflict was unnecessary: "There was never a war more easy to stop than that which has just wrecked what was left of the world from the previous struggle."[3] If Churchill was correct, why did the war occur? How did the victors' understanding of the war's origins influence the system of world order that the victors struggled to put into place once the fighting ended? What lessons did they learn about building world order from the failures of the Versailles settlement and the League of Nations?

....

THE ORIGINS OF THE SECOND WORLD WAR

Germany's defeat in the First World War and its humiliation under the Treaty of Versailles did not extinguish its aspirations for global status and influence. On the contrary, they intensified them. Beginning in the 1930s, Germany, joined by Italy and Japan, began pursuing foreign policies that pitted them against an unlikely combination of great powers who united despite their incompatible ideologies—communism in the case of the Soviet Union and democratic capitalism in the case of Britain, France, and the United States. To appreciate how the horrific clash between these two coalitions shaped the structure of world order during the second half of the twentieth century, we must first recall the atmosphere that prevailed prior to the onset of the war.

As described in the previous chapter, following Germany's surrender in 1918, a constituent assembly meeting in the city of Weimar drafted a constitution that replaced the old imperial system with a federal republic containing a president (head of state), a chancellor (head of government), and a parliament based on proportional representation. Many Germans had little enthusiasm for the so-called Weimar Republic. Not only was the new government linked in their minds to the demeaning Treaty of Versailles, but it also suffered from being associated with the country's economic woes. Well before the 1929 New York stock market crash, Germans endured unemployment and monetary turmoil. Once panic seized Wall Street, their financial situation deteriorated further as jittery Americans began recalling short-term loans to Germany and erecting **tariff** and **nontariff barriers** to foreign imports. Liberal economists, echoing Woodrow Wilson's call in his Fourteen Points speech for removing barriers to free trade, insisted that restrictions on international commerce, such as the U.S. Tariff Act of 1930 (also known as the Smoot-Hawley Tariff Act, after its sponsors, Senator Reed Smoot of Utah and Representative Willis Hawley of Oregon), would hinder economic recovery. On the one hand, the cost of imports from foreign producers would increase, raising prices for both consumers purchasing commodities from abroad and firms relying on foreign parts and equipment in their manufacturing process. On the other hand, the market for exports would decline as other countries retaliated by imposing countervailing tariffs on goods imported from abroad. Despite these warnings, the appeal of **protectionism** grew as the Great Depression worsened. Government officials imagined they could build strong, self-sufficient economies by subsidizing strategically targeted enterprises and protecting these companies from foreign competition. With country after country adopting **beggar-thy-neighbor policies**, trade contracted, businesses failed, and jobs disappeared. Caught in the throes of a deepening economic crisis, many Germans sought deliverance in the promises of demagogues on the far ends of the political spectrum. In the parliamentary elections of 1932, over half of the electorate supported extremist parties, the largest of which was the Nazi Party (or National Socialist German Workers' Party).

In an attempt to relieve the mounting political stress, President Paul von Hindenburg appointed the Nazi leader Adolf Hitler to the chancellorship on January 30, 1933, and scheduled new parliamentary elections. Less than a month later, the Reichstag (Parliament) building burned down under mysterious circumstances. Hitler used the fire to justify an emergency edict allowing him to suspend civil liberties and smother his political adversaries. Once all meaningful political opposition had been silenced, Nazi legislators passed an enabling act that suspended the constitution and granted Hitler dictatorial power.

In his 1924 book *Mein Kampf* ("My Struggle"), Hitler had proclaimed a racist ideology that vilified non-Aryan people. He urged Germany to recover territories lost under the Treaty of Versailles, absorb Germans living in neighboring countries, and colonize Eastern Europe. Conquered lands would be turned into vassal states, providing raw materials and slave labor for the "thousand-year" Reich.

During his initial years in power, however, Hitler cultivated a pacific image, signing a nonaggression pact with Poland, a naval arms limitation agreement with Great Britain, and suggesting a willingness to enter into other accords that would preserve world peace. Yet before long, as outlined in Table 3.1, the goals originally

TABLE 3.1 **MAJOR EVENTS DURING THE DECADE PRECEDING WORLD WAR II**

Date	Event
1929	New York stock market crash
1930	British and French forces evacuate the Rhineland; President Hoover (United States) approves Smoot-Hawley Tariff Act
1931	Manchurian crisis: After seizing Mukden and the surrounding towns in China, Japan proceeds to occupy all of Manchuria
1932	In protest of the Japanese invasion of Manchuria and the creation of the puppet state of Manchukuo, the Stimson Doctrine declares that the United States will not recognize territorial changes made by armed force
1933	Hitler becomes German chancellor; Germany and Japan withdraw from the League of Nations; United States recognizes the Soviet Union
1934	German-Polish nonaggression agreement; Soviet Union admitted to the League of Nations
1935	Ethiopian crisis: Italy invades Ethiopia; Germany repudiates military clauses of the Treaty of Versailles and rearms; the Saar is incorporated into Germany following plebiscite
1936	Germany remilitarizes Rhineland; outbreak of Spanish Civil War; Germany and Japan sign the Anti-Comintern Pact aimed at containing international communism
1937	Italy withdraws from the League of Nations and joins the German-Japanese Anti-Comintern Pact, forming the Rome-Berlin-Tokyo Axis; Sino-Japanese war begins: Japanese attack Shanghai and advance up Yangtze River to seize Nanking
1938	Germany annexes Austria; Munich crisis: Germany annexes the Sudetenland of Czechoslovakia; sporadic hostilities erupt between Japan and the Soviet Union along the Manchurian frontier; Japan seizes Canton
1939	March 15: Germany occupies the regions of Bohemia and Moravia in Czechoslovakia and declares Slovakia a protectorate March 23: Germany annexes Lithuanian city of Memel April 7: Italy occupies Albania April 28: Germany disavows nonaggression agreement with Poland May 22: Germany and Italy sign military agreement August 23: Nazi-Soviet Nonaggression Pact signed September 1: Germany invades Poland September 3: Great Britain and France declare war on Germany

identified in *Mein Kampf* began appearing on his foreign policy agenda. In 1935, he repudiated the military clauses of the Treaty of Versailles; in 1936, he ordered troops into the demilitarized Rhineland; in March 1938, he annexed Austria; and in September 1938, he demanded control over the Sudetenland, a region in Czechoslovakia containing ethnic Germans. At a conference convened in Munich to address the Sudeten German question, British prime minister Neville Chamberlain, as described above, adopted a policy of **appeasement**, believing that agreeing to Hitler's demands would satisfy the dictator's appetite for further German expansionism.

Instead of satisfying Hitler, appeasement encouraged him to press for further revisions in the international status quo. He was joined in this effort by the authoritarian governments that ruled Japan and Italy. The former invaded Manchuria in 1931 and China proper in 1937; the latter attacked Ethiopia in 1935 and Albania in 1939. Furthermore, both Germany and Italy intervened in the Spanish Civil War on the side of the fascists, led by General Francisco Franco.

These acts of aggression paved the way for the century's second massive great-power war. After Germany occupied the rest of Czechoslovakia in March 1939, Britain and France formed an alliance to protect the next likely victim—Poland. They also opened negotiations with Moscow in hopes of enticing the Soviet Union to join them, although their laggardly efforts made little headway. Soviet leader Joseph Stalin remained leery of the capitalists in London and Paris. Given the reluctance of Britain and France to defend Czechoslovakia, and since neither great power was in a geographic position to offer Poland timely military assistance, Stalin doubted that Germany would be deterred. To buy time and prepare for what he saw as an inevitable showdown with the Nazi regime, Stalin signed a nonaggression pact with Germany on August 23, 1939. Certain that the Western democracies would not intervene without Soviet assistance, Hitler invaded Poland on September 1, 1939, launching a devastating air and mechanized land attack called the *blitzkrieg* (lightning war), and the Soviet Union, trusting Hitler's nonaggression pledge, launched an ill-fated invasion of Finland. Britain and France, honoring their promise to defend the Poles, declared war on Germany two days later. World War II had begun.

The war expanded rapidly. Hitler next turned his forces loose on the Balkans, North Africa, and westward. Powerful armored units invaded Norway and raced through Denmark, Belgium, Luxembourg, and the Netherlands. They swept around France's defensive barrier, the Maginot Line, and forced the British to evacuate its large military expeditionary force from the French beaches at Dunkirk. Paris itself fell in June 1940, and in the months that followed, the German air force pounded Britain in an attempt to force it into submission. When the Luftwaffe failed to prevail over the Royal Air Force, Hitler shifted his energies eastward, ordering his troops to attack the Soviet Union in June 1941 under the assumption that a quick victory over the USSR would isolate the British and force them to capitulate.

Germany's military successes provided an opportunity for Japan to move against British, French, and Dutch colonies in Asia, with the aim of replacing Western influence with a Greater East Asia Co-Prosperity Sphere under Tokyo's leadership. Japan followed its earlier conquests of Manchuria and eastern China with pressure on the Vichy French government to allow it to establish military bases in Indochina (now Vietnam, Laos, and Cambodia), from which the vital petroleum and mineral resources of Southeast Asia could be threatened. Concerned that the United States would try to thwart its ambitions, Japan launched a surprise attack on the U.S. naval base at Pearl Harbor, Hawaii, on December 7, 1941. Almost immediately, Germany declared war on the United States. Over the next six months, Japan occupied the Philippines, Malaya, Burma, and the Dutch East Indies (now Indonesia). The military challenges posed by Japan and Germany ended U.S. isolationism as U.S. President Franklin D. Roosevelt forged an alliance with Britain and the Soviet Union to oppose the Axis powers.

In summary, the proximate causes of World War II can be found at the *individual level of analysis*. Adolf Hitler's truculent personality and aggressive tactics ignited a firestorm. As Hitler admitted after Europe burst into flames, "I did not raise the army in order *not* to use it."[4] Astonishingly, many political leaders in the Western democracies thought otherwise, remaining complacent in the face of German rearmament and Hitler's insistence that the status quo was intolerable. Those who remembered the rapid escalation of hostilities during the summer of 1914 and the subsequent horrors of trench warfare were hesitant to respond to Hitler's actions in ways that might incite another conflagration. Trusting that the offensive/defensive balance in military technology favored the defense, they concluded that appeasement was preferable to confrontation.

Several remote, underlying factors also contributed to the onset of war. At the *domestic level of analysis*, internal economic crises, the demise of democratic governance, and a climate of hypernationalism in Germany provided the conditions within which Hitler could rise to power. At the *systemic level of analysis*, the harsh terms imposed by the Treaty of Versailles, the political fragmentation of Central Europe, the failure of the League of Nations, and the collapse of the world economic system created the conditions that made world affairs ripe for another armed conflict among the great powers.

During the war's initial phase, Germany and Japan enjoyed a series of spectacular military successes. The longer combat continued, however, the more difficult it would be for the Axis powers to prevail. Not only did they lack sufficient resources to fight a protracted war on multiple fronts but they also faced opponents that possessed overwhelming superior troop strength and a greater capacity to manufacture armaments. Although the Allies were far from confident of victory, almost immediately they began to search for principles to underpin a postwar order, recognizing that a Versailles-type settlement would be counterproductive. In particular, they were guided by their understanding of both the proximate and remote causes of the war's origins. Rather than trying to appease Adolf Hitler, the Allies considered what the great powers might have done to prevent his acts of aggression. Equally important, they asked how an individual such as Hitler could have come to power in the first place and how he was able to exploit the circumstances of the interwar years to implement his expansionist plans. In their estimation, a durable postwar order required a strategy for containing bellicose dictators like Hitler as well as a set of rules and institutions to prevent such aggressive leaders from surfacing in the years ahead.

PLANNING FOR A POSTWAR WORLD ORDER

The United States and Great Britain were especially cognizant of the need to work together. Four months prior to America's official entry in the war, U.S. president Franklin D. Roosevelt and British prime minister Winston Churchill agreed to the 1941 Atlantic Charter while meeting on a ship off the coast of Newfoundland. Beyond restating many of Woodrow Wilson's ideals—free trade, democratic elections, self-determination, and freedom of the seas—the document affirmed the two leaders' desire to establish a new system of international security once the war ended.

Determining what type of government would be installed in the Axis countries after their defeat was critical to the successful operation of such a system. Following Germany's invasion of the Soviet Union, the prickly question of whether fascism should be replaced by democratic capitalism or autocratic communism threatened to divide Washington and London from Moscow. A partial solution was reached when the Allies provisionally accepted the right of all peoples to choose the type of government under which citizens would live, so long as this principle did not permit another Hitlerite regime from gaining power. The Allies created working committees to coordinate each party's understanding of this principle and to spell out their mutual responsibilities. Despite the outwardly cordial atmosphere of these meetings, uncertainties swirled over the long-term intentions of the "Big Three." Roosevelt insisted that the ideals of the Atlantic Charter were universal; Churchill maintained that they applied to Europe, not the territories of the British Empire; and Stalin suggested that even in Europe they must be adapted to the unique circumstances and historic peculiarities of each country. Tamping down mutual suspicions became a constant challenge. If one party broke ranks and negotiated a separate peace with the Axis powers, its defection would undermine the security of the remaining Allies. To assuage this concern, the United States, Great Britain, the Soviet Union, and twenty-three other states signed the United Nations Declaration on January 1, 1942, which promised to proceed with a common front employing all available resources to defeat Germany, Italy, and Japan, and pledged that no signatory would make a separate peace with their mutual adversaries.

As the prospects for victory in Europe and the Pacific began to improve, the Allies stepped up their consultations, determined not to repeat the failure associated with the Versailles settlement. The American naval victory over Japan in the Battle of Midway (June 4–6, 1942), British success against the Germans in North Africa in the Battle of El Alamein (October 23–November 4, 1942), and Russian triumphs in the Battles of Moscow (October 2, 1941–January 7, 1942), Stalingrad (August 23, 1942–February 2, 1943), and Kursk (July 5–August 23, 1943) injected a bracing dose of confidence into the Allied cause. Another boost to morale occurred during the summer of 1943 when Sicily fell to Anglo-American forces, Benito Mussolini was ousted from power, and Italy's new government signed an armistice with the Allies. (German troops occupying the country continued fighting, however.) Although officials in the White House, on Downing Street, and within the Kremlin differed over the next military moves to take against the remaining members of the Axis, unlike their predecessors in the First World War, they agreed not to wait until the fighting was over to plan for a future world order.

Table 3.2 describes the various meetings that were held to build a consensus on how to restore order to the postwar world. Initially, common ground appeared to exist in the American, British, and Soviet positions, with the 1943 **summit conference** in Tehran representing the pinnacle of collaboration among the three great powers. Upon returning from the conference, President Roosevelt told a national radio audience, "I got along fine with Marshal Stalin. . . . I believe that we are going to get along very well with him and the Russian people—very well indeed."[5] At the Yalta Conference fourteen months later, Stalin echoed Roosevelt's optimism. According to James Byrnes, director of the U.S. Office of War Mobilization, Stalin had been lavish in his praise of the United States; in fact, "Joe was the life of the party."[6] Yet the vague promises of continued unity voiced at these summits concealed many divisive issues, which would result in the party ending with an acute political hangover.

TABLE 3.2 MAJOR ALLIED CONFERENCES AND DECLARATIONS DURING WORLD WAR II

Date	Conference	Issues Considered and Declarations Pronounced
June 12, 1941	London Inter-Allied Meeting	Representatives from Great Britain, Canada, Australia, New Zealand, and South Africa join with the nine governments in exile to sign the Declaration of St. James' Palace, which promises mutual assistance against Germany and cooperation in building enduring peace
August 9–12, 1941	Atlantic Conference	President Franklin Roosevelt and Prime Minister Winston Churchill meet in Placentia Bay, Newfoundland; the Atlantic Charter promulgated, providing a statement of war aims and guiding principles for the Allied powers fighting the Rome-Berlin-Tokyo Axis

(Continued)

TABLE 3.2

Date	Conference	Issues Considered and Declarations Pronounced
December 22–January 14, 1941	Arcadia Conference	Roosevelt and Churchill, along with their senior military advisers, meet in Washington, D.C., to discuss strategy; priority given to the European theater over the Pacific theater, with the further decisions to base U.S. bombers in England and invade North Africa; Declaration of the United Nations issued
January 14–24, 1943	Casablanca Conference	Roosevelt and Churchill call for unconditional surrender of Axis states and agree on an invasion of Sicily and Italy
August 11–24, 1943	Quebec Conference	Roosevelt and Churchill attempt to resolve differences over coordinating military campaign in Italy with a planned invasion of France
October 18–November 11, 1943	Moscow Conference	Joint Four-Nation declaration: governments of the United States, United Kingdom, Soviet Union, and China recognize necessity of creating an international organization to maintain peace and security
November 22–26, 1943	Cairo Conference	Roosevelt, Churchill, and Chinese leader Chiang Kai-shek discuss the war against Japan; Cairo Declaration asserts that Japan would be stripped of all territories that it had seized
November 28–December 1, 1943	Tehran Conference	Roosevelt, Churchill, and Soviet leader Joseph Stalin discuss opening a "second front" in Western Europe
December 2–7, 1943	Second Cairo Conference	Roosevelt and Churchill discuss planned invasion of Normandy
July 1–22, 1944	Bretton Woods Conference	Rules formulated to govern international economic relations; creation of International Monetary Fund (IMF) and International Bank for Reconstruction and Development (IBRD)
August 21–October 7, 1944	Dumbarton Oaks Conference	Proposal for structure of the United Nations drafted

(Continued)

TABLE 3.2 (CONTINUED)

Date	Conference	Issues Considered and Declarations Pronounced
September 11–16, 1944	Second Quebec Conference	Roosevelt and Churchill discuss postwar occupation of Germany and planned invasion of Japan
February 4–11, 1945	Yalta Conference	Roosevelt, Churchill, and Stalin discuss holding war crime trials and the division of Germany into four zones of occupation (U.S., British, French, and Soviet) under unified control commission; Germany slated to undergo demilitarization, denazification, democratization, and decentralization; Polish borders modified; Soviet Union agrees to enter the war against Japan; Declaration on Liberated Europe issued, promising free elections in Eastern Europe after the war
April 25–June 26, 1945	San Francisco Conference	United Nations Charter endorsed; 51 countries become original members of the UN
July 17–August 3, 1945	Potsdam Conference	President Harry Truman, Churchill (later replaced by Clement Attlee), and Stalin meet to implement agreements reached at Yalta on future status of Germany, Poland, and Eastern Europe; bargaining occurs over reparations to be exacted from Germany; Potsdam Declaration calls for unconditional surrender by Japan

Growing Discord Among the Allies

On April 30, 1945, with Soviet forces making their final assault on Berlin, Adolf Hitler committed suicide in his bunker under the Reich Chancellery. A week later, at Allied headquarters in Reims, France, General Alfred Jodl, chief of operations of the German Armed Forces High Command, signed a document agreeing to the complete and unconditional surrender of the Nazi regime's military forces. On August 15, immediately following the devastating atomic bombings of Hiroshima and Nagasaki, Emperor Hirohito announced Japan's unconditional surrender, which was made official on September 2 in a formal ceremony held on the USS *Missouri* in Tokyo Bay. History's most destructive war was finally over; however, many difficult choices remained (see Box 3.1).

Box 3.1   You Decide

In early February 1945, U.S. president Franklin Roosevelt, British prime minister Winston Churchill, and Chairman of the Soviet Union's Council of People's Commissars Joseph Stalin met at Livadia Palace in Yalta, the Crimean seaside retreat of former Tsar Nicholas II. With victory over Nazi Germany in sight, the three leaders would now determine the fate of their common enemy.

Each of the allies had paid a high cost to defeat Hitler, but the Soviet Union's losses were staggering. Estimates place the number of Red Army deaths at approximately 8 million, with almost 19 million civilian deaths. The material destruction was similarly appalling. According to Soviet records, 1,700 cities and towns were demolished, along with 70,000 villages, 31,000 industrial enterprises, over 40,000 miles of railroad track, and some 1,300 bridges. During the war, Stalin acknowledged that whereas Hitler's regime could be destroyed, it was impossible to eliminate the German nation. Thus, the question facing Stalin at Yalta was how to prevent Germany from threatening the Soviet Union in the future.

Two alternatives for reducing Germany's military potential had been circulating among the allies prior to the Yalta conference. One option was dismemberment. The Rhineland, Bavaria, Saxony, and other regions could be reconstituted as independent countries. The advantage of dividing Germany into several smaller states was that none of them could pose a danger to Soviet security. The major drawback was that dissecting Germany might fuel resentment among ardent nationalists, thereby once again raising the odds of a potentially dangerous revanchist movement arising in the decades ahead. Another possible problem was the complexity of extracting reparations from multiple German states rather than a single vanquished country. Still another difficulty concerned the British, who would likely resist the idea as they lobbied the Americans to back their traditional policy of an equilibrium among the continent's great powers, with a resurrected France and a reformed Germany counterbalancing the Soviet Union.

The second option was occupation. Germany would be denazified, lose territory east of the Oder and Neisse Rivers (to Poland), and be partitioned into British, American, Soviet, and French zones of occupation. Once a new German government was established—presumably within the next five years—the final peace treaty would be concluded. From Moscow's perspective, gaining control over an occupation zone offered several benefits. First, it would provide an opportunity to commandeer German industrial equipment in compensation for the damage that had devastated the Soviet economy during the war. Second, it would give Moscow a free hand in recruiting Germans into communist-sponsored, pro-Soviet political organizations.

(Continued)

(Continued)

Third, given the burden of dealing with economic turmoil and a tide of refugees, Britain, France, and the United States might eventually see their occupation zones as a liability and withdraw their troops, furnishing Soviet operatives an opening to penetrate western Germany and influence its political evolution. The downside was the possibility that the Western democracies might combine their occupation zones into a new German state that would align with them against Soviet Union. However, such a merger would be less dangerous than Hitler's Germany because it would not include the eastern region occupied by the Soviet Union.

If you were Joseph Stalin, would you support dismemberment or occupation?

The victors now faced a monumental challenge: How could they construct a peace plan that each of them would accept? Unfortunately, the challenge proved beyond the Allies' capacity, as their mutual suspicions and conflicting aspirations pushed them in divergent directions. Stalin, for example, suspected that his wartime partners delayed opening a second front in France in order to allow the Germans to inflict maximum damage upon the Soviet Union. Churchill, he once observed, "is the kind who, if you don't watch him, will slip a kopeck out of your pocket." Roosevelt is different, he continued, "He dips in his hand only for bigger coins."[7] Western leaders, cognizant of the political repression and brutal purges that Stalin had unleashed on Russian society, had deep misgivings about their ally. Churchill, for example, saw Stalin as a diabolical ruler, but one with whom he could make common cause against Hitler. Commenting on Britain's diplomatic overtures toward the Soviet autocrat after the Nazi invasion of the Soviet Union, Churchill famously quipped, "If Hitler invaded Hell I would make at least favorable reference to the Devil in the House of Commons."[8]

That differences among wary allies should emerge over the precise terms of the peace settlement was not surprising, because changes in global circumstances historically have preceded redefinitions of interests and allegiances. When the American and Russian armies met at the Elbe River less than a week before Hitler's suicide, their common military threat had been destroyed, undermining incentives for subsequent cooperation. Long-gestating apprehensions in Washington, London, and Moscow soon hardened into policy disagreements over the future of the postwar world.

In July 1945, the United States, now represented by President Harry Truman after Franklin Roosevelt's sudden death in April, met with Churchill (who, due to the results of a general election in Britain, was replaced midway through the conference by Clement Attlee) and Stalin in Potsdam, a former residence of Prussian kings located on the outskirts of war-ravaged Berlin. Less cordial than the previous Big Three summit conferences in Tehran and Yalta, the Potsdam conference postponed many important decisions pending a final peace treaty, which was expected to be concluded within the next few years. As agreed at Yalta, Germany's territorial annexations were nullified, Germany and Austria were partitioned into four occupation zones (U.S., British, French, and Soviet), as were Berlin and Vienna, their capital cities (see Map 3.1). The primary issues the three powers took up were reparations, Poland's borders, and Soviet participation

MAP 3.1 EUROPE AFTER WORLD WAR II

The Allied victory in the European theater of the Second World War changed the geostrategic landscape. Germany and Austria were divided into four occupation zones; Poland received a portion of eastern Germany in compensation for the loss of land to the Soviet Union; and the Soviet Union also gained territory from the Baltic states of Estonia, Latvia, and Lithuania as well as from Finland, Czechoslovakia, and Romania.

in the war against Japan. After hard bargaining, some compromises were reached. Each power would take reparations from their own occupation zones, with the Western Allies allotting 15 percent of the industrial equipment from their zones to the Soviet Union in exchange for agricultural goods from its zone, and another 10 percent provided to the Soviet Union in recognition of the massive destruction it suffered during the war. To compensate for land in eastern Poland absorbed by the Soviet Union, Germany was forced to relinquish its eastern territory as the German border with Poland was moved westward. Finally, together with China, the United States and Great Britain demanded that Japan surrender unconditionally or face prompt and utter annihilation.

The issue of Poland's future proved particularly vexing. The Red Army liberated Poland; therefore, Stalin asserted, it was appropriate to impose a government in Warsaw of his choosing. After all, the United States and Great Britain backed Western-style governments in Italy and Belgium, countries that they liberated. A "friendly" government in Warsaw, Stalin argued, would be a buffer against a resurgent Germany, which he expected to materialize within the next fifteen years.

For the Western Allies, however, a communist Poland would call into question the very rationale for the war: Hostilities had begun when Britain and France came to Poland's aid after Hitler's invasion. What would have been accomplished if Poland was saved from the Nazis only to become a Soviet satellite? How could the Western Allies ignore a blatant contravention of the principle of free elections that they had endorsed in the Atlantic Charter and at Yalta in the Declaration on Liberated Europe? Churchill, who had once floated the idea of dismembering Germany, now speculated that a politically reformed Germany was needed to help Britain and France balance against the possibility of future Soviet expansion, especially if the United States, as Roosevelt had suggested at Yalta, removed its troops from Europe within two years after the war's conclusion. Reducing German strength to compensate a communist Poland would make postwar balancing difficult, Churchill concluded, and thus warned against stuffing "the Polish goose so full of German food."[9]

Divergence in the Treatment of Germany

During the final phase of the war, the Allies adopted four principles to govern their treatment of Germany. First, they would demilitarize Germany, insisting on complete disarmament and the dismantling of German industry so that the country's scientific and engineering talents could not be used for weapons production. Second, they would eradicate the remnants of Nazi ideology, holding German leaders accountable for war crimes at a special court established at Nuremberg. Third, they would undertake a program of democratization to eliminate militaristic doctrines and prevent the rise of autocratic leaders. Finally, they would promote decentralization to inhibit the concentration of economic power in monopolistic arrangements. Although the United States, Great Britain, and the Soviet Union differed over how these principles would be implemented, efforts were made to smooth over any disagreements in the belief that Allied unity was a prerequisite for eradicating the last vestiges of Hitler's regime.

Yet once the Axis powers had been defeated, the façade of Allied unity started to crumble. Discord emerged soon after the fighting ended. In a speech delivered in Moscow on February 9, 1946, Stalin blamed the war on world capitalism and accentuated the virtues of Soviet communism. Speaking in Fulton, Missouri, a few weeks later, Churchill warned that an "iron curtain" had descended across Europe, placing the central and eastern regions of the continent under the Kremlin's control. In this uneasy environment, American foreign policymakers began modifying their thinking about a retributive approach to the peace settlement. The signal of the U.S. change of heart was conveyed dramatically by Secretary of State James F. Byrnes during comments made in Stuttgart on September 6, 1946. U.S. policy toward Germany, he informed the audience, would emphasize rehabilitation and reconciliation, with the United States assisting in Germany's reconstruction.

Nowhere were the consequences of the wartime partnership's erosion more evident than in the creation of the Federal Republic of Germany (West Germany) and the German Democratic Republic (East Germany). Setting up two separate states was not a part of the victors' original peace plan. They had agreed to treat Germany as a single state, with an Allied Control Council in charge. However, the decision to divide Germany into four zones of occupation, with the military commanders-in-chief of each victor given complete administrative authority and each occupying power controlling reparations in its respective zone, had the unintended consequence of preventing any treatment of Germany as a single unit. Four years later, as friction among the victors increased, the United States, Britain, and France combined their zones in the west to form the Federal Republic of Germany, and the Soviet Union established the communist Democratic Republic of Germany in its zone.

Resuscitating Japan

In the Far East, Japan was compelled to relinquish all territory acquired by force since 1895. In return for declaring war on Japan and moving against Japanese forces in Manchuria and Korea, the Soviet Union received the four Kuril Islands, or the Northern Territories as Japan called them, and Korea was divided into Soviet and U.S. occupation zones at the 38th parallel (see Map 3.2). Much to Stalin's irritation, however, Moscow was denied a significant role in occupied Japan, since its military had not reached Japan's home islands by the time the country surrendered.

The new U.S. policy of assisting in the recovery of Germany was replicated in the conciliatory posture adopted toward Japan. General Douglas MacArthur, the commander of U.S. occupation forces, built a reform and recovery program on the proposition that America's long-term interests in the Pacific would be impaired by humiliating the Japanese. Thus, while MacArthur directed the

MAP 3.2 EAST ASIA AFTER WORLD WAR II

Following the Second World War, the United States occupied Japan and the Soviet Union obtained control over the southern portion of Sakhalin Island and the Kuril Islands. The Soviets also occupied the Korean Peninsula north of the 38th parallel, while the United States occupied the south. Although it was assumed that Korea would quickly be united, Moscow and Washington were unable to agree on a unification plan, which resulted in the formation of two separate states: the Democratic People's Republic of Korea in the north and the Republic of Korea in the south. Elsewhere, former colonies eventually became independent states.

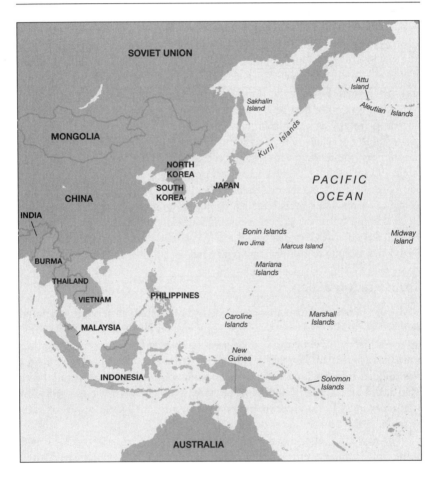

Source: Nau, Perspectives on International Relations 6e, p. 137.

occupation forces to destroy Japan's military power and punish individuals who committed war crimes, he also ordered them to overhaul the country's authoritarian political and economic systems. Permitting the emperor to retain his title as a figurehead in order to facilitate Japanese compliance, MacArthur's occupation forces dismantled the country's feudal system and drafted a new constitution that established a parliamentary form of government, instituted procedures to protect civil liberties, and pledged Japan would "forever renounce . . . the threat or use of force as a means of settling disputes." American-sponsored reforms also redistributed land from baron families to tenant farmers, promoted women's rights, and encouraged the formation of trade unions.

Behind the democratic values inspiring these reforms was an ulterior motive: The United States supported Japan's economic recovery because it feared that a weakened Japan could fall under the influence of the Soviet Union. Reconciliation and resuscitation served U.S. interests as well as its ideals. The American postwar plan arose from a combination of Washington's faith in liberal democracy and its need for a strong Japan that would perform as a faithful ally.

Dealing With Italy

Italy, too, was originally targeted for punitive treatment, although the perpetrators of Italian aggression were no longer in office when the war ended. In July 1943, Mussolini was removed from power and imprisoned in the Apennine Mountains. However, German commandos freed the former dictator in a daring raid, and Hitler installed him as the leader of the Italian Social Republic, a puppet state in the areas of northern Italy still occupied by Germany. As the war drew to a close, Mussolini was captured and executed by enraged Italian partisans, therein taking much of the heat out of the debate over how to treat Italy. At Potsdam, the Council of Foreign Ministers was assigned the task of negotiating the peace settlement with Italy and states aligned with the Axis powers (Romania, Bulgaria, and Hungary), but it remained deadlocked during its September 1945 meeting in London. Ultimately, Italy was forced to relinquish its colonial holdings and cede territory on the Adriatic Sea to Yugoslavia and the Dodecanese Islands to Greece.

Unparalleled in scope and unprecedented in destructiveness, the Second World War transformed the structure of the international system, changing its configuration from a multipolar to a bipolar distribution of power, following what some scholars characterized as a brief interlude of American unipolar dominance.[10] Whereas significant military capabilities were spread among several great powers before the war, now they were concentrated in the hands of two superpowers. The United States and the Soviet Union towered above all other countries. Germany and Japan lay in ruins, Italy was enfeebled, France wrestled with its military humiliation, and Great Britain stood weakened and weary. As a result, officials in Washington and Moscow would shape the form and substance of the postwar world order.

SPHERES-OF-INFLUENCE VERSUS UNIVERSALIST MODELS OF WORLD ORDER

Lacking the glue of a common external threat, the Grand Alliance of World War II splintered amidst distrust, apprehension, and recrimination. All alliances are inherently fragile, and even wartime partners quarrel when their interests diverge. The preeminent status of the United States and the Soviet Union at the top of the international hierarchy gave the leaders of each state reason to be wary of the other's intentions. Nevertheless, a military confrontation was not preordained. After victory had been achieved, new efforts were made to construct rules for continuing engagement. They proceeded fitfully, however, with zigs and zags that often resulted in contentious issues being postponed without resolution.

The pivotal question around which these efforts revolved was whether a spheres-of-influence or universalist conception of world order would prevail. To advocates of a spheres-of-influence peacekeeping scheme, each great power should be accepted by the others as preeminent in a neighboring geographic region that it considers to be of vital interest. The most famous example of a sphere-of-influence deal during the Second World War was the "percentages" agreement that Churchill reached with Stalin in October 1944. Since both Great Britain and the Soviet Union had interests in the Balkans, Churchill proposed a secret arrangement to avoid friction between the two countries. After some haggling between British foreign minister Anthony Eden and Soviet foreign minister Vyacheslav Molotov, the final agreement allocated 90 percent predominance to the British in Greece; 90 percent predominance to the Soviets in Rumania; and 80 percent in Bulgaria and Hungary; and the British and Soviets shared 50 percent influence each in Yugoslavia. Although Churchill and Stalin were comfortable with a sphere-of-influence approach to building world order, Roosevelt, Secretary of State Cordell Hull, U.S. ambassador to the Soviet Union Averell Harriman, and several of the president's other key foreign policy advisers demurred that spheres of influence violated the principles of the Atlantic Charter and would likely condense into competitive blocs. Rather than carving the world into spheres of influence and relying on a balance of power to maintain the postwar order, they wanted to entrust international security to a peacekeeping organization with universal jurisdiction. Precisely how that organization should be crafted remained an issue of contention. Sharp differences existed among the Allies. Russian participation was indispensable, but it would be difficult to secure since Stalin preferred the practical arithmetic of spheres of influence to the abstract algebra of universalism.

The Concept of a Great-Power Concert

President Roosevelt's initial thinking on how to structure a global peacekeeping organization was inspired by the Concert of Europe, a system of regular consultation among the victorious monarchies after the Napoleonic Wars. Under what Roosevelt called his "Grand Design," international security would depend on a new great-power concert, with the United States, Great Britain, the Soviet Union, and eventually China serving as "Four Policemen" that jointly enforced the postwar peace. As depicted in Figure 3.1, he expected these states to act

FIGURE 3.1 THE STRUCTURE OF A GREAT-POWER CONCERT

A concert of power is a directorate composed of great powers for the purpose of jointly managing world affairs. It is predicated on the assumptions that the great powers understand their interests would be advanced by holding periodic meetings to encourage mutual self-restraint and by collaborating to prevent disputes among other states from escalating to wars that could draw them into conflict. The concept of a "concert of power" did not originate with U.S. president Franklin D. Roosevelt's Grand Design. As early as the fourteenth century BCE, Egypt, Hatti (located in central Turkey), Mittani (northern Syria), Babylonia (southern Iraq), and Assyria (upper Tigris Valley) formed a loose consortium of kingdoms that was a rough precursor of a great-power concert. Similar arrangements arose in other cultures at various times. In ancient China, Duke Huan of Ch'i and his chancellor Kuan Chung foreshadowed the idea of a concert by organizing a league composed of the leading states of their day. In the illustration below, a directorate of Great Powers A through D would police international conflict. Minor powers, represented in the figure by the smaller circular forms, would not play a regulatory role.

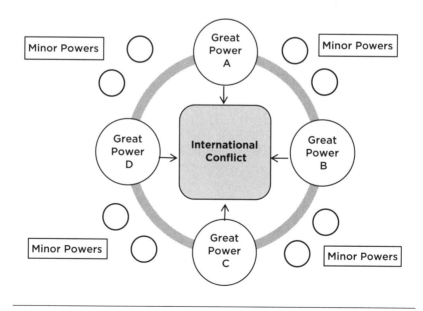

responsibly and selflessly, assisting in emergencies and arresting potential threats. The problem, his advisers pointed out, was that the Grand Design would degenerate into four exclusive spheres of influence if the policemen behaved egoistically, cordoning off areas of vital interest. For Roosevelt's policemen to be compatible with an open, universal approach to world order, they would have to function as members of an executive committee that worked within a broader, more inclusive assembly of nations. As Secretary of State Hull explained to Congress during the autumn of 1943, once such a general international organization was established, "there would be no longer a need for spheres of influence, for alliances, for balance of power,"[11] or for any other special security arrangements.

Roosevelt gradually warmed to the idea of embedding his proposed great-power concert within a global organization—a United Nations—that would replace the old, discredited League of Nations. Such an organization, he told the Congress shortly before his death, "ought to spell the end of . . . the spheres of influence, the balances of power, and all the other expedients that have been tried for centuries—and have always failed."[12] Unanimity among the great power victors was more important to him than the format under which they would cooperate. Equally imperative was convincing Americans to remain engaged in world affairs. Washington, he insisted, needed to take the lead in keeping the wartime coalition together and not withdraw into isolationism as it had after the First World War.

Roosevelt's Policemen and the UN Security Council

Almost from the onset of hostilities, various individuals and nongovernmental groups had begun drafting blueprints for a worldwide organization that would maintain peace and security after the war. Official planning intensified following the 1943 Moscow Conference, when the United States, Great Britain, the Soviet Union, and China issued the Joint Four-Nation Declaration calling for the establishment of a general international organization with universal membership and global scope. At the 1944 Dumbarton Oaks Conference, the great powers delved into the technicalities of how the organization would be structured, and several months later at the Yalta Conference they dealt with voting procedures. Finally, after additional preparatory work by innumerable jurists, scholars, and diplomats, 3,500 delegates and staff representing fifty countries met in San Francisco to hammer out the charter of the United Nations, which was signed on June 26, 1945.

Unlike the League of Nations, which was hastily created after World War I, the United Nations evolved through a lengthy planning process that took place while hostilities were underway. Whereas the league's legitimacy in the eyes of the defeated states was undercut by its linkage to the Treaty of Versailles, the UN remained independent of any peace terms that might subsequently be imposed on the Axis powers. Cognizant of the institutional deficiencies of the league, the UN founders also took steps to strengthen the organization's design. In contrast to the League Covenant, the UN Charter carefully delineated the responsibilities of the organization's principal organs, emphasized majority rule, and made provisions for working conjointly with a network of autonomous specialized agencies that focused on issues ranging from agriculture, labor, and industry to health, education, and culture. Although the league supported committees and conferences that worked on nonmilitary issues, the United Nations, through its numerous programs and funds, research and training institutes, and functional and regional commissions, was far better equipped to tackle a wider array of pressing social, economic, and environmental problems.

The framers of the United Nations Charter expected the Security Council to become the UN principal organ, giving it "primary responsibility for maintaining international peace and security" under Article 24 of the charter. A revised version of Roosevelt's concert of great-power policemen, the Security Council originally consisted of five permanent members (the United States, Great Britain, the Soviet Union, France, and China) with the right to veto substantive decisions, and six nonpermanent members elected for staggered two-year terms by the General Assembly, the UN main deliberative body. As specified in Article 39, the Security Council had the authority to "determine the existence of any threat to peace, breach of the peace, or act of aggression" and, according to Articles 41 and 42, to decide what diplomatic steps, economic sanctions, or military actions should be taken to maintain or restore international peace. Decisions on these matters required seven affirmative votes and the concurrence of the permanent members.

Owing to the veto right, any of the five permanent members could unilaterally block the Security Council from taking collective measures to suppress aggression and remove threats to peace. The rationale behind the veto held that no great power would be willing to join an international organization that allowed a majority vote by smaller states to countermand its national security interests. Recalling the difficulties that the league faced without a full complement of great powers, the charter's framers concluded that a failure to accord special status to those at the apex of the international hierarchy might alienate the very states that the nascent organization most needed to uphold the postwar peace.

THE POLITICAL ECONOMY OF WORLD ORDER

Armed conflict between states emanates from a complex combination of proximate and remote causes. Having just fought German Nazism, Italian Fascism, and Japanese militarism, it is not surprising that the architects of the post–World War II international order saw predatory states as a proximate cause of war. To keep future aggressors in check, they sought to continue Allied collaboration by establishing the United Nations and outfitting it with a Security Council, whose nucleus consisted of the great powers who had worked together to defeat the Axis countries. Enforcing the postwar peace, so their thinking went, required a consortium of the powerful that could stand up to any imaginable threat.

Besides creating an organization to curb an important proximate cause of war, steps were taken to reduce the probability that the remote underlying conditions that gave rise to political extremism in Germany, Italy, and Japan would reappear (see Figure 3.2). Foremost among these conditions was economic nationalism—policies adopted by many countries in the 1930s that favored **autarchy** over open markets and protectionism over free trade. According to the prevailing interpretation of the interwar period, economic nationalism had contributed to the severity of the Great Depression, which in turn fostered the conditions that led to political extremism. To prevent this from happening again, American policymakers pushed for rules and institutions that would buttress world order by stemming economic nationalism.

According to what has become known as **hegemonic stability theory**, the international economic system needs a leader to set standards of conduct, to persuade other countries to adhere to the rules, and to shore up the system during times of adversity. Great Britain played this role during the century following the Napoleonic Wars, but it was unable to continue after being

FIGURE 3.2 THE AMERICAN FRAMEWORK FOR WORLD ORDER

As the Second World War drew to a close, U.S. policymakers envisioned a framework for world order that contained economic and political countermeasures to what they assumed were the primary remote and proximate causes of the war. The economic rules and institutions were designed to inhibit economic nationalism, which they thought inhibited the growth of wealth and created the conditions that allowed political extremists like Hitler to gain power. The political rules and institutions were meant to deter and, if necessary, defeat bellicose leaders like Adolf Hitler, who were seen as the main perpetrators of aggression. Owing to the discord between the United States and the Soviet Union after the war, the economic elements of the framework were largely confined to countries in North and South America, Western Europe, and East Asia.

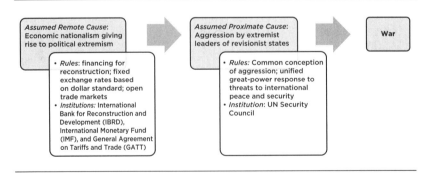

weakened by World War I. Although the United States appeared the logical successor to Britain as the world economic leader, Washington refused to exercise leadership during the interwar years. Seeing this as a mistake, U.S. policymakers, in the aftermath of the Second World War, took on the leadership role that their predecessors had failed to shoulder. Possessing nearly 80 percent of the world's currency reserves, producing roughly 50 percent of the world's manufactured goods, and accounting for more the 40 percent of the world's income, the United States embraced the creed that peace and prosperity worked in tandem and that prosperity depended on an open global marketplace. America was confident at the time that it had the capabilities to take the reins of global leadership, in part because it enjoyed a brief unipolar period of primacy when no other great power was able to challenge its hegemonic status.

Nevertheless, the United States was initially reluctant to actively flex its muscles for fear that its wartime allies would resist any serious American effort to manage postwar international affairs. It preferred diplomatic bargaining to the unilateral exercise of power. For example, in July 1944, the United States hosted representatives from forty-four states allied in the Second World War against the Axis powers at the New Hampshire resort community of Bretton Woods to negotiate a new set of rules and institutions to govern international economic relations. The immediate problem they faced was reconstruction. The war had devastated Europe. To speed its recovery, the International Bank for Reconstruction and Development (IBRD) was established to provide financing for rebuilding the continent's infrastructure.

Prior to World War II, the international community lacked institutional mechanisms to manage the exchange of money across borders. When the delegates from the Allied countries met at Bretton Woods, they were acutely aware of the need to create a reliable way to determine the value of countries' currencies in relation to one another, and they agreed to a set of concepts to define monetary rules to help regulate trade and financial exchanges that crossed national borders. Recognizing that a shared system and vocabulary were necessary preconditions for trade, the delegates agreed that the postwar monetary regime should be based on **fixed exchange rates**. Backed by a vigorous and healthy economy, a preset relationship between gold and the dollar (pegged at $35 per ounce of gold), and a U.S. commitment to exchange gold for dollars at any time (known as "dollar convertibility"), the U.S. dollar became recognized as a "parallel currency," accepted in exchange markets as the reserve used by monetary authorities in most countries and by private banks, corporations, and individuals for international trade and capital transactions. Additionally, the delegates to Bretton Woods created the International Monetary Fund (IMF) to maintain currency exchange stability by promoting international monetary cooperation and orderly exchange arrangements, and by functioning as a lender of last resort for countries experiencing financial crises.

A final major outcome of the Bretton Woods Conference was a recommendation to reduce impediments to free trade, which resulted in a proposal to create an International Trade Organization (ITO) with regulatory authority. When bargaining over its composition and powers dragged on, a group of states craving immediate action agreed to a series of bilateral tariff concessions known as the General Agreement on Tariffs and Trade (GATT). Although GATT was thought of as a temporary arrangement, when a final agreement on the ITO proved elusive, GATT provided a mechanism for continued multilateral negotiations on reducing tariffs and other trade barriers. Never intended to be a formal organization with enforcement powers, it emphasized resolving commercial disputes through negotiations among the parties to the agreement.

While the results of the Bretton Woods Conference added an economic dimension of the postwar world order, its impact was circumscribed by the refusal of the Soviet Union to participate. Votes in the IBRD and IMF were weighted based on the size of each state's monetary contributions, providing a larger voice to wealthier states. Given the economic preeminence of the United States, Washington would provide the bulk of the financial resources for the organizations and would therefore control them. Finding this unacceptable, Stalin rejected IBRD and IMF membership, dashing hopes for an integrated global economy.

A WORLD DIVIDED

On the day before his suicide, Adolf Hitler predicted that the "laws of both history and geography" would compel the United States and the Soviet Union to engage in "a trial of strength."[13] Shortly after the war ended, strident rhetoric in Washington and Moscow suggested that the ominous prediction voiced deep within the bowels of the Reich Chancellery might come to pass. U.S. president Harry Truman, who had been thrust by Roosevelt's untimely death into an international arena with which he had limited knowledge and scant experience, felt that America's agreements with the Soviet Union had been a one-way street, with the Russians deriving most of the benefit. Confident that the Soviets could be chastened by economic pressure, Undersecretary of State Joseph Grew and other key figures in the Truman administration convinced the president to curb postwar assistance to its former wartime ally. To the ever-suspicious Stalin, the termination of American aid under the Lend-Lease program and its snubbing of the Soviet's request for a reconstruction loan were the opening salvos in a campaign to compel Moscow to be more acquiescent. Admonishment accompanied the economic pressure. In a meeting with Soviet foreign minister Molotov on April 23, 1945, Truman berated the stunned Russian, provoking him to protest that he had never been treated with so much disrespect in his life. While Truman and advisers such as Ambassador Averell Harriman and Secretary of the Navy James Forrestal agreed that it was time to get tough with the Russians, the brusque Soviet demeanor at the 1945 London and Moscow Foreign Ministers' Conferences hinted that the Kremlin was not about to roll over.

As Stalin explained to members of his inner circle, "In dealing with such partners as the U.S. and Britain we cannot achieve anything serious if we begin to give into intimidation and betray uncertainty. To get anything from this kind of partner, we must arm ourselves with the policy of tenacity and steadfastness."[14]

At the same time that relations among the former wartime allies began cooling, a new challenge arose. The successful test of a nuclear explosive in Alamogordo, New Mexico, on July 16, 1945, heralded a change in the distribution of military power between the United States and the Soviet Union. For officials in Washington, the bomb eliminated the need for the Red Army to enter the war against Japan by offering the prospect of a swift, decisive victory without a costly invasion of Japan's home islands. For officials in Moscow, the bomb erased the Soviet advantage in ground forces and opened the country to the prospect of atomic blackmail. Whether or not Truman hoped to intimidate the USSR by unleashing the weapon on a spent Japan during the waning days of the war, the atomic bomb complicated relations between the United States and Soviet Union. "Before the atom bomb was used, I would have said, yes, I was sure we could keep the peace with Russia," General Dwight Eisenhower observed after traveling to Moscow at the end of the war. "Now I don't know . . . People are frightened and disturbed all over. Everyone feels insecure again."[15]

Expecting that the United States would try to gain political leverage from its new weapon, and aware that Washington had few bombs in its arsenal, Stalin publicly asserted that nothing had really changed. "Atomic bombs," he proclaimed, "are meant to frighten those with weak nerves."[16] Meanwhile, he accelerated Soviet nuclear research and development, believing that the Soviet Union was at risk until its scientists produced a Russian bomb. "Hiroshima has shaken the whole world," he confided to the physicist Igor Kurchatov. "Provide the bomb—it will remove a great danger from us."[17]

American estimates of when the Soviet Union would develop the atomic bomb varied wildly, ranging from five to twenty years. Assuming that sooner or later the U.S. nuclear monopoly would end and a dangerous arms race would likely ensue, a study directed by Under Secretary of State Dean Acheson and Tennessee Valley Authority chairman David Lilienthal proposed placing nuclear weapons under international control. In 1946, President Truman appointed financier Bernard Baruch to shepherd a modified version of the proposal through the United Nations. Under this plan, an International Atomic Energy Authority (IAEA) would incrementally acquire control over all fissile materials and production plants related to nuclear energy. Furnished with the authority to conduct unrestricted worldwide inspections, it could impose sanctions on states engaged in prohibited activities, which would not be subject to a veto. Once the IAEA was fully functioning, the United States vowed to eliminate its nuclear arsenal.

Alarmed that the Americans would retain their inventory of atomic bombs while his country would be shorn of the veto and have its nuclear research facilities monitored by an international agency, Andrei Gromyko, the Soviet representative to the United Nations, made a counterproposal: Immediately destroy all existing stockpiles of atomic bombs, ban the production of new weapons, and develop a system of supervision some time later. Predictably, Washington was loath to relinquish its nuclear advantage without an absolute assurance that the Soviets were not themselves building atomic bombs. With Moscow rejecting the Baruch Plan and Washington discounting the Gromyko Plan, the two countries remained at loggerheads and were unable to reach an agreement on the control of atomic weapons.

In summary, the United States and the Soviet Union, former partners in war, ceased to remain allies and became foes. The consequences for world order were enormous. Without the foundation of great-power unity, the viability of the UN Security Council for upholding the postwar peace declined. Without full great-power participation, the scope of the economic rules and institutions conceived at Bretton Woods also contracted. Instead of a universal, open system of political and economic order, the world split into rival armed camps. "Let us not be deceived," warned Bernard Baruch in a speech delivered to the South Carolina legislature on April 16, 1947, "we are today in the midst of a cold war." His description instantly caught on and was widely used to characterize the generally frigid relations between the United States and its chief great-power rival, Soviet Union, over the next four and a half decades.

KEY TERMS

appeasement 51

autarchy 68

beggar-thy-neighbor policies 49

fixed exchange rates 69

hegemonic stability theory 68

nontariff barriers 49

protectionism 49

summit conference 54

tariff 49

PART II

The Fitful Evolution of the Contemporary World Order

4 The Cold War and Its Consequences

There are two great peoples which, starting from different points of departure, advance toward the same goal—the Americans and the Russians. Each will one day hold in its hands the destinies of half of mankind.

—ALEXIS DE TOCQUEVILLE,

FRENCH SOCIOLOGIST

On June 18, 1946, Richard C. Hottelet, Moscow correspondent for the Columbia Broadcasting System (CBS), was granted an interview with Maxim Litvinov, the Union of Soviet Socialist Republics (USSR, or Soviet Union) former commissar of foreign affairs. Urbane, insightful, and well versed in Kremlin politics, Litvinov appeared distressed over the evolution of East-West relations. For months he had urged his government to continue its wartime collaboration with members of the Grand Alliance. International order, argued the savvy old Bolshevik, depended on the Soviet Union, United States, United Kingdom, and China working together, playing a "genuinely guiding and decisive role" in world politics. "Only the great powers," he insisted, "are able to act effectively against a big aggressor . . . and they can not be replaced by any union of small states."[1] But now that the common threat of Nazi Germany had been defeated, Litvinov feared that great-power cooperation would collapse.

A few months earlier, Soviet leader Joseph Stalin had implied as much in a speech delivered at the Bolshoi Theatre in central Moscow. Declaring that wars were inevitable due to the nature of the capitalist world economy, he suggested that the Soviet Union had to rely on itself for security. Only by rapidly increasing our strength, Stalin insisted, "can we be sure that our Motherland will be insured against all contingencies."[2]

Resigned to Stalin's dismissal of his appeal for an "amicable agreement" with the West, Litvinov confided to Hottelet that the Kremlin had an "outmoded" conception of security. The more territory that the Soviet Union controlled, the safer its leaders would feel. This was understandable, he admitted, given the devastation suffered by the country during the war. However, when combined with an ideology that assumed communism and capitalism were incompatible, any Soviet attempts to gain control over neighboring countries would lead to a military confrontation with its former allies. Even if Washington acquiesced to all of Moscow's territorial demands, Litvinov told his astonished interviewer, more demands would come. Under the emergent geopolitical conditions, genuine partnership was impossible. In his estimation, the best that could be hoped for was a "prolonged armed truce."[3]

....

THE ORIGINS OF THE COLD WAR

Reflecting on the prospects for constructing a durable world order following the Second World War, Harry Hopkins, an adviser to U.S. president Franklin Roosevelt, described the optimism permeating the White House. "The Russians had proved that they could be reasonable and farseeing," he said. "There wasn't any doubt in the minds of the President or any of us that we could get along with them peacefully for as far into the future as any of us could imagine."[4] Yet, as Maxim Litvinov had predicted, discord soon surfaced. Lacking the glue of a common external threat, the Grand Alliance of World War II dissolved amidst distrust, apprehension, and bitter recriminations. Harry Truman, Roosevelt's successor, insisted that "unless Russia is faced with an iron fist and strong language, another war is in the making."[5] U.S. secretary of state James F. Byrnes agreed: "The only way to negotiate with the Russians is to hit them hard."[6]

The rupture in U.S.-Soviet relations occurred bit by bit, ultimately producing a schism that threatened to undermine the framework of world order that had been carefully worked out in San Francisco at the 1945 United Nations Conference on International Organization. As the secretary-general of the new organization, Trygve Lie of Norway, lamented in late 1947, "The very cornerstone of the U.N., Big Power cooperation and understanding, is being shaken."[7]

How did the falling-out between Washington and Moscow happen? What caused their estrangement? These questions are debated to this day because the historical record lends itself to different interpretations. One interpretation claims that the Cold War arose from diverging strategic interests. The positions of the United States and the Soviet Union at the top of the international hierarchy made rivalry and suspicion inescapable. As direct competitors for global influence, they pictured their interaction as a zero-sum game, presuming that gains by one side would yield losses for the other. According to this reading of the evidence, both the American and the Soviet governments fought the Cold War primarily to secure their political interests, not to promote their political ideals. After all, the United States and the Soviet Union had managed to transcend incompatible ideologies when they allied against the Axis powers in World War ll. Following the war, a power vacuum created by the decline of Europe's traditional great powers—Britain, France, and Germany—drew them into conflict with each other, and as they competed, only then were ideological justifications used to rationalize their mutual hostilities.

A second interpretation holds that the Cold War was simply an extension of the superpowers' mutual disdain for each other's political and economic systems. An inordinate fear of communism led the United States to embrace the **domino theory**, which held that the fall of one country to communism would trigger the fall of others, until the entire world came under Soviet domination. To prevent this from happening, U.S. officials tried to buttress tottering foreign governments so the first domino wouldn't fall. At home they attempted to eradicate inroads—real and imagined—that the Soviet Union may have made within the United States. Sen. Joseph McCarthy, R-WI, for example, led an infamous "witch hunt" for communist sympathizers he claimed had infiltrated the U.S. government. Hollywood production companies blacklisted writers suspected of harboring sympathy for communism, and average American citizens were often required to take loyalty oaths where they worked. Almost everywhere, communism became synonymous with treasonous, un-American activity.

The Soviet Union also couched its Cold War rhetoric in terms of ideology, objecting to the capitalist system that Washington allegedly planned to impose on the entire world. Indeed, many Soviet officials echoed former leader Vladimir Lenin's prediction: "As long as capitalism and socialism exist, we cannot live in peace: in the end, either one or the other will triumph—a funeral dirge will be sung either over the Soviet Republic or over world capitalism."[8] From Moscow's perspective, the Western powers' lenient treatment of Germany and Japan after the war was part of a plan to encircle the Soviet Union with enemies in order to prevent the spread of communism. And conversely, from Washington's perspective, the Soviet Union was suspected of trying to foment "proletarian revolutions" in areas that it liberated during the war, as revealed by the collaboration between the Soviet secret police and local communist political parties, and by Soviet support for removing millions of ethnic Germans, Poles, and Ukrainians from Soviet-occupied countries where they had resided for centuries.[9]

Ideological incompatibility impeded political compromise, locking the United States and the Soviet Union into a long, bitter struggle. Their messianic, diametrically opposed philosophies converted conflicts of interest into confrontations between good and evil. Like in the religious wars of the past, both sides saw their foe's beliefs as existential threats.

A third common explanation of the Cold War is rooted in psychological factors, particularly in misperceptions of each other's motives. Distrustful people are prone to see virtue in their own behavior and malice in those of their adversaries. Policymakers in Washington and Moscow operated from the same "inherent bad faith" image of their rival's intentions, and this hindered postwar cooperation. When such **mirror images** exist, conflict is likely because each side sees its own proposals as helpful but its adversary's responses as obstinate. "*They* arm for war, whereas *we* arm for peace; *they* intervene in other countries to subjugate them, whereas *we* do so to preserve their freedom."[10] Moreover, as perceptions of duplicity become accepted, **self-fulfilling prophecies** can arise. Suspicious of the other side, national leaders become fixated on possible intrigues, see crises as tests of resolve, and exaggerate the susceptibility of their opponent to coercion. By assuming that an adversary is malicious, and acting on that assumption, the target is prone to respond in kind, reacting belligerently, which brings about the outcome that was originally expected. From this perspective, the Cold War was not simply a product of divergent national interests, nor was it merely attributable to incompatible ideologies. Instead, it was a conflict steeped in reciprocal anxieties bred by the way policymakers on both sides misinterpreted each other's intentions.

Additional factors beyond those rooted in interests, ideologies, and images undoubtedly combined to transform a wartime alliance into a trial of strength. Whatever the reasons for its genesis, the Cold War complicated the task of establishing a stable world order. To understand the actions that shaped this great-power conflict, we must go beyond the origins of the Cold War and examine the course of Soviet-American relations from 1946 through 1991.

THE COURSE OF THE COLD WAR

The Cold War was, as Maxim Litvinov had foreseen, an armed truce between the two most powerful victors in the Second World War. Their competition persisted more than forty years, with episodes of acute tension punctuated by periods of relative moderation, and dangerous confrontations interspersed with guarded cooperation. One way to examine how this rivalry evolved is to divide it into the three major phases shown in Table 4.1.

Confrontation, 1946–1962

Following a brief period of wary cooperation during World War II, mutual antagonism began developing between the United States and the Soviet Union, with each side blaming the other. W. Averell Harriman, the U.S. ambassador to the Soviet Union, warned of a "barbarian invasion of Europe,"[11] and Andrei Zhdanov, a close associate of Joseph Stalin, identified American imperialism as the major threat to world peace.[12] George F. Kennan, then a diplomat in the American embassy in Moscow, sent to Washington his famous "Long Telegram" assessing the sources of Soviet conduct. Kennan's ideas were circulated widely in 1947, when the journal *Foreign Affairs* published his views in an article signed simply "X." In it, Kennan argued that Soviet leaders were deeply insecure, and their suspicions of other states would lead to an activist—and perhaps aggressive—foreign policy. However, the United States had the power to resist Soviet pressure and increase the strains under which their leaders would have

TABLE 4.1 A CHRONOLOGY OF THE COLD WAR

Confrontation	
1946	Joseph Stalin's February 9 speech at the Bolshoi Theatre seen in the West as an aggressive pronouncement; Winston Churchill delivers "Iron Curtain" speech; George Kennan sends "Long Telegram" from Moscow
1947	Truman Doctrine announced; Marshall Plan proposed
1948	Coup in Czechoslovakia; Berlin crisis
1949	The North Atlantic Treaty Organization (NATO) formed; Soviet Union detonates atomic bomb; Federal Republic of Germany and German Democratic Republic formed; communists under Mao Zedong establish the People's Republic of China
1950	Korean War begins
1952	United States detonates hydrogen bomb
1953	Death of Stalin; Soviet Union detonates hydrogen bomb; armistice reached in Korea
1955	Austria neutralized; Warsaw Pact formed
1956	Nikita Khrushchev denounces Stalin; Hungarian uprising erupts and Soviet Union intervenes
1957	Soviet Union launches Sputnik
1959	Fidel Castro wins control over Cuba
1960	U.S. U-2 spy plane shot down over Soviet Union
1961	Failure of U.S. Bay of Pigs invasion of Cuba; Berlin Wall constructed
1962	Cuban missile crisis
Coexistence	
1963	Limited Test Ban Treaty signed, prohibiting nuclear testing in the atmosphere, in space, and underwater
1964	Gulf of Tonkin Resolution passed in U.S. Congress, escalating U.S. involvement in Vietnam; China detonates atomic bomb
1967	Outer Space Treaty signed, limiting the military use of space; China detonates hydrogen bomb
1968	Nuclear Nonproliferation Treaty signed; Soviet intervention into Czechoslovakia
1970	Soviet Union and Federal Republic of Germany sign Renunciation of Force Treaty
1971	Strategic Arms Limitation Treaty signed
1972	U.S. President Richard Nixon visits China

(Continued)

TABLE 4.1

1973	U.S. troops withdraw from Vietnam
1975	Helsinki Accords signed, United States and USSR pledge to accept European borders and support human rights
Rapprochement	
1979	China and the United States establish diplomatic relations; Shah of Iran overthrown; Soviet Union invades Afghanistan
1983	U.S. president Ronald Reagan proposes the Strategic Defense Initiative
1985	Mikhail Gorbachev becomes the leader of the Soviet Union and initiates the policies of *glasnost* (openness), *perestroika* (restructuring), and *novoe myshlenie* (new thinking).
1986	United States and Soviet Union agree to remove intermediate range missiles from Europe
1989	Soviet troops withdrawn from Afghanistan; Berlin Wall torn down; communist regimes fall throughout Eastern and Central Europe
1990	German reunification
1991	Attempted coup against Gorbachev fails (August); Soviet Union dissolves (December)

to operate, which could lead to a gradual mellowing of Soviet global ambitions. American policy toward the Soviet Union, Kennan concluded, should involve the long-term, patient **containment** of Russian expansive impulses.

President Harry Truman made containment the foundation of American postwar foreign policy. Troubled by political instability in Turkey and Greece, which he attributed to communist meddling, Truman declared to a joint session of Congress: "I believe that it must be the policy of the United States to support free peoples who are resisting attempted subjugation by armed minorities or by outside pressures." Eventually labeled the Truman Doctrine, this declaration outlined the approach to world order that the United States would follow for decades, despite Kennan's complaints that it did not clearly prioritize America's interests, differentiate among various threats, or distinguish between different potential diplomatic and military responses.[13] As applied by Truman and his immediate successors, the strategy of containment sought to prevent the expansion of Soviet influence by surrounding the Soviet Union with military alliances backed with the threat of nuclear retaliation. The Inter-American Treaty of Reciprocal Assistance (1947); the North Atlantic Treaty Organization (NATO, 1949); the ANZUS Pact (Australia, New Zealand, and United States, 1951); and bilateral alliances with Japan (1951), the Philippines (1951), and Spain (1953) were designed to protect noncommunist centers of world industrial capacity. They were soon followed by alliances with states outside of the main strategic theater, such as the Southeast Asia Treaty Organization (SEATO, 1955) and the Central Treaty Organization (CENTO, 1959).[14] Containment was not without detractors, however. Led by John Foster Dulles, who later became secretary of state under President Dwight Eisenhower, many of Truman's critics complained that containment lacked an offensive punch. They advocated a strategy of **rollback**, which called for liberating the so-called captive nations that unwillingly had fallen under Soviet control.

At the same time that the United States was working to contain the Soviet Union, it also provided aid to Europe under the Marshall Plan. The poverty, unemployment, and economic stagnation afflicting the continent after the war were seen by U.S. policymakers as conditions that would make Europeans receptive to communism's appeals. In order to help finance rebuilding efforts, some $15 billion was offered in grants and loans. The Soviet Union and its Eastern European allies were originally invited to participate, but Stalin, believing that the Americans had ulterior geostrategic motives, insisted that the offer be declined.

A seemingly endless series of Cold War crises soon followed. They included the communist **coup d'état** in Czechoslovakia in 1948, the Soviet blockade of West Berlin in June of that year, the communist acquisition of power on the Chinese mainland in 1949, the outbreak of the Korean War in 1950, the Chinese invasion of Tibet in 1950, and several disputes in the Taiwan Straits. Believing that the communist movement was a monolithic conspiracy spearheaded by the Soviet Union to spread its ideology and institutions throughout the world, policymakers in Washington imagined Soviet plotting behind every tremor rocking the geopolitical landscape. The outbreak of the Korean War in 1950 (see Map 4.1), intensified the growing American conviction that the Kremlin was orchestrating every move. According to Edward Barrett, who was the U.S. assistant secretary of state for public affairs, "the relationship between the Soviet Union and the North Koreans [was] the same as that between Walt Disney and Donald Duck."[15]

The Soviets broke the U.S. atomic monopoly in 1949. Thereafter, the risks of massive destruction of each side fundamentally altered the methods of their competition, necessitating restraint in the use of force and a greater reliance on diplomacy. But because the Soviet Union remained strategically inferior to the United States, Nikita Khrushchev (who became first secretary of the Communist Party several months after Stalin suffered a lethal stroke in March 1953) pursued a policy of peaceful coexistence. Nonetheless, the Soviet Union at times sought to increase its power in places where opportunities appeared to exist. As a result, the period following Stalin's death saw many Cold War confrontations threatening to escalate to a full-scale Soviet-American war. Hungary, Cuba, Egypt, and Berlin were among the major flash points.

In 1962, the surreptitious placement of Soviet missiles in Cuba set the stage for the greatest test of the superpowers' capacity to manage their disputes— the Cuban missile crisis. The superpowers stood eyeball to eyeball. Fortunately, a political solution to the standoff was reached when, at the brink of war,

MAP 4.1 THE KOREAN WAR

Prior to the Second World War, Korea was under Japanese control. Following Japan's defeat, the peninsula was divided at the 38th parallel, with Soviet forces occupying the northern half and U.S. forces occupying the southern half. When a Soviet-American commission proved unable to agree on a reunification plan, separate elections were held in the North and the South. The Soviet Union subsequently pulled its troops out of Korea, and a few months later the United States did so as well. During a speech delivered in January 1950, U.S. Secretary of State Dean Acheson omitted South Korea from America's "defensive perimeter" in the Pacific. On June 25, North Korea attacked the South, driving the South Korean army to the port city of Pusan. Following an amphibious landing at Inchon, U.S. reinforcements drove the North Koreans back across the 38th parallel and advanced toward the Yalu River, which prompted China to intervene. After the Chinese pushed U.S. forces back to the middle of the peninsula, a military stalemate ensued, eventually resulting in the signing of a truce in 1953.

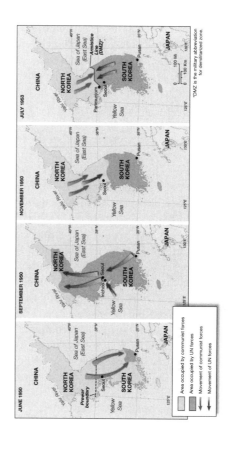

Source: Nau, *Perspectives on International Relations 6e,* p. 173.

Khrushchev blinked, ordering Soviet ships ferrying nuclear missiles to Cuba to turn back. The most dangerous crisis during the Cold War ended. This experience expanded both sides' awareness of the suicidal consequences of a nuclear war and transformed the way that Washington and Moscow would henceforth think about how the Cold War should be waged.

Coexistence, 1963–1978

The looming threat of mutual destruction, in conjunction with the growing parity of U.S. and Soviet military capabilities, made coexistence or nonexistence appear to be the only alternatives for political leaders in Washington and Moscow. At the American University commencement exercises in 1963, U.S. president John F. Kennedy warned that the superpowers were "caught up in a vicious and dangerous cycle in which suspicion on one side breeds suspicion of the other and new weapons beget counterweapons." He went on to signal a shift in how the United States would thereafter interact with the Soviet Union. The Kremlin welcomed Kennedy's overtures, which set the stage for improved relations.

Nevertheless, the superpowers continued their political rivalry. Decolonization—the achievement of independence after World War II by countries that had been colonies of Britain, France, Belgium, and other imperial powers—opened a new arena for competition. Washington and Moscow now vied for influence in the economically less-developed countries of the Southern Hemisphere, often intervening in the internal affairs of Asian, African, and Latin American countries in the hope of curbing their rival's influence. The foremost example occurred during the early 1960s when President Kennedy dispatched military advisers to South Vietnam in support of anticommunist leaders in Saigon, who he thought were fighting a Soviet-supported insurgency (see Map 4.2). Like Korea a decade earlier, Vietnam was perceived as a military front in the fight against the spread of communism. Following Kennedy's assassination, President Lyndon Johnson expanded American involvement by sending more troops, which reached some 543,000 at the peak of American involvement. Johnson's continuous escalation created deep political divisions within the American public, as massive rallies protesting the war and the huge losses of American lives erupted in most U.S. cities.

After Richard Nixon's election in 1968, the United States initiated a new approach to dealing with the Soviet Union that was known as **détente**, and relations between the two countries began to move in a more constructive direction. Under what the Nixon administration dubbed its strategy of **linkage**, cooperation with the Soviet Union in one policy arena (such as trade) would hereafter be tied to acceptable Soviet conduct in other arenas (such as human rights). **Arms control** stood at the center of their activities, with the Strategic Arms Limitation Talks (SALT), initiated in 1969, seeking to restrain a spiraling arms race. Meanwhile, in accordance with what came to be called the Nixon Doctrine, the United States began winding down its costly and unpopular war in

MAP 4.2 THE VIETNAM WAR

Following a protracted anticolonial struggle against France, Vietnam was partitioned during the 1954 Geneva Conference, with the country dividing along the 17th parallel into a communist North Vietnam and a noncommunist South Vietnam. When elections to reunify the country were not held, organized opposition against the South Vietnamese regime intensified. Eventually, the North undertook military operations against the South. Fearing that a communist victory would lead to further gains throughout Southeast Asia, the United States began assisting South Vietnam. Despite the American presence rising to over half a million troops by 1969, the South Vietnamese government was unable to prevail on the battlefield. Direct American military involvement ended following the 1973 Paris Peace Accords, and on April 30, 1975, North Vietnamese forces declared victory after capturing Saigon, the capital of South Vietnam.

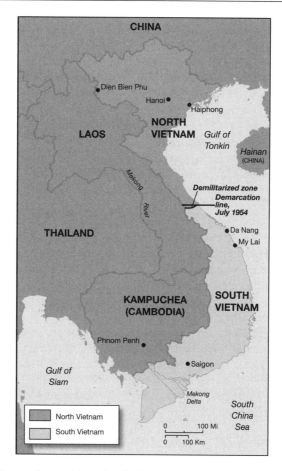

Source: Nau, *Perspectives on International Relations,* 6e, p. 181.

Vietnam by supplanting American combat forces with South Vietnamese troops. In this phase of the Cold War, cooperative interactions between the superpowers became more commonplace than hostile relations. Visits, cultural exchanges, trade agreements, and joint technological ventures replaced threats, warnings, and confrontations.

From Renewed Confrontation to Rapprochement, 1979–1991

Despite the careful nurturing of détente, it did not endure. When the Soviet Union invaded Afghanistan in 1979, President Jimmy Carter defined the situation as "the most serious strategic challenge since the Cold War began." As part of the Carter Doctrine, he announced America was willing to use military force to protect its access to oil supplies from the Persian Gulf. In addition, he suspended grain exports to the Soviet Union and attempted to organize a worldwide boycott of the 1980 Moscow Olympics.

Soviet-American relations deteriorated dramatically thereafter. Carter's successor in the White House, Ronald Reagan, described the Soviet Union as an "evil empire" and asserted that its scheming "underlies all the unrest that is going on." His counterparts in the Kremlin (first Yuri Andropov and then Konstantin Chernenko) responded with equally scathing criticisms of the United States. As the rhetorical salvos became increasingly harsh, Reagan proposed the Strategic Defense Initiative (SDI), a space-based system of lasers that purportedly would destroy Soviet missiles if they were ever launched against the United States. Although the United States lacked the technology to construct a reliable ballistic missile defense at that juncture, some American leaders nonetheless hinted that it was possible to win a "limited" nuclear war against the Soviet Union. Friction between Washington and Moscow increased further when, under the Reagan Doctrine, the United States backed tough talk with renewed military capabilities, pledging support for anticommunist insurgents who sought to overthrow Soviet-supported governments in Afghanistan, Angola, and Nicaragua.

By 1985, superpower relations had become so tense that Mikhail Gorbachev, the new Soviet leader, characterized the situation as "explosive." Exacerbating matters for the Soviet Union, its economy was buckling under the weight of exorbitant military expenditures, bad harvests, and a decline in world petroleum prices. Faced with economic stagnation and declining civic morale, Gorbachev implemented a series of far-reaching reforms to promote political openness (*glasnost*), economic restructuring (*perestroika*), and new thinking (*novoe myshlenie*) on security issues. Meanwhile, in an effort to reduce the suffocating level of military expenditures, he sought a **rapprochement** with the West, proclaiming his desire to end the division of Europe and create a "common home" for all European countries regardless of their political or economic systems. "We realize that we are divided by profound historical, ideological, socioeconomic, and cultural differences," he noted in 1987 during his first visit to the United States. "But the wisdom of politics today lies in not using those differences as a pretext for confrontation, enmity, and the arms race." Not long thereafter, the Soviets ended their aid to Cuba and Central America, withdrew from Afghanistan, and announced unilateral reductions in military spending. Gorbachev also agreed to two new disarmament agreements: the Strategic Arms Reduction Treaty (START) for deep cuts in strategic arsenals and the Treaty on Conventional Armed Forces in Europe (CFE) to reduce the Soviet military presence in Europe. Finally, to nearly everyone's astonishment, Gorbachev declared an end to the Cold War in a December 1988 speech to the United Nations. Ronald Reagan, who by now had come to regard Gorbachev as a partner in the quest for peace, concurred. A month later Reagan proclaimed, "The Cold War is over."[16]

In 1989, the Berlin Wall, long a stark symbol of the division between East and West, was dismantled. On September 12, 1990, the United States, the Soviet Union, Great Britain, and France signed the Treaty on the Final Settlement with Respect to Germany, which made the reunification of Germany possible. German leaders agreed to make no territorial claims in Europe; pledged never to obtain nuclear, biological, or chemical weapons; and promised to reduce their 670,000-person armed forces to 370,000 troops (in exchange for the removal of 370,000 Soviet soldiers from Germany). Afterward, Germany and the Soviet Union signed a bilateral treaty under which the two states promised never to attack each other and to cooperate economically for the next twenty years.

When the Soviet Union collapsed at the end of 1991, some people claimed that "Ronald Reagan won the Cold War by being tough on the communists."[17] His firmness allegedly brought the Soviets to heel. However, many policymakers in both Washington and Moscow insist it was not so simple.[18] Several factors contributed to bringing the Cold War to a peaceful conclusion. Foremost among them were Gorbachev's initiatives, not Reagan's toughness. Indeed, Reagan later gave credit to Gorbachev, and insisted that both sides had won the Cold War. In retrospect, rather than convincing the Kremlin to give up, Reagan's early hard-line posture stiffened the resolve of Soviet hard-liners, complicating matters for would-be reformers. According to Anatoly Dobrynin, the Soviet ambassador to the United States, had Reagan not abandoned his adversarial approach in favor of pragmatic engagement with Gorbachev "we would have been forced to tighten our belts and spend even more on defense."[19] Whatever the full explanation for the Cold War's termination, the peaceful end of this long, acrimonious great-power struggle spared humanity from a future teeming with risks of another catastrophic great-power war.

THE CHARACTERISTICS OF THE COLD WAR

During the course of the Cold War, several patterns characterized U.S.-Soviet relations. The first was oscillation in the behavior of the two superpowers. A high level of conflict was interspersed with short-term periods of relaxed tensions, implying that the foundation for deep, long-term cooperation between Washington and Moscow was fragile and that a peaceful conclusion to their competition remained uncertain.

Another striking pattern was the extent to which the foreign policy exchanges between the two competitors were reciprocal. An action-reaction syndrome existed throughout the Cold War. Periods when the United States made cooperative initiatives toward the Soviets were also the periods when the Soviets undertook friendly actions toward the United States. Similarly, periods of American belligerence were periods of Soviet animosity. This tit-for-tat pattern of interaction suggests that great-power competitors tend to treat each other as they are treated and that it took both adversaries to peacefully end their rivalry.

The third pattern concerned the willingness of officials in Washington and Moscow to spend staggering amounts to gain the upper hand over their counterparts. Spurred by codes of statecraft that emphasized closing windows of vulnerability and operating from a position of strength, the two sides became trapped in a vicious cycle animated by a simple creed: (1) Don't negotiate when you are behind; why accept military inferiority? and (2) Don't negotiate when you are ahead; why relinquish military superiority? Guided by this mind-set, the defense establishments of both states labored to build an ever-widening range of sophisticated weapons. The Soviet Union devoted 20 percent or more of its gross national product (GNP) to the military sector,[20] while the United States spent an estimated $10 trillion to contain the Soviet Union, an expenditure nearly "enough to buy everything in the United States except the land."[21]

A final pattern arose from how the Soviet-American rivalry affected both states. Noting that the Soviet Union occasionally experimented with decentralized market incentives, while the United States increasingly turned to strong central governance, some scholars proposed a **convergence theory**, which postulated that the two sides would grow more alike over time, as each reluctantly adopted aspects of their adversary's systems in order to compete more efficiently. One area where some rough parallels were said to have developed was in their military-industrial complexes.[22] Since Stalin's day, when successive five-year plans emphasized steel production and heavy industry, the command economy in the Soviet Union was geared to military requirements. Something similar was allegedly happening in the United States. "The conjunction of an immense military establishment and a large arms industry," warned President Dwight Eisenhower in his January 17, 1961, farewell address, was "new in the American experience" and had the potential to endanger the country's economic growth, civil liberties, and democratic processes, creating a massive debt that could leave the country "heavily fortified with nothing left to defend."

Putting these events into a long-term perspective, several distinct patterns in U.S.-Soviet relations unfolded during the nearly five decades of the Cold War. Conflict and suspicion generally prevailed over cooperation and trust, undermining the prospects for a world order anchored in the universalism that U.S. president Franklin Roosevelt had espoused during the latter years of the Second World War. In its place, a rigid two-bloc system took root, balanced by the military capability of each superpower to assure any potential aggressor of its own destruction.

THE COLD WAR WORLD ORDER

Once the Grand Alliance of World War II fractured, the United States and the Soviet Union confronted the challenge of developing rules to prevent their rivalry from escalating to a showdown that might result in mutual annihilation. Fortunately, the challenge was met. A set of rules gradually emerged, through trial and error, and disputes between the White House and the Kremlin never spiraled into all-out warfare. Among the implicit rules underlying this **security regime** were an acceptance of separate spheres of influence, avoidance of direct military face-offs, maintenance of a distinction between conventional and nuclear weapons, and abstention from the use of weapons of mass destruction. These rules were associated with two features of postwar world politics: bipolarity and nuclear deterrence.

The Stability of Bipolar Systems

World War II radically changed the distribution of military and economic capabilities among the world's leading states. Of those perched atop the international hierarchy in 1939, Germany, Italy, and Japan were defeated, France was humiliated, and the United Kingdom's resources depleted. Power was now concentrated in the hands of the United States and the Soviet Union. Prewar multipolarity had given way to postwar bipolarity.

Some international relations theorists thought that a bipolar system would be more stable than the previous multipolar system. In their estimation, the incidence of major war would be lower in a world of two superpowers because each counterbalanced the other. Furthermore, with only a single peer rival to monitor, the chances that one side might underestimate the strength or resolve of the other would decrease, therein reducing the odds that hostilities might arise out of miscalculation. The downside of bipolarity was that with the attention of the two rivals riveted almost exclusively on one another, thorny issues could not easily be sidestepped, deflected, or postponed. The superpowers would become fixated on the things that divided them, spawning a struggle for primacy, where the gains made by one side would be seen as losses by the other.

Events in the last months of World War II suggested another consequence of having overwhelming power concentrated in two rivals. Despite the promise of universalism that was embodied in the Atlantic Charter (1941) and the Declaration of the United Nations (1942), both Washington and Moscow began establishing spheres of influence as they attempted to consolidate their positions in countries that they liberated from Axis control. "Whoever occupies a territory," explained Joseph Stalin, "imposes on it his own social system . . . as far as his army can reach."[23] Driven by an American fears of Soviet expansionism into Western Europe and an equally strong Soviet desire to build a buffer zone in Eastern Europe that would impede another invasion of the USSR, the two superpowers constructed "alliances of position" to draw boundaries around areas of vital interest.[24]

Alliances are formal agreements among sovereign states for the purpose of coordinating their behavior under certain specified circumstances. The degree of coordination may range from a detailed list of military forces that will be furnished by each party in the event of war to the more modest requirement that they will consult with one another should hostilities erupt. Traditionally, alliances were formed and dissolved according to the strategic needs of the moment. However, the NATO and the Warsaw Treaty Organization, the primary alliances of position constructed during the Cold War, were not the supple, short-term coalitions that historically were used to address disequilibrium in the balance of power. As illustrated in Figure 4.1, they were blocs—groups of secondary powers clustered around one of the two superpowers.

FIGURE 4.1   THE COLD WAR BIPOLAR SYSTEM

Bipolar systems vary along two dimensions. The first pertains to the relative strength of the bloc leaders, who can be equal (Leader A = Leader B) or unequal (Leader A > Leader B) in their overall capabilities. The second dimension refers to the rigidity of each bloc's structure, which can be tight or loose. The tighter the structure, the less latitude that bloc members have to deviate from the policies of the bloc leader. In a *symmetrical* bipolar system, the two bloc leaders are roughly equal and supervise blocs that are structurally similar. The form of bipolarity that existed throughout most of the Cold War was *asymmetrical*. First, as depicted in the figure below, the United States (represented by Bloc Leader A) possessed greater capabilities than the Soviet Union (Bloc Leader B) due to its larger, more innovative economy. Second, their blocs were structurally different, with the one led by the United States granting more leeway to its members than the tighter bloc headed by the Soviet Union.

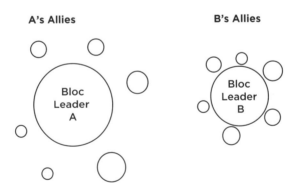

Political blocs are Janus-faced organizations. From an individual member's perspective, they appear overbearing due to the limits placed on national autonomy. The more tightly a bloc is structured, the greater the degree of external penetration experienced by its members and the less latitude they have on whether to conform with the bloc leader's foreign policy. The Warsaw Pact, for example, was far tighter than NATO, as shown by Soviet military interventions in Hungary (1956) and Czechoslovakia (1968) that arrested political rebellions that ran counter to Moscow's interests.

When viewed from a wider perspective at the systemic level of analysis, however, the clarity of purpose that typifies political blocs can promote stability inasmuch as they restrain crisis-provoking behavior by potentially unruly allies. According to evidence from one data-based study, the Cold War evolved into a **long peace** partially because alliances of position permitted the superpowers to keep bloc members in check by dampening conflicts that otherwise might have flared up.[25]

The Cold War alliances of position contributed to world order in other ways as well. First of all, they clarified the political landscape by providing simple, unambiguous lines of demarcation around areas where Washington and Moscow had strong interests. When superpower spheres of influence were clear, neither side mounted a significant challenge to its rival; where they were vague (as in the case of South Korea after U.S. secretary of state Dean Acheson's "defensive perimeter" speech), recklessness and opportunism often overcame caution and prudence.

In addition to coordinating expectations between the superpowers, another contribution that Cold War alliances made to world order was to reassure states that were apprehensive about their security. NATO, for example, helped allay the fears of Europeans who were concerned about facing the Soviet Union and a rearmed Germany alone. As famously described by Lord Ismay, the organization's first secretary general, the purpose of NATO was "to keep the Russians out, the Americans in, and the Germans down."

The long peace of the second half of the twentieth century had multiple roots. Alliances of position contributed by helping prevent potential disputes over areas of vital interest from accumulating in recurring crises of accelerating frequency, where states use more coercive tactics in each sequential encounter. Another contribution was made by nuclear weapons.

The Deadly Logic of Nuclear Deterrence

Bipolarity, with its counterpoised superpowers and political blocs, was a prominent feature of the post–World War II world. Nuclear weapons were even more salient. Whereas the largest conventional weapons of the Second World War delivered the power of 10 tons of TNT, the atomic bomb that leveled Hiroshima on August 6, 1945, had the power of over 15,000 tons of TNT. Soon increasingly more destructive weapons were developed, including a Soviet bomb with a yield of over 50 megatons (million tons) of TNT. As these awesome weapons increasingly filled the U.S. and Soviet arsenals, a "balance of terror" superseded the prewar balance of power.

The principal assumption underpinning the balance of terror is that nuclear weapons are so devastating that they make it irrational to employ war as an instrument of foreign policy. If a state has the willingness and unquestioned capacity to respond to an attack with a retaliatory strike that obliterates the aggressor, deterrence theory postulates that adversaries will be dissuaded from striking. The frightening costs of nuclear war simply outweigh any conceivable benefits. As memorably expressed by former British prime minister Winston Churchill in a speech to the House of Commons on March 1, 1955: In a nuclear-armed world "safety is the sturdy child of terror, and survival the twin brother of annihilation."

Deterring aggression by threatening dreadful punishment requires a **second-strike capability**—the ability to inflict intolerable damage on an opponent even after being hit first. To maintain a credible second-strike capability, the United States and the Soviet Union deployed a **triad** of land-based intercontinental ballistic missiles (ICBMs), submarine-launched ballistic missiles (SLBMs), and long-range bombers, believing that all three could not be wiped out simultaneously in a first-strike attack. If one part of the triad survived, it had enough firepower to rain ruinous damage on the attacker. Defense planners used the term **mutual assured destruction (MAD)** to describe a strategic balance where both superpowers had credible second-strike capabilities (see Figure 4.2). Regardless of which great power struck first, the other side could destroy the attacker. When each side in a bipolar rivalry can eradicate the other after absorbing a first strike, the doctrine of MAD posits that the terror of utter devastation preserves the peace between them. As former Soviet leader Nikita Khrushchev reportedly put it, "If you reach for the push button, you reach for suicide." Thus, as a strategy for preventing war, MAD rests on mutual vulnerability, so that any aggressor tempted to launch a nuclear first strike can expect a devastating response and will resist that temptation if it wishes to survive. This is dependent, of course, on nuclear powers being headed by rational, calm and collected leaders.

The balance of terror between the United States and the Soviet Union never gave way to nuclear war, but it had serious drawbacks. While it might be believable to threaten nuclear retaliation for an attack on one's homeland (direct deterrence), would it be convincing to do so for an attack against an ally (extended deterrence)? The United States, for instance, could credibly threaten the Soviet Union with nuclear destruction if it attacked New York City, but would the Soviets believe that America would carry out a counterattack if Frankfurt were targeted? Would the United States risk Soviet retaliation by responding with nuclear weapons to an attack on its German ally? Deterrence breaks down as credibility weakens. Since the stakes for the United States differ in these two situations, the credibility of the American threat is not the same. Thus, throughout the Cold War, the United States repeatedly signaled to the

FIGURE 4.2 THE BALANCE OF TERROR

As illustrated below, some policy analysts extend the logic of balance-of-power theory to nuclear deterrence. From their point of view, imbalances, situations where only one side in a strategic rivalry possesses a second-strike capability, are dangerous because the stronger side may be tempted in an acute crisis to launch a preemptive nuclear strike, knowing that its rival could not retaliate. Conversely, in situations characterized by balance, where both sides have a second-strike capability, neither state has an incentive to strike first because both can retaliate with devastating counterattacks.

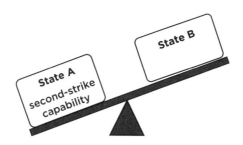

Strategic Imbalance: Only State A Can Retaliate after a First Strike

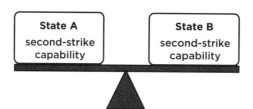

Strategic Balance: Both A and B Have the Capability to Retaliate after a First Strike

Soviets that it placed a high value on its pledge to defend the liberty of NATO allies. As President John F. Kennedy put it in his inaugural address, America would "pay any price, bear any burden, meet any hardship, support any friend, oppose any foe to assure the survival and success of liberty."

Other problems also exist. Perhaps the most important center on the massive buildup of arms that accompanied the adoption of nuclear deterrent strategies by the superpowers during the Cold War. Worried about their vulnerability to a nuclear attack, both superpowers coveted absolute security. Yet every upgrade in their weapons inventories only created greater insecurity for their rival, which prompted it to upgrade as well. Washington and Moscow were trapped in a costly, self-reinforcing arms race that unnerved officials in both capitals and shifted resources away from programs designed to ameliorate pressing domestic problems. Following the "Hot Line" agreement of 1963, which established a direct radio and telegraph system between the two governments, American and Soviet leaders reached a series of arms control agreements aimed at lowering tensions and building a climate of trust that would facilitate negotiating further agreements. The SALT treaties of 1972 and 1979 were emblematic of this joint effort to regulate nuclear weaponry without destabilizing the strategic balance.

Although it is difficult to precisely determine the causal connection between nuclear weapons and the long peace, circumstantial evidence indicates that they helped prevent the Cold War from turning "hot." Documents from the Cuban missile crisis indicate that fear of annihilation had a sobering effect on those looking into the nuclear abyss.[26] Nuclear weapons provided an incentive for the White House and the Kremlin to establish a set of norms to regulate their competition. Just as the alliances of position led to the formation of tacit rules of prudence regarding spheres of superpower influence, the environment of MAD prompted Washington and Moscow to establish rules that encouraged both sides to maintain a sharp distinction between conventional and nuclear weapons and avoid direct military confrontations.

BEYOND THE COLD WAR

In 1835 the French political sociologist Alexis de Tocqueville had predicted that the Americans and Russians would eventually hold sway over the destinies of half of mankind.[27] Just over a century later, they stood like titans above the other members of the state system. Although their interests and ideals collided, they maintained an armed truce, avoiding a nuclear showdown that arguably would have brought humanity to the brink of extinction. The peaceful conclusion of their Cold War suggests something quite different about world politics than the experience of the twentieth century's two previous world wars: hegemonic rivalries are not doomed to end in violence.

The epic struggle for global leadership, known as the Cold War, was the longest era of great-power peace since the birth of the modern world system. When viewed in historical perspective, this was a remarkable achievement. Given the experience of the past five centuries, the probability of no war occurring between great powers during a forty-year period would be roughly .005.[28] Nevertheless, it is worth bearing in mind that this long peace was anything but stable: In all, 251 international crises erupted and one of every five reached full-scale hostilities, with millions of deaths occurring in countries that were not great powers.[29] War may not have broken out among the great powers, but it happened with alarming frequency among everyone else.

The surprisingly peaceful end to the Cold War changed world politics in profound ways. With the dissolution of the Soviet Union, no peer competitor faced the United States. To some, this signified the universalization of liberal democracy as the final form of government,[30] and offered a unique opportunity to implement major elements from the plan for world order advocated by Woodrow Wilson at the end of the First World War. Many of Wilson's liberal-idealist recommendations moved to the top of the U.S. foreign policy agenda, as subsequent American administrations pushed for free trade, the spread of democracy, and the strengthening of international institutions.[31]

Still, practical questions remained. Following the breakup of the Soviet Union, the Russian Federation began moving toward liberal democracy and a market economy. From the Wilsonian perspective, making successful transitions to democracy and capitalism would enhance the prospects for a peaceful post–Cold War world order. As the sole remaining superpower, what should the United States do to support Russia's dual transitions (see Box 4.1)? What would be the appropriate type of assistance? How much assistance was warranted?

Box 4.1   You Decide

On December 25, 1991, Mikhail Gorbachev appeared on a nationwide televised broadcast to announce his resignation as the president of the USSR. Following his speech, the USSR was formally dissolved, and the tricolor flag of the Russian Federation was raised over the Kremlin, replacing the red Soviet flag with its famous hammer and sickle. The Russian Federation, the largest of the fifteen former constituent republics of the USSR, inherited 76 percent of the former Soviet Union's territory and 51 percent of its population. It also inherited a disintegrating economy, a collapsing health care system, and an alarming demographic crisis.

Boris Yeltsin, president of the Russian Federation, faced a series of daunting problems as he navigated the transition from communism and a command economy to democracy and a market economy. Unemployment was high, workers with jobs were not receiving wages, the prices on consumer goods had climbed over twentyfold, and manufacturers relied on barter to obtain supplies and equipment. By 1995, industrial production declined to roughly half of what that had been in 1991, life expectancy for males was the lowest in the industrial world, and the fertility rate dropped below what was needed to maintain a stable population. Outside observers wondered what would become of Russia. Some of them expected that the country would muddle along under a weak central government; others feared that growing dissatisfaction might spark a return to communism;

(Continued)

(Continued)

and still others worried that a hardline, ultranationalist would gain power. None of these scenarios seemed promising to those who saw the Cold War's peaceful end as a unique opportunity to build a new world order.

Imagine that it is the early 1990s and you are a foreign policy adviser to a U.S. president seeking your advice on how America should deal with Russia. A wide range of options are under consideration. At one end of the spectrum are triumphalist policies that would exploit Russia's weakness, treating it as a defeated nation with no substantial security interests beyond its borders. At the other extreme are accommodating policies that would attempt to build Russia into a strategic partner, writing off Soviet-era debts and helping fund Russia's enormous capital needs. Between these extremes are several other options based on mixed strategies. What would you propose? What would be the implications of your proposal for building a stable post–Cold War world order?

Political realists were skeptical of this new version of Wilsonianism. As they saw it, American preeminence was merely a pause in the broad sweep of history, a momentary interruption in the endless global struggle over status and influence. Despite the confluence of overwhelming military and economic might on American soil after the demise of the Soviet Union, history had not ended. Nationalist ambitions and great-power competition would return.[32] In time, Russia, China, and other great powers would vie with the United States for power and position. This argument did not gain traction in Washington after the collapse of the Soviet Union, however. Believing that they had won the Cold War, America's leaders chose instead to follow Harry Truman's advice: "The United States should take the lead in running the world in the way the world ought to be run."[33]

KEY TERMS

arms control 82

containment 79

convergence theory 86

coup d'état 80

détente 82

domino theory 76

linkage 82

long peace 89

mirror images 76

mutual assured destruction (MAD) 90

rapprochement 84

rollback 80

second-strike capability 90

security regime 87

self-fulfilling prophecies 77

triad 90

America's Unipolar Moment

5

The crisis in the Persian Gulf, as grave as it is, also offers
a rare opportunity to move toward . . . a new world order . . .
freer from the threat of terror, stronger in the
pursuit of justice, and more secure in the quest for peace.

—GEORGE H. W. BUSH,

U.S. PRESIDENT

Early on the morning of August 2, 1990, columns of T-72 tanks from Iraq's elite Republican Guard crossed their country's southern border and raced down a six-lane highway toward Kuwait City. Alleging that his military had been invited by Kuwaiti revolutionaries to help liberate the tiny, oil-rich emirate from the corrupt Al-Sabah family, Iraqi president Saddam Hussein declared that he would annex Kuwait and threatened to turn the territory into a graveyard if anyone tried to stop him (see Map 5.1). No one dismissed his threat. Not only did Iraq possess the world's fourth largest army, it also was well-equipped, seasoned by eight years of war with Iran, and possessed the ability to mount a tenacious defense. According to the conventional wisdom, the Iraqis could only be evicted from Kuwait by a costly, protracted war.

Despite apprehension over the toll of waging war against Iraq, America's response to the invasion was strong and unequivocal. U.S. president George Herbert Walker Bush, a pilot whose aircraft had been shot down during battle in World War II, saw the crisis through the lens of the 1930s. Iraq's aggression, he declared, was "a throwback to another era, a dark relic from a dark time."[1] In his eyes, Saddam Hussein was like Adolf Hitler, a rapacious tyrant bent on conquering defenseless neighbors. "A half century ago," Bush told those attending the 91st Veterans of Foreign Wars (VFW) National Convention, "the world had a chance to stop a ruthless dictator and missed it. I pledge to you: We will not make that mistake again."[2]

MAP 5.1 THE PERSIAN GULF REGION

Iraq is situated in the strategic center of the oil-rich and politically unstable Middle East—a region composed of states with a history of recurrent rivalries and episodic warfare. The Persian Gulf War erupted after Iraqi leader Saddam Hussein sent his army into Kuwait in 1990 to obtain territory that he claimed was within the traditional boundaries of his country.

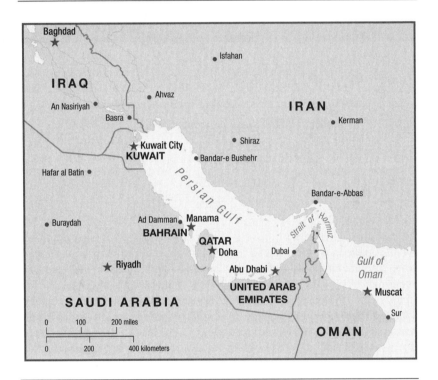

The president's lofty rhetoric masked his concern over maintaining access to Middle Eastern oil, a commodity on which daily life in the twentieth century had become dependent. While Bush preferred to emphasize the importance of upholding international law, he admitted in a speech to Pentagon employees on August 15 that energy resources were also on his mind. As one of his advisers quipped, he wouldn't get involved if Kuwait exported oranges.[3] What especially troubled Bush was the possibility that Saddam Hussein might also attempt to subjugate Saudi Arabia, which would give him control of almost half of the planet's known petroleum reserves. If he succeeded, much of the industrialized world would be beholden for its energy needs to a callous, untrustworthy dictator. The ramifications were unsettling. Deputy Secretary of State Lawrence Eagleburger summarized the administration's thinking: It was "absolutely essential that the U.S.—collectively, if possible, but individually, if necessary—not only put a stop to this aggression but roll it back."[4]

Washington's immediate response to the invasion centered on military containment and economic **compellence**. To contain Iraqi aggression, President Bush forged a large multinational coalition to deter Baghdad from undertaking further expansion, and Secretary of Defense Dick Cheney secured permission from King Fahd to allow elements of the U.S. Rapid Deployment Force (RDF) to be stationed in Saudi Arabia. To compel Iraq to withdraw from Kuwait, American diplomats lobbied the United Nations to organize a global arms and economic embargo against Saddam Hussein's regime. On August 6, the UN Security Council adopted Resolution 661, which spelled out a list of **economic sanctions** to be levied against Iraq; furthermore, in Resolution 665, it called upon member states with a maritime presence in the region to enforce those sanctions by inspecting the cargoes of any ships thought to be assisting the Iraqis.

Iraq seemed to be an ideal target for **coercive diplomacy**. Saddam Hussein was politically isolated, sanctions would be applied decisively, and Iraq's economy was vulnerable to external pressure because it exported a single natural resource, imported most of its finished goods, and relied heavily on foreign sources for technical services. Yet there were reasons for skepticism over whether economic sanctions would work. According to one historical survey, they tended to succeed only a third of the time, requiring an almost 2.5 percent impact on the target's gross national product (GNP) for three years to have meaningful results.[5] The longer Iraq endured trade disruptions and economic deprivation, the greater the likelihood that the diverse coalition so carefully assembled by President Bush would erode. Friction from the ongoing Israeli-Palestinian dispute, Islamic fundamentalist resentment over the growing number of non-Arab soldiers in the region, and the staggering cost of maintaining troops in a distant and inhospitable environment were just some of the problems that threatened to weaken coalition resolve as the months wore on. Additionally, because Saddam Hussein remained indifferent to the hardships borne by his own people, there was no guarantee that tightening the economic screws would compel him to withdraw from Kuwait.

By late fall, few American policymakers retained hope that the economic vice around Iraq would induce Saddam Hussein to give up Kuwait. As the White House began finalizing plans for offensive military action, the UN Security Council passed Resolution 678 authorizing member states "to use all necessary means" to expel Iraq from Kuwait if it did not leave voluntarily by January 15, 1991. Meanwhile, a joint resolution was approved in the U.S. Senate by 52 to 47 and in the House of Representatives by 250 to 183 authorizing the president to wrest control of Kuwait from Iraq. "What is at issue," President Bush wrote in a letter delivered to Iraqi foreign minister Tariq Aziz on January 9, "is not the future of Kuwait . . . but rather the future of Iraq."

Eight days later, the Bush administration unleashed Operation Desert Storm, its plan for emancipating Kuwait. In contrast to the incremental-ism that characterized earlier American thinking about **limited war**, Desert Storm was designed to overwhelm the Iraqis in a fast and furious cam-paign. During the 1960s, policymakers in Washington had been seduced by simplistic theories suggesting threats of impending harm after brief pauses in fighting would induce enemy forces to stand down, thus sparing the United States from costly pitched battles. When reflecting on the fail-ure of this strategy in the Vietnam War, the succeeding generation of U.S. military officers doubted that political leaders would be any more success-ful at fine-tuning a program of progressively rising pressure to persuade Saddam Hussein to relinquish territory his army had seized. Rather than attempting to orchestrate an alternating pattern of escalations and pauses, U.S. general Colin Powell's "doctrine of invincible force" sought to marshal all of the resources necessary to crush an adversary straightaway, using mobility and firepower to win a swift and decisive victory. "I don't believe in doing war on the basis of macroeconomic, marginal-analysis models," the general said. "I'm more of the mind-set of a New York street bully: 'Here's my bat, here's my gun, here's my knife, I'm wearing armor. I'm going to kick your ass.'"[6]

Operation Desert Storm unfolded in two phases: a relentless air assault (January 17–February 24) followed by a devastating ground offensive (February 24–28). The objectives of the first phase were to achieve air supe-riority, cripple Iraq's defenses, and destroy its supply network. The second phase involved convincing Saddam Hussein that the ground offensive would be aimed directly at Kuwait City, while in actuality the bulk of America's forces would make an end run deep into Iraq, pivot, and then circle back to outflank and envelop the Iraqis who were dug in for a frontal assault. The combined impact was devastating. Exhausted by weeks of aerial pound-ing and encircled by formidable armored and mechanized infantry divisions, Iraqi soldiers surrendered in droves. Those who tried to fight were pummeled into submission. What Saddam Hussein predicted would be the "mother of all battles" quickly degenerated into the mother of all retreats. The United States and its coalition allies had achieved one of the most lopsided engage-ments in military history. Speaking from the Oval Office on February 27, 1991, President Bush proclaimed a triumph "for all mankind, for the rule of law, and for what is right," and spoke about constructing a new world order. "We must now begin to look beyond victory in war," he explained. "We must meet the challenge of securing the peace."

....

Saddam Hussein had pinned his hopes on a war of attrition, believing that his adversaries lacked the patience and tenacity to fight a protracted war. If U.S. forces could be lured into heavily fortified "killing zones," he assumed mounting casualties would prompt the Americans to yield. Just as they had done in their earlier eight-year war with Iran, the Iraqis constructed an elaborate system of minefields, bunkers, antitank guns, and fire trenches all surrounded by concertina wire. Slowed by these barriers, a direct American assault would come under a heavy artillery barrage, followed by a counterattack by mechanized divisions of Saddam Hussein's Republican Guard. Rumors circulated in Washington that the Pentagon ordered sixteen thousand body bags in preparation for the war.

Much to the astonishment of onlookers, the United States and its coalition partners won a resounding victory with minimal casualties. Journalists likened the action to a computer game. By taking advantage of navigational data from global positioning satellites and the lethal accuracy of heat-seeking sensors and laser-guided munitions, coalition forces ravaged the Iraqis with wave after wave of swarming aircraft. On the ground, sophisticated American technology allowed nimble armored units to outmaneuver the Iraqis, fire accurately while on the move, and attack at night. It was a war of twenty-first-century electronics against twentieth-century mechanics.

American prowess on the battlefields of the Persian Gulf War signaled to the other great powers that a new era had dawned. Unipolarity was superseding the Cold War bipolar system. With the collapse of the Soviet Union roughly nine months after a cease-fire was established in Iraq, the United States enjoyed unquestioned dominance. It was no longer a superpower; it had become, in the words of former French foreign minister Hubert Védrine, a "hyperpower." The U.S. military was not just stronger than anybody—it was stronger than everybody. American military expenditures exceeded the combined total of all other great powers. Beyond supporting a formidable strategic arsenal, these funds allowed Washington to build a conventional military capability without peer: On the ground, U.S. forces possessed awesome speed, agility, and firepower; in the skies, they combined innovative stealth technology with precision-guided munitions; and at sea, they faced no serious blue-water challenge. With eight operational Nimitz-class aircraft carriers, over 700 overseas military bases, and unparalleled strategic airlift capability, the United States had the singular capacity to project its power rapidly over vast distances.

Complementing U.S. military muscle was its economic strength. During the opening years of the new century, America accounted for over 40 percent of the world's production and 50 percent of its research and development. In 2004, the United States ranked first in global competitiveness, was home of 29 of the 50 largest companies in the world, served as the source of 62 of the top

100 international brands, and comprised roughly 33 percent of the global gross domestic product (GDP). Remarkably, America's military prowess was being maintained by spending only four percent of its $12 trillion GDP, less than a third of that spent during the Second World War.

Aside from the military and economic sources of its power, the United States wielded tremendous soft power as an open, alluring society located at the hub of global telecommunications. American music, films, and television programs commanded wide attention, and U.S. institutions of higher education attracted students from throughout the world. As a dynamic country that blended personal freedom with cutting-edge technology, the United States was positioned in the immediate aftermath of the Cold War to lead through the attractiveness of its culture.

Astonished by the magnitude and scope of American power, it became fashionable for the foreign policy commentariat to write about "the end of history." Francis Fukuyama, for example, saw the collapse of the Soviet Union as the completion of humanity's political evolution, with Western liberal democracy triumphing as the final form of government.[7] Intoxicated by its victories over communism and Saddam Hussein, a self-congratulatory mood enveloped the United States. "We stand tall and therefore we can see further [than other countries]," boasted Madeleine Albright, President Bill Clinton's secretary of state.[8] Heartened by a conviction that the United States was an "indispensable nation," many people in Washington expected the country's preeminent status to continue indefinitely. According to the leaked draft of a 1992 Department of Defense strategic planning document, one of the aims of various U.S. officials after the Soviet Union dissolved was to prevent the rise of a future great-power competitor. As President George W. Bush explained, "America has, and intends to keep, military strengths beyond challenge, thereby making the destabilizing arms races of other eras pointless, and limiting rivalries to trade and other pursuits of peace."[9]

PRIMACY AND WORLD ORDER

As described in preceding chapters, the architecture of contemporary world order evolved from several sources. One was the Westphalian peace settlement of the mid-seventeenth century, based on international anarchy and state sovereignty. The second source was the set of liberal rules and institutions that were endorsed by the Western Allies at the end of World War II, ranging from the economic agreements of Bretton Woods to the collective security principles embedded in the United Nations system. A third major source was the series of tacit understandings and formal conventions on arms control and related strategic issues that developed between the rival superpowers during the Cold War. On the eve of the twenty-first century, with the United States ensconced at the head of a unipolar global system, government officials in Washington felt they had the leverage to uphold this amalgamated structure of world order.

Periods of international primacy provide opportunities for the dominant great power to induce others to accept its conception of what is fitting behavior and how the international system should operate. In the wake of the Persian Gulf War, American policymakers wanted to entrench the liberal rules and multilateral institutions that successive administrations had endorsed since the Second World War. Open markets and nondiscriminatory trade, augmented by monetary stability and financial assistance for states under duress, continued to be hailed as antidotes to economic depression and political extremism. Furthermore, U.S. leaders wished to build on the arms control agreements that were reached over the past few decades. But now that the Cold War was over, decision makers in Washington sought to make several additions to this framework of world order, as chronicled in Table 5.1. First, they strove to bring former adversaries into the fold, gradually making them democratic stakeholders in an expanded liberal world order. Second, they sought to redefine the concept of sovereignty, allowing outside powers to intervene into the domestic affairs of those regimes that were flagrantly violating human rights and civil liberties. Finally, they pushed for a more permissive interpretation of self-defense, which would authorize preventive military action against potential security threats. Let us explore each of these policy initiatives in turn.

TABLE 5.1   MAJOR EVENTS IN THE AFTERMATH OF THE COLD WAR

Date	Event
1991	U.S.-led coalition launches air war on Iraq in Operation Desert Storm on January 17; ground offensive begins on February 24; Iraq accepts cease-fire on February 28
	Slovenia declares independence from Yugoslavia in June and successfully defends its territory against the Yugoslav federal army; Croatia declares independence
	Hard-line opponents of Soviet president and general secretary Mikhail Gorbachev attempt to seize power on August 19; Gorbachev resigns on December 25; independence granted to the former republics of the Soviet Union
1992	Bosnia and Herzegovina declares independence from Yugoslavia; civil war erupts among Bosnian Muslims, Serbs, and Croats; Serbia and Montenegro form a new, smaller Yugoslav federation
1994	North American Free Trade Association (NAFTA) formed; Rwandan genocide

(Continued)

TABLE 5.1 (CONTINUED)

Date	Event
1995	The presidents of Serbia, Croatia, and Bosnia meet in Dayton, Ohio, and sign a peace agreement
1999	The Rambouillet peace talks between Serbs and Kosovar Albanians collapse; North Atlantic Treaty Organization (NATO) air strikes against Serbia begin on March 24 and continue until June 10; UN Interim Administration Mission in Kosovo (UNMIK) is established on June 13 and the NATO-led Kosovo Force (KFOR) is assigned peacekeeping duties
2001	Al Qaeda operatives crash hijacked airliners into the World Trade Center and the Pentagon on September 11; United States responds by launching Operation Enduring Freedom on October 7 against Al Qaeda and Taliban positions in Afghanistan
2003	U.S.-led invasion of Iraq begins on March 19; Baghdad falls on April 9, ending the government of Saddam Hussein; Iraqi insurgency begins
2008	Global financial crisis; Russo-Georgian War
2010	Anti-government protests erupt in Tunisia in December and spread across North Africa and the Middle East during the following year China declares that the South China Sea is an area of core interest
2011	NATO-led coalition undertakes military intervention in Libya on March 19; civil war begins in Syria; Al Qaeda leader Osama bin Laden killed
2013	China announces that it is establishing an air defense identification zone in the East China Sea
2014	Crimean Peninsula annexed by Russia; armed conflict erupts between Ukrainian government and pro-Russian separatists in the eastern part of the country
2015	Full diplomatic relations reestablished between the United States and Cuba; United States and five other great powers reach an agreement with Iran on limiting that country's nuclear program

DEMOCRATIC PEACE THEORY AND AMERICAN FOREIGN POLICY

Widening the liberal order to include countries recently ruled by communist governments with command economies posed an enormous challenge. In addition to privatizing their state-owned enterprises, they had to embrace democratic values and support efforts to construct a civil society. Increasing citizen involvement in public affairs seldom unfolds in a smooth, linear process. Democratization takes time and relapses are common. Sometimes countries shed autocracy only to become populist regimes, adopting the trappings of democratic rule but spurning civil liberties. Although they may hold regular elections, participation and contestation are limited, and few restraints exist on executive power. For American policymakers, backsliding toward authoritarianism would undermine the stability of the post–Cold War world order. Democratization, they concluded, was the key to future peace and security.

As we saw in Chapters 1 and 2, liberal theory assumes that the type of political regime governing a country has a significant impact on its international behavior. Believing autocracies are prone to wage war, Wilsonian liberals at the end of World War I called for replacing the kaiser in Germany, insisting that a democratic regime would be more peaceful than its authoritarian predecessor. Were they right? Are democracies less apt to start wars than other governments?

Today social scientists possess a large body of research that supports **democratic peace theory**. Although constitutionally secure democracies experience foreign conflict as often as nondemocracies and are only slightly less likely than nondemocratic states to initiate wars, they almost never wage war against one another.[10] Scholars advance two overlapping explanations. In the first place, the shared norms of peaceful conflict resolution within democratic political cultures foster a non-zero-sum view of politics and a spirit of compromise. In the second place, institutional checks and balances combine with the hurdle of enlisting public support to constrain decision makers in democratic states from rashly launching large-scale foreign wars. Disputes between mature democracies rarely result in the use of armed force because each side respects the legitimacy of the other and expects it to adopt amicable methods of conflict resolution.

Democracy Promotion as a Goal of U.S. Foreign Policy

A corollary to democratic peace theory postulates that the amount of war globally would diminish as the proportion of democratic states within the international system grew. The claim resonated with Bill Clinton, who had surprisingly defeated George H. W. Bush in the 1992 U.S. presidential election. Democracy promotion—working to increase the ratio of open to closed polities worldwide—ultimately became a cornerstone of his administration's foreign policy. "The best strategy to ensure our security and build a durable peace," he declared in his 1994 State of the Union address, "is to support the advance of democracy elsewhere." Providing technical assistance and other forms of aid to **nongovernmental organizations** that were trying to strengthen civil society in countries previously controlled by authoritarian regimes would enlarge the zone of peace. As Anthony Lake, Clinton's first-term national security adviser, put it, "The successor to a doctrine of containment must be a strategy of enlargement— enlargement of the world's free community."[11]

Democratic peace theory also appealed to President George W. Bush. Following the terrorist attacks on September 11, 2001, when Al Qaeda operatives flew hijacked airliners into the World Trade Center and the Pentagon, Bush announced his "forward strategy for freedom," whose objective was to bring about regime change in autocratic states that were regarded as hostile and dangerous. U.S. national security, he believed, would benefit if these countries became democracies. "We are led, by events and common sense, to one conclusion," Bush declared on January 20, 2005, in his second inaugural address. "The survival of liberty in our land increasingly depends on the success of liberty in other lands." Spreading democracy throughout the world is "the calling of our time." The goal of U.S. foreign policy must be to "support the growth of democratic movements and institutions in every nation and culture."

Democracy promotion coincided with a long-standing missionary impulse to spread America's civic culture, exporting representative government and converting others to liberal values. Ever since John Winthrop declared in 1630 that the immigrants to the New World would establish a "city on the hill," many Americans believed that they were fated to become a moral beacon for humanity. The United States was different from other countries; it was the "First Universal Nation," animated by a unique set of ideals and institutions that others would emulate. When Benjamin Franklin wrote in 1777 that "our Cause is the Cause of Mankind," he foreshadowed Woodrow Wilson's 1919 proclamation that "the idea of America is to serve humanity." It was this same messianic spirit that led Harry Truman to proclaim that "the United States should take the lead in running the world the way the world ought to be run."

"Exceptionalism"—the belief that the United States is not an ordinary country—embodies the conviction that Americans have a higher purpose to serve in the world. Theirs is a special charge to champion freedom and expand liberty. Earlier in U.S. history, most of America's political leaders thought that purpose was served best by remaining aloof from the rest of the world and serving as an example of how a free society should conduct its domestic affairs. Now, with the United States standing at the pinnacle of world power, its leaders embraced an activist foreign policy that promoted democratic values throughout the world. With the Soviet Union gone, senior members of the Clinton administration believed that America had a unique opportunity to solidify democratic gains in countries that had formerly been behind the Iron Curtain.

Consolidating Fledgling Democracies

When Bill Clinton became the U.S. commander in chief on January 20, 1993, the idea of bringing the newly formed democracies of Central and Eastern Europe into the North Atlantic Treaty Organization (NATO) had already been circulating in Washington. After debating for nearly a year about whether this would antagonize Russia, Clinton decided to proceed with the Partnership for Peace (PfP) initiative, which established a mechanism for bilateral cooperation between NATO and over twenty European and central Asian countries, most of which had been Warsaw Pact members or republics within the former Soviet Union. For the Russians, who staunchly opposed the NATO expansion and believed that Soviet leader Mikhail Gorbachev had agreed to German reunification based on the understanding that it would not push NATO defenses forward, the PfP plan seemed to provide a pan-European structure that would give Moscow a voice in geostrategic deliberations over the future of Europe. Clinton's foreign policy team had a different view. They conceived of PfP as a way to channel Eastern Europe's nascent democracies into the Atlantic Alliance.[12]

Whereas Russian leaders initially interpreted PfP as an alternative to NATO enlargement, they soon realized that it actually was the precursor to a bigger American-led bloc. Suspicious that NATO remained a mechanism aimed at isolating and containing Russia, many officials in Moscow believed that their counterparts in Washington were taking advantage of Russia's momentary weakness rather than sincerely working to build a new, inclusive structure for European security. In a speech delivered in Budapest on December 5, 1994, Russian president Boris Yeltsin harshly criticized NATO expansion, though he refrained from taking any actions to dissuade neighboring countries from **bandwagoning** with the United States. After the Czech Republic, Hungary, and Poland acquired NATO membership in 1999, five years later Bulgaria, Estonia, Latvia, Lithuania, Romania, Slovakia, and Slovenia were added to the alliance. Embittered by what he perceived as brazen encroachments by NATO into Russia's sphere of influence, Yeltsin's successor, Vladimir Putin, described the collapse of the Soviet Union in his 2005 state of the nation address as the "greatest geopolitical catastrophe" of the twentieth century. At the 2007 Munich Conference on Security Policy, he elaborated on his interpretation of the post–Cold War world, calling unipolarity unacceptable, describing NATO expansion as a provocation, and complaining that placing frontline military forces along Russia's border created new divisions across the continent.

Despite protests that the United States and its NATO allies had been condescending toward Russia and generally ignored its security interests, at the alliance's Bucharest conference in 2008, NATO leaders proceeded to invite Albania and Croatia to begin accession talks, held out the prospect of accession talks to the former Yugoslav Republic of Macedonia, welcomed Montenegro and Bosnia and Herzegovina to develop Individual Partnership Action Plans (IPAP), encouraged Serbia to do the same, and supported the aspirations of Georgia and Ukraine for eventual membership. From Moscow's point of view, the United States did not grasp that Russia was no longer the chaotic, revenue-strapped country of the early 1990s. Russia once again began to act as an assertive, self-confident great power, and vociferously proclaimed that it would not countenance further NATO expansion into former Soviet republics.

Expanding NATO, cautioned George Kennan, "would be the most fateful error of American policy in the entire post–Cold War era." It would "inflame the nationalistic, anti-Western and militaristic tendencies in Russian opinion" and "restore the atmosphere of the Cold War to East-West relations."[13] His prediction came to pass in the small, mountainous country of Georgia. Ever since Mikheil Saakashvili became its president, Georgia had adopted a pro-American foreign policy. While not a military threat to Russia, the November 2003 "Rose

Revolution" (so named because anti-government protestors carried roses) that brought Saakashvili to power was perceived to be a political threat. Kremlin leaders saw it (and similar protest movements in Ukraine and Kyrgyzstan) as foreign-sponsored efforts to instigate regime change, which, if not stopped, might one day destabilize Russia.

On August 8, 2008, after military units of the Republic of Georgia attacked South Ossetia, a secessionist region that had been seeking to withdraw from Georgia and align itself with Russia, Moscow intervened, routing the Georgian army and subsequently recognizing the independence of South Ossetia and Abkhazia, another breakaway region. In justifying Russia's actions, President Dmitry Medvedev emphasized that "Russia, just like other countries in the world, has regions where it has its privileged interests." Moscow could not idly stand by, he explained, while events in Georgia endangered Russian citizens in the area. Implicit in his comments was a message that the Kremlin would not acquiesce to further NATO expansion eastward.

RETHINKING STATE SOVEREIGNTY IN AN ERA OF GLOBALIZATION

The second major addition that the United States advocated for the post–Cold War world order called for a reconceptualization of state sovereignty. Until the fifteenth century, most civilizations remained relatively isolated from one another. Circumscribed by slow, costly, and often dangerous transportation routes, international intercourse tended to occur within self-contained regions of the world. Except for intermittent trade, occasional waves of migrants, and periodic clashes with invaders, contact with distant nations was rare.

By the late twentieth century, the process of **globalization** began changing age-old conceptions about geographic distance and international frontiers. Advances in telecommunication technology were reshaping the world. Markets, for example, no longer corresponded with national boundaries. Rather than commodities being produced by and for people living within a single territorial state, they were increasingly made by people living in different parts of the world for a global marketplace. Cross-border financial flows—borrowing, lending, investing, and currency trading—were also rapidly expanding, leading many economists to ask whether it was still meaningful to think of the nation-state as the basis for organizing economic activity. Concurrently, ethicists wondered whether it made sense to think about sovereignty, nonintervention, and **human rights** from a Westphalian perspective.

From the end of the Thirty Years' War through the Second World War, the twin principles of sovereignty and nonintervention framed how people thought about human rights in international politics. Sovereignty denoted that no authority stood above the state, and nonintervention meant that states could manage affairs inside their borders without external interference. Rights, from this standpoint, were prerogatives granted by rulers to their subjects, whose plight was a matter of domestic politics, not the concern of outsiders. How a state treated its citizens was its own business.

Whereas human rights were rarely part of traditional diplomatic discourse, by the second half of the twentieth century international society began to recognize the inherent moral status of humans and the concomitant obligation of states to protect that status. Pundits and policymakers now questioned the relevance of a framework of world order built upon Westphalian footings (see Box 5.1). Was sovereignty sacrosanct? Did it safeguard rogue leaders who abused the civil liberties of their citizens? What could foreign powers do if a state failed in its responsibility to protect its population?

Box 5.1 You Decide

The Republic of Somalia, a poor, predominantly agricultural country located on the Horn of Africa, was commonly described as a "failed state" during the latter part of the twentieth century. It descended into civil war in January 1991, when the government of Mohamed Siad Barre was ousted by a coalition of rebel groups, who subsequently clashed with each other over which clan-based warlord would seize political control. As factional conflict increased, economic disruption and famine spread throughout the country. Responding to reports of mass starvation, on December 3, 1992, the UN Security Council passed Resolution 794, which characterized the situation as a "threat to international peace" and authorized the secretary-general "to use all possible means to establish as soon as possible a secure environment for humanitarian relief operations." In a televised speech to the nation on the following day, U.S. president George H. W. Bush announced that he was sending troops to Somalia to open supply routes that would allow food to reach those who were suffering. While avowing that "some crises cannot be resolved without American involvement," Bush underscored the limited objectives of the mission. American forces would be deployed to provide humanitarian assistance, not to pacify the country.

Despite Bush's reluctance to police Somalia, the U.S. military soon found itself patrolling the capital city of Mogadishu and disarming gunmen. When Bill Clinton replaced Bush in the Oval Office, he began reevaluating America's role in the region, weighing the alternatives for dealing with the disintegrating Somali state. Three options appeared viable. First, he could order the U.S. troops to continue guarding relief convoys but stipulate that they not take forceful action against militias from the warring clans. Second, he could expand the mission beyond humanitarian relief by attempting to capture the warlords who were carving the country into

(Continued)

(Continued)

personal fiefdoms. Third, he could withdraw American combat forces and place Somalia's security and well-being in the hands of the United Nations. Each option had potential advantages and drawbacks. The first option would keep supplies flowing to people in need, but it would not remove those who were undermining the country's stability. The second option would directly target the perpetrators of Somalia's political chaos but could grow into an open-ended military operation with significant American casualties. Finally, the third option would prevent the United States from wading into a military quagmire, but it was unlikely that UN forces would be able to maintain peace.

Lurking beneath these options were several thorny questions. Do national leaders have a moral obligation to ameliorate acute deprivation in other countries? What duties does the preeminent power in a unipolar world have for providing humanitarian assistance and peacekeeping forces to failing states? As the architect of the current world order, was the United States responsible for enforcing internationally recognized human rights? The answers to these questions were not self-evident to Clinton and his staff. Controversy abounded. If you were a high-ranking adviser to the president, how would you answer them? Which option would you recommend?

One response to these questions was that Westphalian principles of state sovereignty were still germane. From the perspective of **communitarianism,** human rights were a matter of national jurisdiction. National leaders did not have duties to people outside of their country and should not intervene into the domestic affairs of other states. In a world populated by diverse cultures, where no widely accepted basis existed for choosing among different value systems, communitarians held that references to universal moral obligations were problematic.

Another response came from adherents to **cosmopolitanism,** who insisted that national leaders had a moral obligation to alleviate human suffering no matter where it occurred. All individuals, solely by virtue of being human, had inalienable rights that warranted international protection. If a national leader had the power to prevent insufferable harm from traumatizing people living in another country, action should be taken on the grounds of common humanity. Not only was **humanitarian intervention** legally justified but it was morally necessary in situations where governments flagrantly violated the human rights of their citizens.

While communitarian theories had their adherents, following the Cold War many people gravitated toward the cosmopolitan view that all individuals held fundamental rights and sovereignty should not shield national leaders from outside efforts to stem flagrant violations of those rights. Their stance rested on three propositions: (1) human rights are an international entitlement; (2) governments committing grave violations of human rights lose their legitimacy and forfeit protection under international law; and (3) the international community has legal and moral obligations to stop human rights violations. During the first quarter century of its existence, the UN developed a detailed list of the inherent rights possessed by all human beings. The most important legal formulation of these rights is expressed in the so-called International Bill of Human Rights, the informal name given to the Universal Declaration of Human Rights (which was passed by a vote of the UN General Assembly in 1948), the International Covenant on Civil and Political Rights, and the International Covenant on Economic, Social, and Cultural Rights (which were both opened for signature in 1966 and entered into force a decade later). Although Article 2 (7) of the UN Charter prevents members from interfering in the domestic matters of other states, the UN Charter's legal protection does not extend to **genocide** or other horrific abuses of human rights that are shocking to the conscience of the international community.

Human Rights and the Disintegration of Yugoslavia

During the Clinton administration, American policymakers applied this cosmopolitan, post-Westphalian line of thought to the Balkans as Yugoslavia began disintegrating. Yugoslavia initially had been stitched together after the defeat of the Central powers in the First World War with the formation of the Kingdom of Serbs, Croats, and Slovenes. Renamed Yugoslavia in 1929, the new country faced several grave problems. Externally, its boundaries were challenged by Italy in the west and Bulgaria in the east. Internally, it was divided by heritage, religion, and alphabet: Serbs had lived under Ottoman rule, they were Orthodox Christians, and they used the Cyrillic alphabet; Croats and Slovenes had lived under Austro-Hungarian rule, they were Roman Catholics, and they used the Latin alphabet. Further complicating matters, parts of Yugoslavia contained significant Muslim populations, composed of the descendants of people who had converted to Islam during the centuries of Ottoman rule. Sharp disagreements over how the country should be governed magnified these divisions. Reeling from ethnic discord and political bickering, Yugoslavia collapsed soon after the Germans invaded in April 1941.

The country was reconstituted after the Second World War as the Socialist Federal Republic of Yugoslavia. Throughout the war, a resistance movement known as the Partisans conducted a guerrilla campaign against German garrisons. Led by Josip Broz (who used the pseudonym "Tito"), they proposed building a political system that would transcend the territory's historical divisions. When the fighting ended, Tito established a federation composed of six equal republics: Serbia, Croatia, Slovenia, Bosnia and Herzegovina, Macedonia, and Montenegro. To assuage the feelings of Hungarian and Albanian minorities, two "autonomous regions" were created within the Serbian Republic: Vojvodina and Kosovo, respectively (see Map 5.2). The ethnic composition of the republics

MAP 5.2 THE DISINTEGRATION OF YUGOSLAVIA

The Yugoslav state forged by Tito after World War II began disintegrating a decade after his death. In 1991, Slovenia and Croatia declared their independence. They were followed later that year by Macedonia and by Bosnia and Herzegovina the subsequent year, which then experienced a civil war among Muslims, Croats, and Serbs living in the territory. During April 1992, the two remaining republics of Serbia and Montenegro formed the Federal Republic of Yugoslavia, the remnant of the much larger Socialist Federal Republic of Yugoslavia established by Tito. Armed conflict in the province of Kosovo between the Serbian government and ethnic Albanians began escalating during 1996 and led a military intervention by the North Atlantic Treaty Organization (NATO) three years later.

Source: Data courtesy of the University Libraries, The University of Texas at Austin.

varied widely. Whereas 93 percent of Slovenia's population was Slovenian, only 43 percent of Bosnia and Herzegovina consisted of Bosniaks (as the Slavic Muslims of the region were called), while another 34 percent were Serbs, and roughly 17 percent were Croats. In addition to variations in the ethnic composition of the republics, levels of economic development also differed. The northern third of the country (Slovenia, Croatia, and the autonomous region of Vojvodina within Serbia) had twice the per capita income of the rest of Yugoslavia, an inequality exacerbated by the desire of northerners to invest their earnings locally rather than have them used to subsidize the less industrialized southern republics.

Civil War in Bosnia

During his years in power, Tito used a blend of personal diplomacy, political decentralization, and brute force to muzzle ethnic discord. However, following his death in 1980, the Socialist Federal Republic of Yugoslavia began falling apart. Having borrowed heavily to finance salary increases for state employees and projects that duplicated in one republic what already existed in others, policymakers in the capital city of Belgrade faced rising inflation and declining productivity. Owing to a wave of regional grievances that accompanied the economic downturn, the Slovene and Croatian parliaments declared independence from Yugoslavia in June 1991. Belgrade responded by sending armored units into the breakaway republics. A negotiated settlement ended hostilities between the Slovenes and the Yugoslav National Army in July, and a cease-fire was reached with the Croats six months later. However, Macedonia declared independence in December, and armed conflict erupted in Bosnia and Herzegovina the following year.

On April 27, 1992, the two remaining republics—Serbia and Montenegro—created a new federation known as the Federal Republic of Yugoslavia. This third incarnation of Yugoslavia possessed approximately 45 percent of the population and 40 percent of the territory of Tito's Socialist Federal Republic of Yugoslavia, with Serbia accounting for roughly 94 percent of the new federation's inhabitants and 87 percent of its area.

Almost immediately, the Federal Republic of Yugoslavia became embroiled in the civil strife that was tearing Bosnia apart. With sizable Serb and Croat minorities living among a largely Muslim population, Bosnian leaders had feared that the republic would be dismembered by the pull of **irredentism**, with Serbia absorbing territory populated by Bosnian Serbs and Croatia incorporating territory inhabited by Bosnia Croats. In a futile attempt to prevent partition along ethnic lines, they declared independence. Bosnia's Serbs responded by proclaiming the formation of their own state, which they called the Serb Republic of Bosnia. Hostilities soon followed. By early 1993, two-thirds of Bosnia was under Serb control and the capital city of Sarajevo suffered a brutal siege. Meanwhile, Bosnian Croats began attacking Muslim positions around the medieval city of Mostar.

During the summer of 1995, Bosnian Serbs seized the Muslim town of Srebrenica, which had been declared a "safe area" by the UN Security Council. Over the next week, they massacred 7,000 inhabitants in the most gruesome mass execution in Europe since World War II. As the world recoiled in horror, several developments began to turn the tide of battle. First, the Croat minority in Bosnia agreed to join with Bosnia's Muslims in a coalition that would fight alongside the Republic of Croatia against the Serbs. Second, the combat effectiveness of the Bosnian and Croatian armies began improving: The former was now obtaining desperately needed weapons from Iran, while the latter was receiving military training from retired American officers of Croatian descent. Third, to supplement the economic sanctions already in place against Yugoslavia, increased diplomatic pressure was brought to bear on Belgrade by the so-called Contact Group (the United States, Great Britain, France, Germany, and Russia) to restrain the Bosnian Serbs. Finally, on August 30, over sixty NATO warplanes began a massive assault on Serb positions around Sarajevo.

As a result of these developments, the Bosnian Serbs faced a joint Croat-Bosnian offensive in August and September, which pushed the Serbs out of the Krajina region of Croatia and toward Banja Luka, the largest Serb city in Bosnia. By October, the United States concluded that the time was ripe for a cease-fire. A rough balance of power existed among the combatants and disagreements between the Croats and Bosnian Muslims threatened to jeopardize their fragile coalition. By stopping the fighting before anyone had to capitulate, peace talks could commence without a shroud of humiliation draped over one or more of the combatants. None of them had achieved all they might have wished on the battlefield, but they were not so dissatisfied with the military status quo that they would balk at negotiating a peace agreement.

In November 1995, at Wright-Patterson Air Force Base on the outskirts of Dayton, Ohio, President Alija Izetbegovic of Bosnia and Herzegovina, Franjo Tudjman of Croatia, and Slobodan Milošević of Serbia met to sign a peace accord. Under the terms of the agreement, a single Bosnian state was established. It possessed a central government in Sarajevo and two regional entities: a Muslim-Croat Federation encompassing 51 percent of the country's territory and a Serb Republic of Bosnia comprising 49 percent of the territory. An International Protection Force (IFOR) of 60,000 NATO troops would oversee the disengagement of the rival armies and their withdrawal to predesignated locations. In addition, free elections would be held within nine months, displaced persons were allowed to recover lost property, and all citizens were guaranteed the right to move freely throughout the country. These accords did not provide the foundation for a stable, multiethnic Bosnia, however. Hardly anyone felt allegiance to the state cobbled together at Dayton. Washington had the clout to pressure Bosnians, Croats, and Serbs to sign an agreement, but it underestimated the allure of nationalism and the difficulty of transplanting liberal principles to foreign soil. Being a unipolar power did not facilitate state building in a land whose culture and history differed profoundly from the American political experience.

Humanitarian Intervention in Kosovo

At the same time that the United States was trying to end the civil war in Bosnia, conflict erupted in Kosovo, where ethnic Albanians began pressing for independence. An autonomous province within Serbia, Kosovo was seen by Serbs as their ancient homeland and the heart of the Serbian Orthodox Church. Roughly the size of Connecticut, it contained the Patriarchate of Pec and many other important religious sites, including the Monastery of Michael the Archangel near Prizren and the fourteenth-century Gracanica and Decani Monasteries. Following the victory of the Ottoman Empire over the Serbs in 1389, many Serbs migrated to lands north of Kosovo and ethnic Albanians began moving into the region. By the last decade of the twentieth century, 90 percent of Kosovo's 2 million inhabitants were Albanians, who had the highest birth rate in Europe and a population largely under the age of thirty.

Friction between Serbs and Kosovo's ethnic Albanians had existed since the founding of Yugoslavia. After Tito's death, it threatened to tear the country apart. On April 24, 1987, Slobodan Milošević, the head of the Serbia branch of the League of Yugoslav Communists, traveled to Kosovo to hear grievances from Serbs living in the province. Assembled where the epic battle had been fought against the Ottomans centuries earlier, the Serbs clashed with local Kosovo Albanian police. Milošević, in a brief but electrifying speech, told the crowd, "No one will ever beat a Serb again." His popularity soared. In May 1989 he was elected to the presidency of Serbia and, a few months later, he rescinded the provisions of the 1974 Constitution that had provided autonomy to Kosovo. Predictability, ethnic Albanians assailed Serbs living in the province. Milošević, who as president of Serbia dominated the newly formed Federal Republic of Yugoslavia, then proposed to force the Albanians out of Kosovo, a policy known euphemistically as "ethnic cleansing."

Although some Kosovar Albanians believed that the best way to oppose Milošević was through passive resistance, others disagreed. In May 1993 several of them gunned down a group of Serb police officers in Glogovac. The incident was the opening salvo in a guerrilla campaign waged by the Kosovo Liberation Army (KLA). For the next two years, the KLA launched sporadic attacks against Serbs, provoking reprisals against villages suspected of sheltering the insurgents, which radicalized even more ethnic Albanians. Beginning in the late spring of 1998, the intermittent sniping and skirmishing of previous years escalated to fierce fighting. After weeks of KLA gains, the Serbs launched a counteroffensive that drove the guerrillas back into hiding. The fighting displaced some 200,000 ethnic Albanians, forcing many to seek refuge in the hills along Kosovo's border with Albania.

Responding to images of burning homes and frightened villagers on the nightly news, the UN Security Council passed Resolution 1199, which insisted that the Federal Republic of Yugoslavia cease all hostilities affecting the civilian population and alluded to the possibility of further action if it did not obey. NATO made similar demands. When violence erupted again in early 1999, members of the Contact Group summoned the Serbs and Kosovar Albanians to peace talks in Rambouillet, a small town located about thirty miles from Paris. The peace proposal offered to the delegates at Rambouillet called for the disarmament of the KLA, the withdrawal of Yugoslav military units from Kosovo, deployment of a NATO-led peacekeeping force, restoration of Kosovo's autonomy, and a referendum in three years on the region's political future. Much to the surprise of the United States, neither side accepted the proposal. With negotiations at an impasse, the talks were suspended for nineteen days and then resumed in Paris. Tremendous pressure was placed on the Kosovar Albanians during the recess to accept the peace proposal. Although they eventually relented, the Serbs remained intransigent. In a final effort to convince the Serbs to accept the peace proposal, U.S. envoy Richard Holbrooke flew to Belgrade to meet with Slobodan Milošević. If anyone had a chance to salvage the situation, it was Holbrooke. Labeled "the Muhammad Ali" of diplomacy by other foreign service officers for being able to wear down even the most difficult opponent, he bluntly informed the Serbian leader that unless he accepted the Rambouillet proposals, NATO would bomb Serbia. Speaking in a firm deliberate tone, Holbrooke promised, "It will be swift, it will be severe, it will be sustained."[14]

In a televised address to the nation on March 24, President Bill Clinton argued that "ending this tragedy was a moral imperative." The United States had learned a lesson in Bosnia: Firmness saves lives. "We must apply that lesson in Kosovo," he continued, "before what happened in Bosnia, happens there, too." Clinton's advisers believed that NATO airstrikes against the Bosnian Serbs during the summer of 1995 forced them to negotiate at Dayton. Another dose of air power would presumably compel Milošević to accept the Rambouillet accords.

The NATO air campaign lasted for 78 days. The United States flew 60 percent of the more than 37,000 sorties against the Federal Republic of Yugoslavia and was responsible for over 90 percent of the electronic warfare missions and over 95 percent of the cruise missiles that were fired. In addition to attacking Serbian military units, the portfolio of targets included oil refineries, radio and television broadcasting facilities, key elements in the transportation infrastructure, and the national power grid. Once the grid went down, Milošević's support began to erode as the civilian population became increasingly demoralized.

Following intense negotiations, Milošević agreed to terminate hostilities. The war did not end with Serbian officials from the Federal Republic of Yugoslavia accepting the same proposal they previously rejected at Rambouillet. The United Nations rather than NATO assumed political authority over Kosovo. Following the withdrawal of Yugoslav military forces, civil administration in the province was turned over to the United Nations Interim Administration Mission in Kosovo (UNMIK), and peacekeeping was undertaken by a 45,000-strong Kosovo Force (KFOR), a NATO-led body that included contingents from twenty non-NATO countries, including Russia. Within days of the establishment of KFOR, hundreds of thousands of ethnic Albanians began returning to Kosovo while Serbs, threatened by KLA members bent on revenge, departed. Unrest continued to plague Kosovo as the economy sputtered, organized crime became rampant, and different factions of ex-KLA guerrillas fought among themselves.

Milošević remained in power when the war ended, but he was indicted by the International Criminal Tribunal for the former Yugoslavia (ICTY), a court in The Hague, Netherlands, created by the UN Security Council to prosecute those who committed war crimes, crimes against humanity, and genocide during the armed conflicts that led to the breakup of Tito's Socialist Federal Republic Yugoslavia. After being defeated in the fall 2000 presidential election and subsequently linked to the theft of state funds, Milošević was taken into custody by Yugoslav authorities and transferred to The Hague to stand trial. Although he died before a verdict was reached, Carla del Ponte, the ICTY chief prosecutor, noted that the indictment of an incumbent head of state for war crimes conveyed an important post-Westphalian principle: National leaders could not evade legal accountability for their actions by invoking state sovereignty.

Others drew a different lesson from the U.S. experience in Bosnia and Kosovo. They believed that too many policymakers in Washington concluded that America only had to throw its weight around to get results. These observers drew a straight line from the Balkans to Iraq.[15]

ANTICIPATORY SELF-DEFENSE AND PREVENTIVE WAR

Promoting democracy and reconceptualizing state sovereignty were not the only modifications in the post–Cold War order that the United States sponsored while it stood at the pinnacle of world power. It also sought to redefine the concept of self-defense.

Following Al Qaeda's 2001 attacks on New York and Washington, American aircraft and special operations forces struck the Taliban regime in Afghanistan, which had harbored Osama bin Laden and furnished his operatives with a place to train future terrorists. Suspicious of possible ties between Al Qaeda and Saddam Hussein, President George W. Bush next turned his sights on Iraq. When the 1991 Persian Gulf War ended, Saddam Hussein was allowed to remain in power, ostensibly because the United States did not want to become entrapped in a prolonged occupation of a fragmented, unstable country. The 9/11 attacks prompted a reevaluation of that decision. Modern technology allowed transnational terrorist networks to strike almost anywhere with devastating consequences. Saddam, it was now feared, was developing weapons of mass destruction and might provide them to Al Qaeda. Without fixed territory or a population to protect, Osama bin Laden could not be deterred by threats of retaliation; consequently, Bush advocated a third amendment to the prevailing ideas about world order—changing the way that the international community interpreted self-defense. Identifying Iraq as a potential source of terrorist activity, he ordered a massive air campaign against Baghdad on March 19, 2003. In short order, the U.S. military removed Saddam Hussein from power, dismantled his security apparatus, and began redesigning the Iraqi political system. America, the Bush administration explained, had acted in anticipatory self-defense.

Since the earliest days of the modern international system, self-defense has been understood as a sovereign right, one that every state possessed in order to protect itself in the rough and tumble world of international politics. Specifying when this right could be invoked has always been controversial, however. International law authorized states to use armed force once they had been attacked, so long as their military actions were proportionate and they avoided targeting noncombatants. But was force also warranted against potential future dangers? Was it lawful to assail threats that are not wholly formed? Most legal analysts agreed that it was acceptable to preempt an impending strike. If a state had insufficient time for an effective nonmilitary response, national leaders need not wait until an advancing enemy had crossed their country's borders before taking military action. Preemptive defense, as U.S. secretary of state Daniel Webster put it in the 1837 *Caroline* incident, was justified in situations of "instant, overwhelming necessity" that leave "no choice of means, and no moment for deliberation."[16]

The horrific events of September 11, 2001, led the Bush administration to push for a more proactive conception of self-defense. **Terrorism** was no longer a rare and relatively remote threat. Not only did groups like Al Qaeda have global reach, but stealth, ingenuity, and fanaticism made them frighteningly lethal. Emphasizing the peril posed by violent extremists armed with weapons of mass destruction, Bush argued for the right to take preventive military action against any states that supported, trained, or harbored terrorists. Whereas **preemption** involves the use of force to intercept a military strike that is about to occur, a **preventive war** entails the use of force to eliminate any possible future strike—even if there is no reason to believe that the capacity to mount an attack currently existed. In short, the grounds for preemption lie in evidence of a credible, imminent threat, whereas the basis for prevention rests on suspicions of an incipient, contingent threat.

The logic underpinning Bush's call for preventive, anticipatory self-defense was built on the premise that waiting for dire threats to fully materialize was waiting too long. America could not afford to stand idly in the face of grave and gathering dangers. Even if there was just a 1 percent chance of a catastrophic terrorist attack, insisted Vice President Dick Cheney, the United States had to act as if it were a certainty.[17] As he and others in the administration saw it, absolute proof of an enemy's capabilities and intentions should not be a precondition for preventive military action; that would be too high a threshold in a world where warnings of a devastating attack would be limited and confirmation of the perpetrator's identity unattainable in operational time. As President Bush's September 17, 2002, report, *The National Security Strategy of the United States* concluded, in these circumstances "the best defense is a good offense."

Despite the allure of revising the framework of world order to allow swift, decisive attacks against budding threats, the Bush administration's position on anticipatory self-defense did not gain widespread international acceptance. Critics feared that such a permissive doctrine would set a risky precedent. If mere suspicions about an opponent become a justifiable cause for military action, every truculent leader would have a pretext for ordering first strikes against prospective foes. Critics further argued that preventive wars could easily be triggered by unreliable intelligence reports. Predicting another state's future behavior is difficult because leadership intentions are hard to discern, information on long-term goals may be shrouded in secrecy, and signals about its policy plans may be distorted or missed due to background noise. A major policy dilemma facing national leaders contemplating preventive war is the ratio of "false positives" to "false negatives." How can leaders avoid unleashing preventive wars against states that are wrongly suspected to be planning aggression without foregoing action against states that are indeed planning aggression?

Finally, those opposing anticipatory self-defense also noted that foreign policymakers must be attentive to how addressing one problem may lay the foundation for more challenging problems. The 2003 invasion of Iraq ousted Saddam Hussein, but it unexpectedly entangled Washington in a protracted insurgency that led to numerous casualties, drained resources, and frustrated the U.S. effort to build a new democracy in the volatile Middle East.

THE TWILIGHT OF UNIPOLARITY

Ever since the Peace of Westphalia in 1648, war has been less frequent when an unambiguous rank order existed among the principal members of the international system and a single dominant state held a decisive advantage over its nearest challenger. However, throughout modern history these conditions have been rare and fleeting due to differential growth rates among the major powers. When relative productivity and investment in the dominant state decline, when the costs of maintaining its military superiority and underwriting international institutions soar, and when challengers develop greater capacity to extract resources and become more technologically innovative, unipolarity begins to wane.

Leading From Behind

Changes in the configuration of the global system surfaced as the presidency of George W. Bush drew to a close. America's unipolar moment was ending. The wars in Afghanistan and Iraq had imposed by this time an enormous economic burden on the United States, which was funded through deficit spending rather than bonds or tax increases. Estimates of the war-related costs ranged between $1 trillion and $5 trillion, when such factors as lifetime care of wounded soldiers and the economic value of lost productivity of National Guard and Reserve troops were included in the calculations. Instead of the $5.6 trillion surplus projected by the Congressional Budget Office for the first decade of the new century, the level of federal debt exceeded $8.9 trillion by 2007.

The financial crisis of 2008–2009 added to the country's woes. Plummeting values in the housing market triggered a collapse in financial assets that were collateralized by real estate wealth. The economic carnage spread from highly leveraged investment banks to the insurance industry and commercial banking and then to corporations such as Chrysler and General Motors, which relied on easily accessible consumer credit to sell their products. The Dow Jones Industrial Average lost roughly a third of its value in 2008, household wealth dropped by more than 20 percent, and unemployment climbed to 10 percent. Nor were the effects limited to the United States. Stock markets worldwide tumbled, global foreign direct investment outflows declined by 42 percent, world trade contracted by 9 percent, and total global output as measured by GDP shrank by 2.3 percent.

Ranking as the worst economic downturn since the Great Depression, the financial crisis had far-reaching implications for U.S. foreign policy under President Barack Obama, who had recently been elected. Not only did it erode faith in the American gospel of privatization, deregulation, and open markets, but it led several prominent figures to suggest that a post-American era was emerging.[18] No longer could Washington bankroll world order. It needed to rebalance commitments with capabilities. Worried that the United States was overextended, President Obama sought to convince allies to help shoulder financial burdens at the same time that he tried to engage America's adversaries diplomatically. On the one hand, he encouraged members of the Atlantic Alliance to increase military spending and become more assertive in defending their common values. On the other hand, he strove to reset relations with Russia, reconcile with Cuba and the Muslim world, and pivot toward the ascending nations of Asia. In a speech delivered at West Point on December 1, 2009, Obama said that he would not pursue policy goals that were beyond what could be achieved at a reasonable cost. "We can't . . . relieve all the world's misery," he conceded. International politics is "tough, complicated, messy" and "full of hardship and tragedy." To make headway "we have to choose where we can make a real impact." We must recognize "that there are going to be times where the best we can do is to shine a spotlight on something that's terrible, but not believe that we can automatically solve it."[19] Washington would still play a primary role in setting the global agenda, he reassured the nation, but henceforth it would recognize the limits of military power.

For Obama, overreaching posed more dangers for America than underreaching.[20] Retrenchment, from his perspective, was a pragmatic response to a decade of overreaching. It entailed scaling back, cutting losses, and sharing responsibilities. America would lead by articulating goals, empowering collaborators, and taking measured actions to keep its partners on course. One member of his administration characterized it as "leading from behind"—guiding others like a shepherd herding his or her flock.

An example of this occurred in 2011, when a NATO-led coalition of nineteen states imposed a no-fly zone, naval blockade, and bombing campaign aimed at the regime of Libyan ruler Muammar Qaddafi. Following a rebellion in late 2010 against Tunisian dictator Zine al-Abidine Ben Ali, popular uprisings had spread across North Africa, eventually toppling Egyptian president Hosni Mubarak a few months later. Mubarak's ouster encouraged Qaddafi's political foes, who seized control over several cities in eastern Libya. Fearing the volatile leader's threats to massacre opposition forces, French president Nicolas Sarkozy, backed by British prime minister David Cameron, called for military intervention. While President Obama insisted that the Libyan government refrain from inflicting violence on its opponents, he hesitated to take direct action. Unless there was an existential threat to the United States, Obama believed that it would be best to avoid becoming mired in another war with a Muslim country.

On March 17, 2011, the UN Security Council passed a resolution calling for "all necessary measures" to protect Libyan civilians. The mission soon widened into ousting Qaddafi, with the United States playing a central, albeit somewhat veiled, role. Although American allies flew the majority of the sorties and largely enforced the naval blockade, the United States provided the bulk of intelligence-gathering and refueling aircraft as well as precision-guided munitions and targeting assistance. Qaddafi was overthrown at a relatively low cost to the coalition. Only one aircraft was lost, and no major casualties were incurred. Yet the political results were dreadful. Civil order in Libya disintegrated, convincing Obama that further military involvement in the Middle East should be avoided. Thus, when Syria disintegrated into civil war shortly thereafter, Obama refused to become deeply involved, even when Syrian president Bashar al-Assad crossed his "red line" by using chemical weapons against the rebels.

Financial constraints and apprehension over becoming ensnared in an interminable **asymmetric war** also influenced how the Obama administration tackled the unrelenting conflict in Afghanistan. One approach considered by the White House was a search-and-destroy strategy that attempted to grind down insurgent forces with massive firepower. It was rejected because collateral damage might alienate civilians and strengthen their support for the insurgency. A second approach was a clear-and-hold strategy that assumed protecting the noncombatants within territories liberated from rebel control would be critical for gaining their assistance. Rather than operating out of remote, fortress-like compounds, U.S. forces would live in the neighborhoods they wished to secure, building relationships with locals that allowed them to discriminate between those rebels who could be won over and those who were irreconcilable. Despite seeming to work under the command of General David Petraeus in Iraq, senior officials lamented that this approach was slow and expensive, requiring roughly one soldier or policeman for every fifty civilians. Equally troubling, no successful counterinsurgency in the twentieth century took less than a decade.[21] With the war in Afghanistan costing over $100 billion a year and the Republican-controlled House of Representatives complaining about the national debt, Obama soured on counterinsurgency as a solution to the turmoil in Afghanistan and began looking for a way to draw down U.S. troop strength.

Given the drawbacks of search-and-destroy and clear-and-hold, Vice President Joe Biden advocated a strategy of counterterrorism—eliminating incorrigible militants with special operations forces and precision-guided missiles fired from drones. Though less expensive than the alternatives under consideration, this approach had shortcomings, too. As one presidential adviser observed, it was like exterminating one bee at a time rather than destroying the hive.[22] However, when a team of U.S. Navy SEALs killed Al Qaeda leader Osama bin Laden in May 2011, Obama embraced counterterrorism. According to the 2012 strategic guidance for the Department of Defense, U.S. forces would "no longer be sized to conduct large-scale, prolonged stability operations." Whenever possible, the United States would adopt "low-cost and small-footprint approaches" to achieving its security objectives.[23]

Sustaining the Liberal World Order at a Bearable Cost

Throughout America's unipolar moment, each occupant of the White House tried to enhance the voluntary, rules-based international order that their predecessors had constructed after the Second World War. These efforts were numerous, and most produced positive results. Several arms control agreements were negotiated with the Kremlin to lower the odds that an arms race between the United States and the Russian Federation would escalate to a mutually destructive nuclear exchange. The most important accords were the Strategic Arms Reduction Treaties of 1991 (START I), 1993 (START II), and 2010 (New START), and the Strategic Offensive Reductions Treaty of 2002 (SORT), which cut the number of weapons in each country's nuclear inventory. On the economic front, Canada, Mexico, and the United States signed the North American Free Trade Agreement (NAFTA) in 1993, and two years later the General Agreement on Tariffs and Trade (GATT) was superseded by the World Trade Organization (WTO), which had the authority to enforce trading rules and adjudicate trade disputes. All of these agreements rested on the conviction that world order would be enhanced by framing world politics as a **positive-sum game** and embedding American power within a set of rules that allayed cutthroat competition.

In addition to strengthening the liberal rules-based order, Washington also tried to extend its reach, expanding the zone of free-market democracies and intervening abroad to shore up human rights and the rule of law. Former Soviet republics and members of the Warsaw Pact were brought into NATO, and, although the United States did not stop the 1994 genocide in Rwanda, it inserted itself into the turbulent domestic politics of Somalia, Haiti, Bosnia, Serbia, and Libya. Unchecked by peer competitors following the collapse of the Soviet Union, America redefined its strategic interests broadly. "We're an empire now," proclaimed a senior adviser to President George W. Bush in 2004, "and when we act, we create our own reality."[24]

However, by the end of Bush's second term, American optimism had eroded. Despite Obama's ability to engineer a recovery from the 2008–2009 economic crisis, with thirty-two consecutive quarters of job creation and financial growth, faith in the capacity of the world's preeminent state to accomplish ambitious foreign policy goals unilaterally had faded. The United States remained at the summit of world power, but its comparative advantage over other great powers was clearly receding. Intractable wars in Afghanistan and Iraq, alongside the Great Recession of 2008–2009 and the unprecedented growth of America's national debt, sapped American strength. At the very time that Washington's ability to project American power was declining, great-power challengers were rising. Russia seized the Crimean Peninsula and supported separatists in the eastern part of Ukraine. China declared that the South and East China Seas were areas of "core interest" and began moving military assets into both regions under its security strategy of "active defense" which, ironically, mirrored the "anticipatory self-defense" justification that the United States had voiced when it invaded Iraq in 2003.[25] To many onlookers, the American-led liberal order was unraveling, and in its place the growing rivalry between the United States, Russia, and China threatened to plunge the world into a new Cold War.

As his presidency drew to a close, Barack Obama penned a letter to his successor. "American leadership in this world is indispensable," he counseled. "It's up to us, through action and example, to sustain the international order that's expanded steadily since the end of the Cold War, and upon which our own wealth and safety depend."[26] In the light of Donald Trump's campaign rhetoric, it seemed unlikely that he would heed Obama's advice.

KEY TERMS

asymmetric war 119

bandwagoning 105

coercive diplomacy 97

communitarianism 108

compellence 97

cosmopolitanism 108

democratic peace theory 103

economic sanctions 97

genocide 109

globalization 106

human rights 106

humanitarian intervention 108

irredentism 111

limited war 98

nongovernmental organizations 103

positive-sum game 120

preemption 116

preventive war 116

terrorism 116

The Unraveling Liberal Order

What worried me the most . . . is the fact that the rules-based international order is being challenged.

—DONALD TUSK,

PRESIDENT, EUROPEAN COUNCIL

On December 4, 1918, U.S. president Woodrow Wilson sailed to France aboard the SS *George Washington*, bearing the vision of a liberal, rules-based world order anchored in democracy, free trade, and collective security. Upon his arrival in Paris, he was cheered by enormous crowds eager to voice their gratitude for his role in ending the Great War. Wilson received the keys to the city and had his name spelled out in lights along the route of a parade held in his honor. "Moral force is irresistible," he said when proposing an explanation for his enthusiastic welcome.

Although Wilson's idealistic experiment in global governance failed, elements of his vision were resurrected after the Second World War and successfully implemented in the West during the Cold War. Following the collapse of the Soviet Union, the United States attempted to extend the liberal order throughout the globe. "We have within our grasp an extraordinary possibility that few generations have enjoyed," asserted President George H. W. Bush in the preface to the August 1991 report *National Security Strategy of the United States of America*. We are in a position "to create a new world in which our fundamental values not only survive but flourish."[1]

Optimism over what American global leadership could accomplish did not last, however. A century after Wilson's trip, President Donald Trump traveled to the "City of Light," where he planned to participate in observances marking the 100th anniversary of the end of the First World War. In contrast to the welcome Wilson enjoyed, Trump's reception by Parisians was frosty. The new president's inaugural address, which promised that "From this day forward, it's going to be only America first," struck the French as a repudiation of Wilson's ideals. According to a public opinion survey conducted by the Pew Research Center, on the eve of his trip only 9 percent of French citizens had confidence in Trump to do the right thing in world affairs.[2] For many French, Trump's behavior while visiting Paris reinforced their negative attitudes. He declined to march down the Champs-Élysées with other world leaders, he chose not to visit a World War I cemetery in Belleau, and he skipped the Paris Peace Forum on international cooperation. During a ceremony held at the Arc de Triomphe, French president Emmanuel Macron reminded the assembled dignitaries of the First World War's origins and suggested that some of the conditions that gave rise to its horrors appeared to be reemerging. In a stinging criticism of Trump's foreign policy, Macron declared, "In saying 'Our interests first, whatever happens to the others,' you erase the most precious thing a nation can have, . . . that which causes it to be great and that which is most important: Its moral values."

Macron's speech highlighted the apprehension felt by many Europeans. While annoyed by Trump's "America First" rhetoric, they were more worried that he might unravel the rules-based order that had nurtured peace and prosperity on the continent for decades. What would happen if the rules and institutions that so many people took for granted were rejected? What might follow in the wake of the liberal international order? It would not be surprising for Russia or China to challenge the prevailing world order, explained Donald Tusk, president of the European Council. What alarmed him was that the challenge came from its architect and guarantor—the United States.[3]

....

DONALD TRUMP AND CONSERVATIVE THOUGHT ON FOREIGN POLICY

Unease over the future of the liberal order stemmed from a belief that the world of the early twenty-first century was more secure than previous periods in modern history. Since the end of the Second World War, international trade soared, standards of living rose, lifespans increased, and wars between states were less frequent. Regrettably, violence still occurred, especially within **failing states**. By one account, 254 armed conflicts, most of which were civil wars within states, had erupted between 1946 and 2013.[4] However, peacekeeping efforts had become better at reducing the level of violence and limiting its diffusion to neighboring countries. Despite the many threats menacing the world, the dangers humanity faced in the past seemed far worse.[5]

Nonetheless, disquiet haunted Western capitals. Stunned by the 2008 financial crisis, hamstrung by political polarization and partisan gridlock, and wearied by costly wars in Iraq and Afghanistan, scholars and journalists increasingly questioned whether America would continue to maintain its preeminent position in international politics. Other pillars of the liberal world order also looked rickety. Japan was suffering through a prolonged period of economic stagnation, and the European Union was shaken by a host of problems, including fears that Greece and several other eurozone countries might default on government bonds, difficulties handling an influx of refugees fleeing violence in Africa and the Middle East, and the shock of a June 2016 referendum in the United Kingdom, where 51.9 percent of those voting supported the so-named Brexit proposal for their country to leave the EU. Meanwhile, Russia and China—great powers critical of the liberal order—had become more assertive. Russia seized Crimea, backed separatists and mercenaries fighting in eastern Ukraine, and intervened in the Syrian civil war to support Bashar al-Assad's regime. China, which received "special and differential treatment" as a developing nation when it joined the World Trade Organization (WTO) in 2001, used the lengthy time period it was granted for implementing WTO obligations to support domestic enterprises with government subsidies and restrict imports from foreign firms. These actions, as well as violations of intellectual property rights and pressure on foreign companies to transfer their technology to Chinese enterprises, were tolerated under the assumption that prosperity would eventually engender political reforms and encourage China to assist in upholding the prevailing order. But rather than serve as a junior partner within a U.S.-led system, Beijing began exploring Chinese-style solutions to world problems,[6] eventually calling for a new security architecture. In the words of President Xi Jinping, "the Chinese nation has gone from standing up, to becoming rich, to becoming strong."[7]

The 2016 U.S. presidential election occurred in the midst of these turbulent crosscurrents. Before Donald Trump ever descended a gold escalator in Trump Tower to announce his campaign for the presidency, America's strategic position was eroding. Japan and the European Union were ailing; Russia and China were becoming more strident; and the United States remained mired in costly, seemingly interminable conflicts in Afghanistan, Iraq, Syria, Yemen, and elsewhere. Over the ensuing months, Trump complained that neither the Obama nor the Bush administrations understood the threats facing the United States. Claiming to be a "very stable genius" who knew more about security than generals and more about trade than economists,[8] he ran for the presidency on the premise that he alone could make America great again. "Our foreign policy is a complete and total disaster," Trump proclaimed in a speech delivered in Washington on April 27, 2016. "Reckless, rudderless, and aimless," it has no underlying purpose and is ridiculed by others.

Pollsters and pundits were shocked when Trump, a former real estate developer and reality television celebrity with no government or military experience, won an upset victory, obtaining almost 57 percent of the votes in the Electoral College despite trailing his Democratic opponent by 2.8 million in the popular vote. Equally perplexing was where Trump fit within the spectrum of Republican thinking on statecraft. As someone with a propensity to shift stances and deny positions that he had taken in the past, Trump was difficult to categorize. "I don't like to say where I'm going and what I'm doing," Trump would later explain at an April 7, 2017, news conference. Nor did he want people to know what he was thinking. "I like being unpredictable," he once wrote. "It keeps [people] off balance."[9]

In early twenty-first-century America, conservatives fell into three broad schools of thought.[10] Inspired by Ronald Reagan, *conservative internationalists* supported active engagement in world politics, backing rules and institutions that promoted security, open markets, and the free movement of goods and capital. They saw military strength as a prerequisite for peace, and they sought to expand liberty by increasing the number of democratic states. Whereas a neo-conservative offshoot from this school of thought advocated armed intervention to bring about regime change in rogue states across the globe, most conservative internationalists adopted a less aggressive posture, calling for patient long-term pressure on those repressive governments that bordered free countries.

Internationalists strongly opposed insularity, and although Trump was not a contemporary manifestation of earlier isolationists such as Sen. Henry Cabot Lodge, R-MA, and Sen. Robert Taft, R-OH, his blistering attacks on the inter-nationalist foreign policy agenda led many establishment Republicans to oppose his candidacy. On March 2, 2016, an open letter from 122 Republican national security leaders warned that as president, Trump "would use the authority of his office to act in ways that make America less safe."[11] Not grasping how the liberal international order benefited the United States, Trump would undermine its rules and institutions, which would diminish the country's standing and security. The United States maintained alliances and open commerce not as a "mindless act of charity," explained conservative columnist Charles Krauthammer, but in its "enlightened self-interest."[12] No other great-power democracy would have the willingness and wherewithal to maintain the liberal international order if the United States reduced its global footprint, as Trump often proposed.[13]

Conservative realists, who belong to the second major school of thought, were exponents of the foreign policy crafted by Richard Nixon and Henry Kissinger. In contrast to the assertive promotion of freedom by internationalists, members of this camp prioritized stability and sought to construct a balance of power that would uphold the status quo. Like their internationalist brethren, they valued military strength, though they saw it as a means for deterring threats rather than as a tool for advancing democracy. Despotism, for them, was not sufficient to warrant intervention. Instead of trying to remake other countries in America's image, conservative realists called for using armed force only when there were direct threats to vital American interests.

Although Trump's comments on world politics were peppered with the tropes of power and national interest, it would be an exaggeration to say that he had a clear, consistent realist creed. Like realists, he saw the world as "a vicious place" populated by nations that were shrewd, competitive, and tough.[14] Pursuing relative gain was part of the "elemental nature of international affairs,"[15] where national security hinged on the savvy, unapologetic use of military and economic might, not surrendering to "the false song of globalism."[16] Yet unlike realists, Trump relished disruption and stoked upheaval. Conservative realism values prudence and shies away from radical change. Trump allegedly was not a realist because he lacked this sensibility, which was rooted in a "sense of the tragic," an awareness of "all the things that can go wrong in foreign policy, so that caution and a knowledge of history" shape how one responds to international events.[17] Nor, it was claimed, did Trump appreciate that world politics constituted as much a struggle to realize moral values as it was a struggle for survival. In the words of Hans Morgenthau, a seminal figure in the history of political realism, "In order to be worthy of our lasting sympathy, a nation must pursue its interests for the sake of a transcendent purpose that gives meaning to the day-to-day operations of its foreign policy."[18] Cutting deals, scoffed realists, did not advance a profound, inspiring purpose.

If Donald Trump's worldview did not emanate from conservative internationalist or conservative realist thinking, how should his approach to statecraft best be characterized? Various scholars situate him among *conservative nationalists*, the third major school of Republican thought. Conservative nationalists represent the tradition of American foreign policy most associated with the view of former U.S. president Andrew Jackson.[19] They believe that the United States must be cunning and resilient to thrive in the rough-and-tumble arena of international politics, where threats abound and every great power is a potential adversary. They are deeply skeptical of Wilsonian blueprints for world order, arguing that self-reliance safeguards the nation, not legal rules and institutions. At best, international law and organization are ineffective, lacking the means to protect states from one another; at worst, they are deleterious, lulling states into a mistaken sense of security. In a world where today's friend may become tomorrow's foe, Jacksonians insist that it does not pay to forego what is in a great power's national interest for the benefit of an illusory international community.

THE JACKSONIAN TURN IN AMERICAN FOREIGN POLICY

The post-1945 liberal order reflected American values and power, but it was built on an understanding that the United States would not wield its clout to the detriment of like-minded states. To reinforce this understanding, American actions were regulated by a web of legal rules and **multilateral** institutions that sought to preclude Washington from judging its own cause whenever disputes with international partners arose. Once Trump took up residence in the White House, these regulations were panned. Multilateralism—giving everyone a voice and promoting mutual advantage—ran counter to Trump's approach to negotiation. Only a "chump" would relinquish bargaining leverage, waive opportunities, and allow **free-riding** allies to have input on security matters. As U.S. secretary of state Michael Pompeo complained in Brussels on December 4, 2018, "Multilateralism has too often become viewed as an end in itself," as if "the more treaties we sign, the safer we are supposed to be."

Trump saw the world in transactional terms, placing great stock cultivating personal relationships that he assumed would facilitate making concrete deals.[20]

Date	Event
2017	
January	United States withdraws from Trans-Pacific Partnership
	Mexican president Enrique Peña Nieto cancels meeting with U.S. president Donald Trump in protest over Trump's calls for Mexico to pay for a border wall
	Executive order is issued banning nationals from six Muslim-majority countries from entering the United States
February	Economic sanctions are placed on Iranian companies in the aftermath of its ballistic missile tests
April	United States strikes Shayrat Airbase with cruise missiles in retaliation for Syrian use of chemical weapons
	United States drops most powerful nonnuclear bomb in its arsenal on the Islamic State of Iraq and Syria (ISIS) tunnel complex in Afghanistan
	While in South Korea, U.S. vice president Mike Pence declares end of U.S. "strategic patience" with North Korea
	Tariffs are placed on lumber imports from Canada
May	Trump visits Saudi Arabia, Israel, Italy, and Belgium on his first official foreign tour; while at the North Atlantic Treaty Organization (NATO) meeting in Brussels, Trump criticizes member countries for not spending more on defense and refuses to explicitly support the NATO Article 5 mutual defense clause
June	United States announces intent to withdraw from the 2015 Paris Agreement, which had been negotiated to stem climate change
	Trump supports Arab countries that severed diplomatic relations with Qatar, even though it hosted the regional headquarters of U.S. Central Command
	United States reinstates restrictions on travel and trade with Cuba
July	Trump attends the Group of Twenty (G20) summit in Hamburg and meets with Russian president Vladimir Putin; Congress approves sanctions on Russia over White House objections
August	Trump warns North Korea of "fire and fury" and later says America's military is "locked and loaded"
	United States announces increase in U.S. troops in Afghanistan

(Continued)

TABLE 6.1 (CONTINUED)

Date	Event
September	In speech at the UN, Trump calls North Korean leader Kim Jong-un "Rocket Man" and threatens to "totally destroy" his country if the United States is attacked
October	Trump announces that he will not recertify Iran's compliance with the 2015 nuclear deal
November	New sanctions on North Korea are announced
	Trump elaborates on his "America First" vision at the Asia-Pacific Economic Cooperation summit in Vietnam
December	United States recognizes Jerusalem as Israel's capital and declares it will relocate its embassy from Tel Aviv to Jerusalem
	United States releases the *Nuclear Posture Review*, which names China and Russia as America's main strategic competitors
2018	
January	Trump boasts his "nuclear button" is larger than North Korea's
	Trump administration backs off imposing sanctions on Russia
March	United States imposes tariffs on foreign-made steel and aluminum
April	Trump suggests United States may rejoin Trans-Pacific Partnership
	China imposes tariffs on U.S. products; Trump proposes $100 billion in tariffs on Chinese goods
	Together with France and the United Kingdom, the United States strikes facilities in Syria that are connected to the regime's chemical weapons program
May	Trump announces United States will withdraw from Iran nuclear deal and will reinstate sanctions
	United States announces it will withdraw from UN Human Rights Council
	As part of a new immigration policy by the Trump administration, children are separated from their parents after crossing the U.S. southern border
June	Trump and North Korean despot Kim Jong-un hold summit conference in Singapore
July	Trump calls the European Union a foe
	At a joint press conference in Helsinki, Trump accepts Putin's disavowal of Russian interference in the 2016 U.S. presidential election

(Continued)

TABLE 6.1

Date	Event
October	Trump announces new trade agreement with Canada and Mexico to replace the North American Free Trade Agreement (NAFTA)
	Following the murder of journalist Jamal Khashoggi inside the consulate of Saudi Arabia in Istanbul, Trump supports the Saudis and underscores their importance as a consumer of U.S. arms
November	Trump scolds British Prime Minister Theresa May over her handling of Brexit
December	Trump announces intention to significantly reduce U.S. troop level in Afghanistan and withdraw from Syria
	Partial government shutdown begins after Trump and Congress are unable to agree on funding for a border wall, which Trump had promised Mexico would fund
2019	
January	Trump calls for a space-based missile defense system
February	United States announces intention to withdraw from the Intermediate-Range Nuclear Forces (INF) Treaty; Trump and Kim Jong-un hold a second summit conference in Hanoi, Vietnam, which abruptly ends without any significant agreements
March	America's Kurdish partners in the Syrian Democratic Forces eliminate the Islamic State's caliphate after five years of grueling warfare, losing 11,000 soldiers (the U.S. lost six)
April	Trump vetoes bipartisan resolution to end U.S. military involvement in Yemen
June	Following attacks on oil tankers in the Gulf of Oman and the downing of an unmanned U.S. surveillance drone near the Strait of Hormuz, Trump authorizes and then calls off a military strike against Iran
	Trump briefly meets Kim Jong-un at the Demilitarized Zone separating North and South Korea
July	Over U.S. objections, Russia ships sophisticated surface-to-air missiles to Turkey, generating fears that Turkey would not remain an active member of NATO
August	China retaliates for U.S. tariffs by placing duties on $75 billion worth of goods imported from the United States
	Trump calls for Russia to be readmitted into the Group of Seven (G7)
	Trump cancels a state visit to Denmark because Danish prime minister Mette Frederiksen refused to consider selling Greenland to the United States

(Continued)

TABLE 6.1 (CONTINUED)

Date	Event
September	After a whistleblower working in the U.S. intelligence community complained that Trump pressured the president of Ukraine to investigate former vice president Joe Biden and his son, House Speaker Nancy Pelosi announced that she would open a formal impeachment inquiry
	At the opening session of the 74th annual kickoff session of the United Nations, Secretary-General António Guterres paints a gloomy picture of the global future, a view reinforced by Chinese foreign minister Wang Yi's speech declaring that "the world today is not a peaceful place," and his Russian counterpart Sergey Lavrov's similar assessment that declared "it is getting harder to address [multiple global] challenges from year to year. The fragmentation of the international community is only increasing"
October	The U.S. Department of Commerce reports that the U.S. trade deficit widens to $54.9 billion
	The Trump administration threatens to impose new tariffs on the European Union's $5.7 billion imports to the United States, escalating a long-standing trade dispute that threatens the globe's biggest trading bloc, which, critics warn, could pull the global economy into another worldwide recession
	At a spectacular parade in Beijing, China displays its new Dongfeng nuclear missile, capable of striking the United States from the mainland in thirty minutes, and announces its successful development of robot submarines and supersonic drones
	Trump administration threatens to impose new tariffs by October 18 on the European Union's $5.7 billion imports to the U.S., escalating a long-standing trade dispute that threatens the globe's biggest trading bloc which, critics warn, could pull the global economy into another worldwide recession
	The thirteenth round of U.S.–China trade talks in Washington fails to resolve conflicts
	Trump talks with Turkish strongman Recep Tayyip Erdogan, and immediately Trump orders exit of all U.S. Special Forces in northeastern Syria, leaving Kurdish allies unprotected; House of Representatives votes 354–60 to condemn the U.S. withdrawal
	Trump announces that American troops will continue military operations against the Islamic State (IS) from bases in neighboring Iraq, but Iraq rejects redeployment on its soil, and Trump instead orders U.S. troops and the Army National Guard 30th Armored Brigade Combat team to protect oil fields in eastern Syria from the Islamic State

(Continued)

TABLE 6.1

Date	Event
	Russia and Turkey strike a deal to invade northern Syria to force the Kurds to withdraw
	Saudi Arabia's largest oil-processing plants bombed following earlier attacks on Saudi tankers in the Persian Gulf; Trump deploys an additional 1,500 soldiers to Saudi Arabia
	President Vladimir Putin flaunts Russian influence in Africa, hosting more than 40 African leaders at a first-of-its-kind summit in Sochi
	Trump orders 1,000 troops to join the 500 already stationed in Poland, to serve as a tripwire if Russia were to invade
	The navies of China and Japan stage joint exercises
	Trump declares he wants to rip apart the Open Skies treaty
December	Atlantic Alliance marks its 70th anniversary in disarray, as fears mount of a potential American withdrawal from NATO; U.S. complains about Turkey's purchase of Russian S-400 air defense system
2020	
January	Claiming that an Iranian attack was imminent, the U.S. uses a drone to kill Iranian General Qassem Soleimani; Iran retaliates with missile strikes on two military bases housing U.S. troops in Iraq

According to Trump, the best format for deal making was through **bilateral** bargaining. One-on-one negotiations allowed the dominant party to flex its muscles, extracting concessions from the weaker party and demanding favorable revisions in the agreement whenever conditions change. Bargaining was a test of wills, and projecting strength was the key to success. "Victory, winning, beautiful words, but that is what it is all about," he said in his 2018 commencement address at the U.S. Naval Academy. "You hear lots of people say that a great deal is when both sides win," he remarked on another occasion. "That is a bunch of crap. In a great deal you win—not the other side. You crush the opponent and come away with something better for yourself."[21]

Speaking at Naval Air Station Sigonella in Sicily on May 27, 2017, Donald Trump accentuated the Jacksonian theme of peace through strength. After describing his administration's efforts to boost defense spending, he proclaimed, "We're gonna have a lot of strength, and we're gonna have a lot of peace." But for Trump, strength entailed more than unquestioned military dominance. It also meant walking away from international accords he disliked. "The United States will not be taken advantage of any longer," he told the United Nations General Assembly on September 25, 2018, repeating a litany of complaints against various treaties and executive agreements that he deemed unfair. Repudiating these agreements, however, could unravel the liberal world order constructed over the past seventy years.

Undermining the Economic Pillars of the Liberal Order

As described in Chapter 3, the post–World War II order rested on rules and institutions that addressed what were considered to be the remote, underlying causes of war. Convinced that economic protectionism was a particular danger, the General Agreement on Tariffs and Trade (GATT) and its successor, the WTO, promoted free trade within an open world economy. Many **regional trade agreements (RTAs)** also sought to remove barriers to trade among their members. Not surprisingly, international trade increased rapidly after the Second World War, with the share of exports as a percentage of world gross domestic product (GDP) recording more than a threefold increase by the end of the century. Advances in communications, information technology, and transportation facilitated this surge in globalization, and gradually reshaped long-established patterns of labor, production, and finance. With markets no longer corresponding to national boundaries, corporations began building supply chains that stretched far outside the countries where they were headquartered. Rather than goods being produced by and for people living in a given state, people from multiple different states increasingly produced them. The benefits of globalization were not evenly distributed, however. Whereas Wall Street investors and blue-collar workers in Asia gained, countless manufacturing jobs in the United States disappeared. As more industries were exposed to fierce international competition, domestic protectionist pressures started to rise.

Donald Trump campaigned on a platform of economic nationalism, vowing to tear up bad deals, impose tariffs on wily foreign competitors, and begin winning at trade once again. "We're gonna win so much, you may even get tired of winning," he exclaimed at rallies. Upon taking office, Trump immediately withdrew from the Trans-Pacific Partnership (see Table 6.1), a multinational trade agreement endorsed by the Obama administration to counter China's growing economic clout throughout the Pacific Rim. Poised to withdraw from the North American Free Trade Agreement (NAFTA) as well, he ultimately realized that the impact on Midwest agriculture and corporate supply chains would be so severe that it was better to renegotiate the agreement. But after months of bargaining, the new 2020 United States-Mexico-Canada Agreement (USMCA) looked like the old NAFTA, with only a few minor changes, such as giving the United States greater access to the Canadian dairy market.

Trump also took aim at the European Union, calling it an economic foe and supporting those in the United Kingdom who favored withdrawing from the organization. In addition, he slammed the WTO, launching blistering attacks on members that ran large trade surpluses with the United States or depressed the value of their currencies to make their exports less expensive. Americans needed protection from foreign competition, members of the Trump administration insisted. Domestic manufacturing was under assault; jobs had been stolen. For too long the United States "enriched foreign industry at the expense of American industry" and "made other countries rich while the wealth, strength, and confidence of our country has disappeared over the horizon."[22] Tariffs, the president thought, would solve the problem by stopping cheap foreign goods from pouring into the United States; therefore, he slapped duties on agricultural produce, solar panels, washing machines, steel and aluminum imports, and a wide range of Chinese products. Little forethought was given to the likelihood that targeted countries would respond in kind with tariffs against U.S. imports or to what impact foreign retaliation would have on the U.S. economy. Acting as though he had no knowledge of the disastrous trade wars of the 1930s, Trump tweeted this on March 2, 2018: "Trade wars are good, and easy to win."

Trump's focus on bilateral deficits in the trade of goods ignored sweeping changes that had transformed America. The service sector now dominated the U.S. economy. Trade in *both* goods and services were not taken into account when estimating the trade deficits that worried his administration. America was no longer a country of smoke stacks and assembly lines; it had become a land of cloud computing and digital networks. Yet Trump and his closest economic advisers—National Economic Council chair Lawrence Kudlow, Office of Trade and Manufacturing Policy director Peter Navarro, and trade representative Robert Lighthizer—stubbornly clung to their protectionist vision of international economics. Pronouncing climate change a hoax, the Trump administration withdrew from the Paris Agreement, arguing that the fossil fuels were essential for making America great again. Meanwhile, as Washington retreated from multilateralism, other states began negotiating free-trade agreements without the United States, and, as America abdicated its role as the leader of the global economy, China saw an opportunity to fill the vacuum.

Undermining the Security Pillars of the Liberal Order

Besides tackling the underlying economic sources of great-power conflict, the rules and institutions of the post–World War II order also focused on what was thought to be the foremost proximate cause of war—aggression by predatory states. The United Nations, which was supplemented during the Cold War by the North Atlantic Treaty Organization (NATO) and other alliances formed to deter potential aggressors, provided mechanisms for consultation, peacekeeping, and coordinating the expectations of rival powers. However, just as he had derided the economic pillars of the American-led liberal international order, Donald Trump disparaged its security pillars. In a December 26, 2016 tweet, he grumbled that the United Nations "is just a club for people to get together, talk and have a good time." His opinion of NATO was equally dismissive. On several occasions, he declared that the alliance was obsolete, left open whether he would honor the mutual defense commitment embodied in Article 5 of the charter pledging that an attack on any NATO member would be met by a counterstrike by all members, and mulled over the possibility that the United States might pull out of NATO and go it alone. Like previous presidents, Trump complained that most NATO members did not spend enough on defense, though he mistakenly implied that countries paid dues in exchange for U.S. military protection and their repeated shortfalls meant that they owed the United States money. While other NATO members had lower levels of military spending than the United States, that did not mean they were delinquent on payments to Washington. NATO is an alliance not a protection racket, as many foreign policy analysts have pointed out. Each member allocates funds for its own national defense and also pays part of the organization's base budget, apportioned on a formula tied to national income.

Trump's misunderstanding of how alliances function extended to America's military partnerships in Asia, which he also saw as a financial drain. While campaigning for the presidency, Trump asserted that the United States could not afford to be the world's policeman. Building on that theme, he suggested withdrawing U.S troops from Japan and South Korea if Washington was not compensated appropriately, and he proposed that those countries might need their own nuclear weapons for self-defense. Understanding Trump's penchant for personalizing political relations, Japanese prime minister Shinzo Abe traveled to the United States shortly after Trump's election, where he presented the president-elect with a gold-plated golf club and received assurances that Trump would not sacrifice Japan's defense in an effort to control costs.

Whereas Japan feared abandonment, South Korea feared entrapment.[23] With a nuclear armed North Korea developing ballistic missiles capable of striking American soil, Seoul worried that the mercurial U.S. president would drag South Korea into a disastrous confrontation. Throughout Trump's first year in office, he and North Korean dictator Kim Jong-un hurled insults at one another, prompting Trump to threaten to rain "fire and fury" on the North. Thus, most observers were surprised when Trump agreed to meet with Kim in Singapore on June 12, 2018. Although tensions in Northeast Asia decreased, few tangible results ensued. The joint statement issued after the summit contained vague statements in which Pyongyang agreed to "work towards complete denuclearization of the Korean Peninsula" and Washington committed to "provide security guarantees" to North Korea. Kim, however, secured concessions that the North had long sought. The meeting was staged in a manner that presented the two leaders as equals, and Trump (without consulting Seoul) agreed to suspend upcoming military exercises with South Korea, saying they would be provocative. The president left Singapore convinced that North Korea no longer posed a nuclear threat. At a September 29, 2018, rally in Wheeling, West Virginia, Trump confided that he and Kim "fell in love." Despite the purported warm relations between the two leaders, progress on resolving their disagreements remained stalled. Intelligence officials testified on Capitol Hill that Kim was unlikely to dismantle his nuclear arsenal, and a February 2019 summit meeting in Hanoi, Vietnam, abruptly collapsed without any new accords. Still, Trump remained upbeat. When North Korea conducted missile tests in May that National Security Adviser John Bolton believed had violated UN Security Council resolutions, Trump said that he was not bothered and expressed confidence that his personal friendship with Kim would eventually result in a deal. Underscoring the importance of his relationship with the North Korean dictator, the following month Trump responded to reports that Kim's estranged half brother had been a CIA asset by insisting that he would never let American intelligence agencies recruit members of Kim's family as informants.

In summary, Donald Trump is not an isolationist. He has sought to disentangle the United States from its network of alliances but still exert American power abroad. Sometimes exercising power means walking away from an agreement you dislike, as his willingness to pull out of the 1987 Intermediate-Range Nuclear Forces (INF) Treaty and the 2015 Iran nuclear deal indicates. By his reckoning, the allegedly one-sided agreements his predecessors signed had weakened the U.S. economy, which in turn undermined American military strength and led other nations to treat Washington disrespectfully. Seeing politics in transactional terms, Trump imagined that combining outreach to adversaries with a tougher stance toward allies would place the country on a firmer foundation. However, this strategy did not take into account the probability that these actions might embolden America's adversaries and confuse its allies, encouraging them to hedge against the United States by upgrading ties with China and Russia. Secretary of Defense James Mattis summarized this problem in his resignation letter of December 20, 2018. "Our strength as a nation is inextricably linked to the strength of our unique and comprehensive system of alliances and partnerships," he wrote. "We must do everything possible to advance an international order that is most conducive to our security, prosperity and values, and we are strengthened in this effort by the solidarity of our alliances."

POWER WITHOUT PRINCIPLE

In remarks to State Department employees on May 3, 2017, then Secretary of State Rex Tillerson warned against conditioning foreign policy too heavily on noble values, saying that they create obstacles to advancing national security interests. Raw strength, he suggested, provided a firmer foundation for American conduct abroad. The problem with absolutist ethics, he reasoned, was that certain foreign policy actions were warranted even though they might be problematic when evaluated in terms of conventional morality (see Box 6.1). Sometimes no option is unequivocally right, and policymakers must choose a course of action from a group of unpalatable alternatives.

Tillerson's defense of using power politics when responding to the harsh contingencies of international affairs reflected the tone set by the president. A morally lofty posture can cause hesitation in situations where winning demands

Box 6.1   You Decide

Among the greatest controversies in the field of international relations is the debate over the place of moral values and ethical reasoning in world politics. Should considerations of right and wrong influence foreign policy? Or are these concerns irrelevant, or even self-defeating? To delve into these questions, reflect on whether you think that the United States owes any obligations to the Kurdish inhabitants of Syria as a result of their collaboration with America's military during the war against the Islamic State of Iraq and Syria (ISIS).

The Kurds are one of the major indigenous ethnic groups of the Middle East, residing in adjacent parts of Syria, Iraq, Iran, Turkey, and Armenia. Beginning in 2013, the militant extremist group ISIS launched a series of attacks against the Kurdish region of northern Syria. An offshoot of Al Qaeda, ISIS was seen in Washington as a major threat to American interests, which led the United States in 2015 to support Kurdish armed forces, known as the Peshmerga ("Those who face death"), in their conflict with ISIS. With the Kurds doing the majority of the fighting on the ground and the United States providing advisers, arms, and air support, ISIS was eventually ousted from most of the land it once held, although military intelligence indicated that with thousands of fighters still in the region, ISIS cells remained a serious threat that could spark more fighting. In December 2018, Brett McGurk, the special presidential envoy to the coalition confronting ISIS, acknowledged that America's military mission was not over and promised that the United States would remain engaged as part of a long-term campaign to eradicate the terrorist organization. A few days later, however, U.S. president Donald Trump abruptly proclaimed that ISIS had been defeated and said that he was ordering a full and rapid withdrawal of American forces from Syria. Critics of Trump's decision immediately raised several objections, some of which were based on ethical principles.

There are different ways of applying ethical reasoning to foreign policy decisions. One approach, known as *consequentialist ethics*, asserts that the morality of an action depends on the goodness of the results that it produces. Withdrawing U.S. troops from Syria would extricate the United States from a bloody civil war and arguably allow its military resources to be deployed elsewhere. On the other hand, without a significant American presence, the Kurds would be vulnerable to attack by ISIS, by forces under the command of autocratic Syrian president Bashar al-Assad, as well as by the Turks, who claimed that there was a connection between the Kurds in Syria and Kurdish separatists operating in their country. Thus, even though an American military withdrawal could marginally reduce military costs for the United States, it would produce dreadful consequences for the Kurds, resulting in numerous deaths.

Another approach, referred to as *deontological ethics* (derived from the Greek word *deon*, meaning "duty"), argues that the morality of an action depends on whether it is intrinsically right according to some moral rule, not due to the goodness of its consequences. As applied to Syria, this approach to ethical reasoning would counsel Washington to retain a military presence in Syria since U.S. officials had promised that America would stay for the long haul, and keeping promises is the right thing to do. The United States, by this account, has a duty to follow the moral rule of upholding commitments.

Finally, a third approach, *virtue ethics*, asks what a decision maker of admirable character would naturally do in a particular situation in contrast to focusing on the consequences of an action or the duty to do something deemed inherently right. Whereas consequentialists would remain in Syria because it could save Kurdish lives, and deontologists would do so because promises ought to be kept, a virtue ethicist would say that an honorable, morally upstanding nation does not forsake its partners. The Kurdish Peshmerga was a reliable, disciplined fighting force that provided critical assistance to the United States in the struggle against ISIS. Unless the United States wanted to be the kind of country that leaves allies in the lurch, it should not abandon the Kurds.

How important are moral values and ethical reasoning in the formulation and conduct of foreign policy? If you were in a position to make a recommendation on whether or not to withdraw U.S. military forces from Syria, what weight would you give to arguments based on consequentialist, deontological, or virtue ethics?

taking initiatives untethered by ethical considerations, Donald Trump maintained. Now and again unsavory means are necessary for success. In keeping with this line of thought, Trump, customarily downplayed human rights abuses in repressive regimes, frequently complimenting the governing practices of authoritarian rulers such as Egyptian president Abdel Fattah el-Sisi, Philippine president Rodrigo Duterte, and Turkish president Recep Tayyip Erdogan. To be sure, previous presidents had forged marriages of convenience with autocrats, especially when vying with the Soviet Union for geopolitical influence during the Cold War. Nevertheless, Trump has been unique in his admiration of political strongmen, most notably Russian president Vladimir Putin. Trump not only dismissed accusations of oppression in Russia, observing that "our country does plenty of killing," he also backed Putin's denial of Russian interference in the

2016 U.S. presidential election despite findings of the entire complex of the U.S. intelligence community to the contrary, as well as the 2019 conclusion of the Mueller investigation that Russian efforts to manipulate the election in Trump's favor were "widespread and massive."[24]

When seen against the backdrop of Trump's harsh criticism of Canadian prime minister Justin Trudeau, German chancellor Angela Merkel, and leaders in other democracies aligned with the United States, Trump's praise of autocrats has baffled congressional observers from both sides of the political aisle. The United States championed democracy, human rights, and the rule of law throughout the post–World War II era, even using force in ill-conceived attempts to foster regime change in several authoritarian countries. Indeed, as reflected in Ronald Reagan's denial of moral equivalence between open and closed societies, mainstream Republicans have long insisted that a conservative U.S. foreign policy must embody military as well as moral strength.[25] While Trump emphasized the former, he downplayed the latter. He has pursued military superiority while ignoring Reagan's vision of a "shining city on a hill," an America "teeming with people of all kinds living in harmony and peace," an America that "hummed with commerce and creativity," an America where "the walls had doors, and the doors were open to anyone with the will and heart to get here."[26] Why forsake the ideals that have long guided U.S. policymakers? Some think that a September 2018 op-ed essay published in the *New York Times* provides a clue. Written by an official in the Trump administration known only as "Anonymous," it described the president's core problem as amorality: "He is not moored to any discernable first principles that guide his decision making."[27]

Lacking a moral compass, critics charge the Trump administration was steering America into troubled international waters. "The captain of the ship of state is an ill-informed and incompetent skipper lacking accurate charts, an able crew, or a clear destination," writes one respected political realist.[28] Eminent conservatives, such as Max Boot, David Brooks, David Frum, Bill Kristol, and George Will, point out that Trump's chronic lying has undercut Washington's ability to lead on global issues[29] and that his erratic behavior was tarnishing the country's reputation. Mocking Indian prime minister Narendra Modi, hanging up on Australian prime minister Malcolm Turnbull, shoving Montenegrin prime minister Dusko Markovic, and engaging in other acts of incivility toward foreign leaders have eroded America's soft power. For Trump, these complaints are irrelevant. Soft power is toothless. In his estimation, *real* power entails creating fear in others.[30]

Many people who have closely observed Trump describe him as an impulsive, easily distracted president who trusts his instincts and shows scant interest in learning. They report little empathy, negligible self-control, a deep sensitivity to criticism, and a craving for flattery.[31] At a March 2019 retreat in Sea Island, Georgia, hosted by the American Enterprise Institute, former vice president Dick Cheney built on these criticisms when he expressed alarm that Trump spent so little time with his intelligence briefers, a pattern that former Secretary of State Rex Tillerson said resulted in the president being unprepared at summit meetings with foreign leaders.[32] Boasting "I'm the only one who matters,"[33] Trump belittled senior aides and disparaged professionals working in the CIA, FBI, and in the Departments of State and Defense. He often touted a new initiative only to later reverse course. Consistently inconsistent, nothing is final for Trump; anything can be revised on a whim. As an exasperated Chief of Staff John Kelly lamented, "We're in crazytown."[34]

The greatest gift that the World War II generation bequeathed to us, Secretary of Defense James Mattis once told Donald Trump, "is the rules-based, international democratic order."[35] However, by disregarding questions of **grand strategy** in favor of short-term tactical maneuvers, by replacing multilateral collaboration with winner-take-all competition, and by discounting reliable democratic partners while currying the favor of capricious authoritarian regimes, the Trump administration destabilized that order. Any framework of rules and institutions may weaken as international circumstances change, but the president's divisive rhetoric and fickle behavior have damaged the liberal order at the very time that rival great powers are challenging its principles.

The world now stands at a critical juncture. Many possible futures lie ahead; some are attractive, others repellant. Although no one can predict which one will come to pass, it is important to bear in mind that the future is not something that just happens. The great powers heavily shape it with their choices. Given the uncertainties surrounding the rules and institutions of the past seventy years, it is time to assess the options for rebuilding world order. It is to this task that we turn in the next chapter.

KEY TERMS

bilateral 131

failing states 123

free-riding 126

grand strategy 139

multilateral 126

regional trade agreements (RTAs) 132

PART III

Forging a New World Order

7 The Range of Great-Power Choice

*The global situation is more dangerous today than at any time
since the collapse of the Soviet Union. We are experiencing
and epochal shift; an era is ending, and the rough outlines
of a new political age are only beginning to emerge.*

—WOLFGANG ISCHINGER,

CHAIRMAN, MUNICH SECURITY CONFERENCE

With the unraveling of the liberal world order and the return of great-power competition, the international system is undergoing its most profound transformation since the end of the Cold War. Momentous change foments uncertainty. Yet our current situation is not entirely novel. We have entered a new period in global affairs—but one that should be recognizable to those familiar with the patterns of diplomatic history. This is not to deny that some features of contemporary world politics are different from those of the past. Sovereign, territorial states, for example, now share the world stage with nonstate actors, and connectivity among individuals is fast, easy, and ubiquitous.[1] Notwithstanding these and other dizzying changes, an elemental continuity persists: great powers continue to compete over who sets the terms for the rules and institutions that define acceptable international behavior.

Whether world politics becomes more orderly or disorderly in the years ahead will depend on a variety of factors. Foremost among them are the foreign policy choices that the leading great powers make. Despite their complaints about different aspects of the current body of international rules and institutions, none of them have thus far have come forth with a sound proposal for a clear, coherent alternative approach to world order. No designs have been unveiled on what should replace the prevailing rules of the game, or what institutions should supplant those that presently exist. The orientation of the most prominent states has largely been tactical—recommending incremental modifications to the existing global architecture. To some extent, this is understandable. Operating in a complex, confusing world poses formidable challenges, so improvisation and an inclination to muddle through by a process of trial and error should not be surprising. The simple unipolar system of the recent past has given way to a more complicated configuration, and the shifting great-power balance has made crafting a long-term strategy for building a new world order exceedingly difficult. No wonder hesitation and false starts by the great powers are so common.

Nonetheless, one of the most salient properties of the emerging system is readily foreseeable: Military and economic might is increasingly diffused. In contrast to the immediate aftermath of the Cold War, when the United States enjoyed a position of preponderance compared to all other countries, the international system has moved toward a more dispersed distribution of power. The United States still sits atop the global hierarchy, but competitors are gaining ground. What remains unclear is how this trend will reshape international life. How will the military and economic ascendance of China, Russia, and possibly other states transform world politics?

....

VIEWING SYSTEM TRANSFORMATION IN HISTORICAL CONTEXT

The global pecking order is changing. National trajectories suggest that tomorrow will not look like today. What impact will seismic shifts in relative capabilities have on world order? Will the international system be thrown into chaos? Or will it settle into a new equilibrium? Many factors will affect the answers to these questions. Two of the most important are the nature of the transition process and the type of structure that materializes in its aftermath.

The Process of Power Transition

The diffusion of strength among the world's leading states raises concerns because while there have been many periods of power transition in the past, some previous transitions have been more war-prone than others. For example, although a declining Great Britain at the turn of the twentieth century clashed with a rising Germany, the British accommodated themselves to a rising United States despite a century of animosity with the Americans. Historians give various reasons for London's unsuccessful efforts to reach an understanding with Berlin while establishing an amicable relationship with Washington. Germany was a nearby threat, the United States was far away; Germany possessed a different cultural identity than Great Britain, the United States shared many commonalities; and whereas Germany seemed inclined to overturn the British-led order, the United States appeared to be a responsible stakeholder. Power transitions, in other words, are not destined to end in hostilities. War is common, but under certain conditions declining great powers and ascending challengers have shown a capacity to avoid a military showdown. If a declining hegemon is focused on other pressing problems, it will generally postpone confronting its challenger right away in order to defer paying the costs of taking immediate action to preserve its primacy. At the same time, if an ascending challenger is largely satisfied with the existing world order, it can remain patient, recognizing that pragmatic cooperation will yield long-term benefits.[2]

Yet even when power transitions do not culminate in war, they often spawn instability. As countries once dominated by a waning great power begin to exercise greater independence, allegiances fracture, alignments shift, and competitors jockey to take advantage of political opportunities. Changes in global status encourage states to rethink interests and objectives, redefine friends and foes, and recalibrate policies and programs. It is rare for defensive coalitions to continue if during a power transition the preeminent great power ceases to be menacing.[3] As illustrated by the behavior of Warsaw Pact members after the collapse of the Soviet Union, following power transitions some states are likely to abandon their former bloc leader and realign with its great-power rival.

Instability can also arise if a power transition alters the prevailing normative climate, turning relatively restrictive rules of the game in a permissive direction. Many legal scholars maintain that commitment norms are the bedrock of international law. Two such norms have vied for acceptance throughout the history of the modern state system. The first norm, *pacta sunt servanda* ("agreements must be kept"), declares that international accords create binding obligations between the signatory parties. The second, *rebus sic stantibus* ("things standing thus"), is more permissive. Interpreted in its most narrow sense, this injunction permits one party to an agreement to withdraw if conditions change after the accord was signed. Interpreted in its broadest sense, it permits withdrawing if the accord is later deemed by one of the parties to be detrimental to its fundamental interests, which some leaders define so widely that they include almost any justification.

During turbulent times, the temptation to jettison previous commitments by appealing to the norm *rebus sic stantibus* can be enticing. According to the logic of realpolitik, international commitments are situational: Fulfilling an agreement is contingent on whether it serves key national interests at the moment. No matter how carefully a treaty may have been negotiated, sooner or later unanticipated events usually arise. When new circumstances make adherence to a commitment onerous, hard-boiled practitioners of power politics are prone to claim that states should have the leeway to extricate themselves from its provisions. A permissive conception of promissory obligation grants tremendous freedom of maneuver to national leaders, but it also breeds uncertainty and can lead to miscalculations about the reliability of allies and assurances voiced by adversaries. Research indicates that as the normative climate of world politics grows more permissive, trust erodes, serious interstate disputes multiply, and armed conflicts increase.[4]

In summary, not every power transition ends in war. However, to the extent that the process intensifies great-power competition and fosters permissive norms that allow commitments to be repudiated, power transitions create instability. Recognizing this problem, diplomatic efforts have been undertaken after every hegemonic war in the modern era to put international affairs on a secure normative and institutional footing. That happened after the Thirty Years' War (1618–1648) when the Peace of Westphalia gave states sovereign control over their internal and foreign affairs. It occurred on the heels of the wars of King Louis XIV of France (1688–1713); when the Treaty of Utrecht designated the balance of power as the primary mechanism for preserving peace; and again after the Napoleonic Wars (1792–1815) when the Congress of Vienna endorsed the Concert of Europe, a system of regularized great-power consultation aimed at jointly managing the balance. Likewise, World War I (1914–1918) ended with an attempt to implement collective security after the Versailles peace conference, and World War II (1939–1945) concluded with another stab at collective security, when the United Nations superseded the League of Nations.

Every one of these attempts to establish common rules and limits had unique features that embodied the geostrategic thinking of its age. Each of them also reflected the existing configuration of power. A consensus on what was acceptable international conduct emerged because the principal centers of power accepted the arrangements as legitimate. Achieving that consensus required the would-be architects of international order to work within the parameters set by the structure of the state system.

The Parameters of System Structure

The choices great powers make on how to establish order following major changes in the distribution of their relative capabilities are influenced by the process of power transition and the structure of the system that emerges in its wake. The degree of instability in the transition process and the redistribution of international power that follows in its aftermath both affect great-power decisions about the ordering rules and institutions they ultimately support.

Figure 7.1 portrays several different ways that the state system may be configured if American unipolarity continues to fade. One possibility is the advent of a Chinese-centered system, reminiscent of the sixteenth century, when the Ming dynasty (1368–1644) reigned as the most powerful state in the world, overshadowing every other country in population, wealth, and military might.[5] A second possibility is the emergence of Sino-American bipolarity, where China and the United States become the world's dominant power centers. The third possibility is some form of multipolarity, with China, the United States, Russia, and conceivably the European Union and Japan having significantly more military and economic strength than the other members of the state system. Finally, the last possibility is nonpolarity—a condition where no dominating power centers exist. Let's briefly examine each of these possibilities.

FIGURE 7.1 SCENARIOS FOR THE GLOBAL FUTURE

Foreign policy analysts often construct scenarios that range from descriptions of what could possibly emerge in world affairs to what is more likely to define the future global playing field. Some scenarios are predicated on simple extrapolations from current conditions, while others imagine sharp discontinuities between the present and the future. One of the benefits of imagining alternative world futures is that it helps clarify assumptions about which global trends are transient and which will have a long-lasting impact as well as how the most significant trends interact with one another. This diagram presents four plausible scenarios regarding how the state system may be reconfigured in the aftermath of American unipolarity.

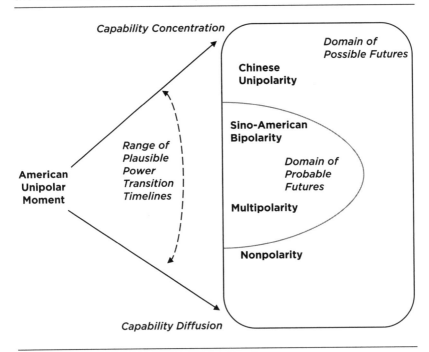

Chinese Unipolarity

At the beginning of the twenty-first century, China's gross domestic product (GDP) was 39 percent of that of the United States, based on **purchasing power parity (PPP)**. By 2016, China's GDP had climbed to 114 percent of that of the United States. The **scenario** that envisions China as a future unipolar power begins with the assumption that China's economic growth will continue.

The scenario then builds upon evidence that while the United States has grown weary from protracted warfare, is staggering under mounting debt, and has seen its international reputation erode, China has become more assertive, criticizing American military interventions, touting itself as an alternative model of economic development, and promoting new international organizations, such as the Asian Infrastructure Investment Bank as well as the New Development Bank.

China's exponential economic growth has amplified its power and influence. Driven by productivity increases and large-scale capital investment, China's annual GDP growth has averaged over 9 percent since the end of the Cold War, accounting for 18.3 percent of the global GDP on a PPP basis in 2017, compared to 15.3 percent for the United States. China—home to one in five people in the world—has become the world's largest manufacturer and, with the highest gross savings as a percentage of GDP among the world's major economies, has also developed into a major global lender. Beijing's Belt and Road Initiative, a program of financing and building infrastructure projects in Asia, Africa, and Europe that is estimated to exceed $4 trillion, will create huge economic opportunities for Chinese firms and boost the country's influence abroad.[6] Over eighty countries are participating in this intercontinental project, which amounts to 63 percent of the world's population, with a collective total of 29 percent of global output.[7]

Paralleling China's rapid economic growth is a comprehensive, multifaceted effort at military modernization, which has made considerable progress in anti-satellite weaponry, intermediate-range ballistic missiles, and area denial capabilities. China has vastly increased defense outlays during the past decade, spending an estimated $228.2 billion in 2017, second only to the $597.2 billion spent by the United States.[8] The thinking behind China's growing military expenditures was summarized in a document on geopolitical strategy published during 2015 by China's State Council Information Office. "Profound changes are taking place in the international situation," it observed, and China is in "an important period of strategic opportunities for its development." Although the document's authors presumed that a hegemonic war was unlikely, they anticipated increased "international competition for the redistribution of power, rights, and interests."[9] In his report to the Nineteenth Party Congress in October 2017, Chinese President Xi Jinping built on this expectation, setting the goal of achieving a fully modernized Chinese military by 2035.[10] Toward that end, China has developed a new generation of mobile missiles with **multiple independently targetable reentry vehicles (MIRVs)** and has begun work on a long-range stealth bomber, a domestically designed aircraft carrier, and **hypersonic weapons**. However, lagging in logistics and power-projection capability, it will be some time before China can reach parity with the United States, let alone ascend to preeminence in a new unipolar system.

Several additional factors raise doubts about the prospects for China achieving unipolar preeminence. Economically, political leaders in Beijing face serious problems with corruption, regional inequalities, and reducing the nation's substantial debt while simultaneously pushing banks to loan more to inefficient state-owned companies. Politically, the Chinese are experiencing an international backlash over their territorial claims in the South China Sea, their endeavors to extradite citizens from Hong Kong for trial on the mainland, their repression of Muslim Uyghurs in the western region of Xinjiang, as well as over suspicions that 5G telecommunications technology sold by the Chinese firm Huawei might be used for government espionage. Demographically, China must grapple with the consequences of an aging population and shrinking labor pool. Environmentally, China is beset with water shortages and staggering levels of air and water pollution from a heavy reliance on coal for generating electricity. While these problems may be manageable in the long term, they currently impede realizing the dream of uncontested primacy. Rather than a Chinese-led unipolar system, Sino-American bipolarity or some form of multipolarity that includes Russia are more probable global futures.

Sino-American Bipolarity

To question the likelihood of Chinese unipolarity in the near future is not to discount the importance of China's growing stature on the world stage. A bipolar system anchored by China and the United States is a distinct possibility, though it would differ from the Soviet-American standoff that existed during the Cold War.[11] In contrast to the Soviet Union, China is becoming an economic peer of the United States—a stature that could change if the escalating threat of a Sino-American trade war disrupts its economic growth and undermines the massive flows of trade and finance with the United States. If a trade war decouples the Chinese and American economies, the world would be split into rival trading blocs, forcing other countries to choose between Beijing and Washington.

Sino-American bipolarity would differ from Soviet-American bipolarity in other ways, too. China has neither tightly coupled allies like the Soviets had with the Warsaw Pact, nor would it pose a direct military threat to Washington's erstwhile European allies, although China would wrangle with them over access to foreign energy resources, raw materials, and export markets. Furthermore, unlike during the depths of the Cold War, when ideological enmity contributed to a zero-sum bargaining on international issues, Chinese-American relations could resemble a **mixed-motive game**, where rather than taking diametrically opposed positions, the two rivals could both see incentives for reaching agreements on shared responsibilities for global governance.

Multipolarity

Some variant of multipolarity is also more probable in the immediate future than China standing alone at the helm of world affairs or sharing top dog status with the United States in a bipolar distribution of power. Recall from Chapter 1 that multipolarity is typically defined as a global system containing more than two prominent states that are far stronger than any other great power. Different forms of multipolarity are possible. The great powers in a multipolar system may be roughly equal in their overall capabilities, or there may be asymmetries in the distribution of their capabilities. For instance, China and Japan are both considered great powers, but China's military and economic might outstrips Japan's strength. As shown in Figure 7.2, two alternative multipolar futures commonly discussed today consist of several unequal power centers. One contains three such centers and the other, five.

When three overwhelmingly powerful states dominate the international system, a condition of **tripolarity** exists. Such triangular systems are thought to

FIGURE 7.2   TWO HYPOTHETICAL FORMS OF MULTIPOLARITY IN THE TWENTY-FIRST CENTURY

Multipolar systems vary in size. Tripolarity, where military and economic capabilities are concentrated in the hands of three international actors, and quintipolarity, where five actors dominate the world stage, are often postulated as the most likely forms of multipolarity to emerge in the first half of the twenty-first century.

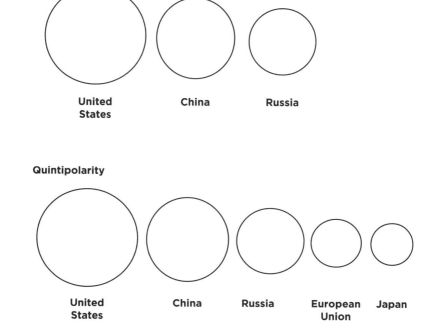

Tripolarity

United States   China   Russia

Quintipolarity

United States   China   Russia   European Union   Japan

be stable as long as the preeminent powers are approximately equal and remain impartial toward one another. Theoretically, each state would maintain responsibility for its own region and consult with the others on matters affecting them all. Volatility arises whenever two of the great powers align against the third, which tends to occur when the colluding states seek to overturn the status quo, or when their individual rankings are lower than the other great powers.[12] The odds of a preventive attack are remote in the nuclear age, but all three of today's leading great powers are likely to suspiciously regard one another as rivals. The United States, China, and Russia are the most likely centers of power in a twenty-first-century tripolar system. With each having global interests and none possessing the ability to override the others, establishing rules and institutions that provide incentives for them to cooperate would help avert any effort to carve the world into competing blocs. Some theorists doubt this will happen, arguing that tripolar variants of multipolarity are inherently unstable.[13]

Another form of multipolarity that many observers consider possible would contain more than three potent powers. As typically envisioned, power would be distributed among them in a stepwise manner, with the United States leading the pack, followed in sequence by China, Russia, the European Union, and Japan. This is not the only possible configuration. Some commentators on world affairs, pointing to the rise of illiberal anti-European parties on the European continent and the turmoil surrounding the disputes disrupting cooperation between London and Brussels, question whether the European Union will remain an important actor in global affairs. Others, emphasizing the power potential of other countries, expand the list of upper-echelon states to include India and Brazil. Regardless of the precise number of power centers, the political dynamics of a world with more than three would be increasingly complex as each new great power is added to the top strata of the global hierarchy. If five or more principal states prove unable to establish working relationships among themselves, the system could devolve into rival camps.

In addition to varying in size, multipolar systems also differ in the degree to which they experience **polarization**—the propensity of the great powers to coalesce into countervailing blocs (see Figure 7.3). Historically, rigid polarized systems have been catalysts to the onset of war.[14] Each pole in a polarized system focuses intently on the others, which are assumed to be too formidable to discount and too cunning to ignore. Whenever a world of many great powers has split into opposing coalitions, it has become less likely for contestants in one policy arena to collaborate on other issues. Gains made by one side tend to be been seen as losses by the other, ultimately raising the odds of disagreements growing into military showdowns from which neither coalition is inclined to retreat.

Nonpolarity

Finally, **nonpolarity** describes a situation where national capabilities are spread even more widely than in a multipolar system.[15] In a unipolar system, one preeminent state holds more than 50 percent of the power within the system;

FIGURE 7.3 ALLIANCES, POLARIZATION, AND THE AGGREGATION OF CAPABILITIES

Polarization transforms the environment within which great powers operate. Through alliances, the distribution of capabilities becomes aggregated into blocs of military might much larger than would have been the case had each state relied only on its own wherewithal. Note how in the upper diagram each of the five great powers (A, B, C, D, and E) is independent. They all are potential collaborators or opponents on any given issue. When the system becomes polarized, as illustrated in the lower diagram, the military capabilities of A, D, and E are combined, as are those of B and C. In addition to creating powerful coalitions, polarization reduces policy flexibility. State C, for instance, is unlikely to support state D on an issue that matters to State B. When polarization occurs, the state system takes on a character that is different from what would exist had the great powers remained independent and thereby more capable of shifting alignments when circumstances change and new issues arise.

Multipolar System with Uncommitted Great Powers

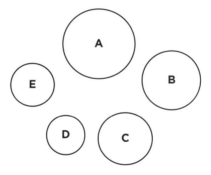

Multipolar System with Polarized Great Powers

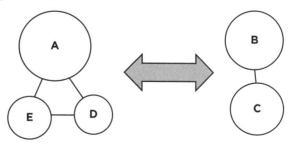

in a bipolar system, the two foremost states each hold at least 25 percent of available power, and together both possess more than 50 percent; and in a multipolar system, each principal state holds no more than 25 percent, and in the aggregate these states together command at least 50 percent of such power. But in a nonpolar distribution, military and economic capabilities are dispersed so broadly that the strongest states collectively comprise less than 50 percent of available power.[16] In short, power is atomized in nonpolar systems—dispersed among a welter of state and nonstate actors.

At various times throughout history, nonpolar systems have ensued following the breakdown of unipolarity. Ancient Mesopotamia, for example, splintered into a kaleidoscope of small, bickering states after the Akkadian Empire collapsed (c. 2150 BCE), and China experienced similar fragmentation during its Spring and Autumn period (770–476 BCE) after the demise of the Western Zhou dynasty. Although these and other examples from antiquity suggest that a nonpolar system could emerge, it is unlikely to happen in the near future unless the planet experiences rapid, severe climate change or some other global catastrophe abruptly modifies the earth's environment. In the absence of a cataclysm, great powers will continue to dominate the geopolitical landscape. To be sure, nonstate actors—transnational ethnopolitical and religious movements, issue-advocacy groups, multinational corporations, and terrorist and criminal networks—will play bigger roles in international affairs; however, it is very likely that great powers will continue for the foreseeable future to exert disproportionate influence on the architecture of the future world order.

For most people, the future is a mysterious place filled with endless surprises. The utter complexity of world politics makes it difficult to foresee how international developments will unfold. While there is a broad consensus that the international system is undergoing a long-term power transition, it remains unclear how evolving global trends will interact to influence the future course of world affairs. The most probable outcomes posit either U.S.-China bipolarity or a triangular form of multipolarity that includes Russia in the roster of top-tier states. Each of these alternative futures presents challenges. How the great powers respond today will shape the contours of world order tomorrow.

GREAT-POWER OPTIONS FOR SHAPING WORLD ORDER

As military and economic capabilities become more diffused, will great-power competition intensify? How can the great powers avoid becoming divided into antagonistic blocs? What organizing principles can help stabilize their relations? What are the best options for cultivating world order?

Although elements of the American-led liberal world order have unraveled under the presidency of Donald J. Trump, many parts remain intact because they serve a broad set of common international interests. The post–World War II order is a complex, multilayered conglomeration of rules and institutions that spans a wide array of issues. Insofar as rising states continue to support some liberal principles but not others, what is likely in the years ahead is renovation and refurbishment rather than demolition and replacement.[17]

FIGURE 7.4 UNILATERALISM, BILATERALISM, AND MULTILATERALISM
In the upper illustration, State A conducts its foreign policy unilaterally, interacting with States B, C, D, and E without consultation or the involvement of other countries. The middle illustration depicts a special bilateral relationship between States A and B, who adopt a common stance when engaging with States C, D, and E. The lower illustration portrays multilateralism, where States A through E are linked by indivisible interests and generalized principles based on nondiscrimination and the reciprocal treatment of parties to international exchanges.

Unilateralism

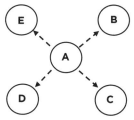

Bilateral Special Relationship

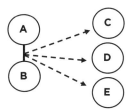

Multilateralism

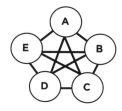

How might the current order be renovated? What options do the great powers have? Three general courses of action exist: (1) the great powers can pursue unilateral action, (2) they can cultivate specialized bilateral ties with other states, or (3) they can engage in some form of multilateral collaboration. Of course, each option has many possible variations, and the foreign policies of most great powers in the past have contained a mixture of acting single-handedly, joining with a partner, and cooperating globally. What matters most for international stability is the relative emphasis placed on "going it alone" versus "going it with others" and whether joint action is defined in inclusive or exclusive terms.

Unilateral Options

"Every nation for itself," British foreign secretary George Canning reportedly said upon taking office in 1822. His unilateralist sentiments are attractive to the leaders of some great powers today since they embody autonomy and self-reliance. The capacity to act independently is attractive because international consent is not required before acting; costly efforts to coordinate policies are not necessary. Standing alone avoids entangling foreign commitments, freeing states from obligations that may become too heavy to bear. By approaching issues independently on a case-by-case basis, unilateralism speaks to many of the time-honored maxims about statecraft that have evolved from realist thinking: "Be flexible," "Don't take a fixed position when circumstances may change," "Trust your own power not the promises of others," and, as Hans J. Morgenthau, the dean of classical realism, insisted, "Never put yourself in a position from which you cannot retreat without losing face and from which you cannot advance without grave risks."[18]

Several different policy postures are compatible with acting unilaterally, including retreating into isolationism, exercising hegemonic leadership, and playing the role of a **balancer** striving to maintain rough parity between opponents. *Isolationism*—withdrawing from active participation in world affairs—necessitates charting a country's foreign policy course alone. Isolationism is counterproductive for a great power, however. Retreating from active international involvement opens the door for rivals to step into the void and expand their influence. It also imperils efforts to benefit from rewarding transnational exchanges or to deal with climate change and the many other nonmilitary threats to global security that do not observe national borders but require international collaboration for their management.

Another posture congruent with unilateralism is *hegemonic leadership*. When power is concentrated in the hands of a single leading state, it is positioned to take advantage of its uncontested status by ignoring the interests and security concerns of other countries. The consequences for weaker states depend on the goals to which such a leader aspires. If it acts coercively, undertaking policies aimed only at national self-aggrandizement, then the security and welfare of others will be put at risk. Conversely, if it acts benevolently, providing

public goods for all countries, then others can benefit from the hegemon's leadership. In such instances, states at the pinnacle of world power can readily turn their initiatives into multipartite endeavors. Simply by declaring an intention to act, they can marshal a "coalition of the willing." After all, "no one wants to be left at the dock when the hegemon is sailing," explained syndicated columnist Charles Krauthammer.[19]

Still another foreign policy posture grounded in unilateralism is that of a *balancer* that seeks to maintain an equilibrium among the other contending great powers (recall Figure 2.2). Independence is essential when playing this role. A balancer must be unencumbered by ties to other countries so it can throw its weight against any potential aggressor. From the sixteenth through the early twentieth centuries, the British acted as the holder of the European balance, asserting that they had no eternal allies and no perpetual enemies, just a permanent interest in preventing the balance from tipping too far one way or the other and plunging all into armed conflict. Prime Minister Winston Churchill summarized Britain's role as a balancer in the following way: "For four hundred years the foreign policy of England has been to oppose the strongest, most aggressive, most dominating Power on the Continent. . . . It would have been easy and must have been very tempting to join with the stronger and share the fruits of the conquest. However, we always took the harder course, joining with the less strong Powers, made a combination among them, and thus defeated the Continental military tyrant, whoever he was, whatever nation he led."[20]

By only projecting its power abroad when an aspiring hegemon threatens to disrupt the balance of power in a vital region of the world, a balancer can ostensibly hold down its defense spending, since it does not garrison large, quasi-permanent military bases on foreign soil. Instead, a balancer keeps its forces over the horizon, deploying them only when the leading states of that region are unable to counterbalance one another, and when aggression by the would-be hegemon seems imminent.[21]

The problem with playing the role of a balancer in the twenty-first century is that classical balance-of-power logic has been overtaken by advances in cybertechnology. Aggression may not come through **kinetic military action** but through cyberattacks on a country's infrastructure. As borders have become permeable and tracing the perpetrators of cyber operations more challenging, it is difficult for states to balance power in a manner they once could, with an independent, stand-alone balancer shifting sides among opposing great powers to deter a potential aggressor. Yet old habits die hard. Balance-of-power reasoning continues to influence the thinking of many great-power military planners, even if it has become increasingly anachronistic.

To sum up, unilateral policies have advantages as well as drawbacks (see Box 7.1). Going it alone maximizes freedom, but it can leave a state exposed. Placing faith in the goodwill of other states is risky, yet the alternative can be even more hazardous without the strength to stand unaided in the face of adversity. Independence enables policy adjustments to be readily made as global circumstances change, but budding problems may be too big for any single great power to handle. When the benefits of unilateralism sink below its costs, some states try to cultivate a special relationship with another great power.

Box 7.1 You Decide

Picture yourself as the newly elected president of the United States. You have invited your national security adviser and secretary of state to the Oval Office to provide recommendations on how you might increase U.S. national security. You are especially interested in whether they believe that America in the twenty-first century still needs a vast network of military alliances, most of which were formed during the Cold War to deter a Soviet threat that no longer exists. Are these alliances necessary today? Do their costs outweigh their benefits?

The national security adviser speaks first. He does not mince his words. "Mr. President, you command the most awesome military force in world history. No other state would dare to attack us. But to maintain our edge in the years ahead, we need to increase military spending, expanding our nuclear arsenal and upgrading our ballistic missile defense."

"Alliances are of decreasing relevance. Most of our allies contribute little to American national security. They drain our resources and entangle us in affairs that are none of our business. Yet we have treaties with dozens of countries that oblige us to come to their aid if they are attacked. What do we gain from these commitments? Why should we protect countries that are unwilling to spend serious money on their own defense? Despite all that we have expended on collective defense, I'm not sure we can count on the majority of our allies when the chips are down. In a crisis, they'll pursue their own interests and leave us out to dry."

Next, the secretary of state offers her advice. "Mr. President, America needs friends now more than ever. Adding nuclear weapons to our arsenal will not address the complex problems of climate change, failing states, and global terrorism. Nor is it clear that we are even close to having the technology to intercept ballistic missiles. Increasing our nuclear firepower and spending more on missile defense will only make our rivals insecure and trigger an expensive and potentially suicidal arms race. Remember what Ronald Reagan said: 'A nuclear war cannot be won and must never be fought.'"

"If we retreat into 'Fortress America,' we will lose diplomatic influence and squander our ability to shape the global agenda. China and Russia will rush to fill the political vacuum, attempting to convince other countries to join them in constructing a new, post-American world order. Mr. President, please consider strengthening ties with nations that share our values and ideals. Being isolated within a world order that reflects the preferences of rival great powers will surely reduce our security."

As you listen to these divergent recommendations, you, as president, must decide which path will lead to greater security for the United States. What would you choose?

Bilateral Options

An alternative to acting unilaterally is partnering with selected states in a series of bilateral groupings, such as that between Great Britain and the United States throughout the twentieth century. On the surface, this option also appears attractive. Bilateral associations are alluring because they inject predictability into freewheeling balance-of-power politics where any alignment is equally probable. Yet in a world of dispersed power, differentiating friend from foe is exceedingly difficult, particularly because allies in the realm of military security can also be commercial competitors in the global marketplace.

Different types of specialized relationships have existed throughout modern history. Some were informal understandings, such as **ententes** that pledged consultation in the event of certain contingencies. Others were formal agreements, such as defense pacts or **condominiums** crafted to jointly oversee a specified region. Whether they entail tacit understandings or formal treaties, all bilateral partnerships have a common drawback: They promote a politics of exclusion that can breed resentment and a fear of encirclement among those great powers that perceive themselves as the targets of these combinations.

In addition to fueling fears that others are teaming up in opposition, special relationships often give rise to suspicions that one partner is enjoying most of the benefits while the other is shouldering most of the burdens. The post–World War II Anglo-American special relationship exemplified this problem. The relationship was "special" primarily for the British insofar as it gave them the opportunity to exert private, informal influence in Washington, even though their position throughout the world had deteriorated. From the American perspective, Britain was "an ageing, self-satisfied prima donna who insisted on holding the limelight" though its glory had long passed.[22]

Another problem associated with special relationships is the tendency for outsiders to assume that the junior partner has the same preferences as the senior partner and thus will not take independent action. In the aftermath of Prussia's victory over Austria in the Seven Weeks' War of 1866, Otto von Bismarck, the Prussian chancellor, crafted a lenient peace to diffuse any aspirations in Vienna for a war of revenge. Bismarck's conciliatory policy succeeded. Following Prussia's unification with other German states in 1871, the diplomatic paths of Austria and the new German empire were closely intertwined. By the beginning of the twentieth century the relationship was so close that the British Foreign Office assumed that Austria's foreign policy was an extension of Germany's.[23] Not only did this assumption mask policy differences between Vienna and Berlin but it prevented the British from encouraging the Austrians to sever their dependence on Germany.

Still another problem with special relationships is that they can take on a life of their own, growing into something quite different from what was envisioned by their founders. In 1904, for example, Britain and France, which previously had seen one another as adversaries, reached a series of agreements known as the *Entente Cordiale*. Freedom of action was granted to the British in Egypt and to the French in Morocco, outstanding colonial disputes were settled, as were disagreements over fisheries off the coast of Newfoundland. The two powers also began unofficial meetings on the possibility of joint military action in the event of war with Germany. Over time, these talks acquired moral cogency. British foreign secretary Sir Edward Grey mused that it would be "very difficult" for Britain to stay out of a war between France and Germany. The "constant and emphatic demonstrations of affection (official, naval, political, commercial and in the Press) have created in France a belief that we shall support them in war. . . . If this expectation is disappointed, the French will never forgive us. There would also I think be a general feeling that we had behaved badly and left France in the lurch."[24]

In sum, during turbulent times great powers occasionally seek special bilateral relationships in order to add predictability to their strategic circumstances. The movement away from America's unipolar moment will benefit some states and disadvantage others. Regardless of which great-power competitor gains or loses, maintaining world order will be challenging. Although great-power special relationships can contribute to international stability by establishing tacit, partner-specific understandings between the aligned powers, their downside is that by failing to take all the great and rising powers' security interests into account, they are inherently exclusionary and potentially divisive.

Multilateral Options

Beyond forming special bilateral relationships, great powers have the option of working with multiple states. Some multilateral arrangements have been confined to certain geographic regions; others have been global in scope. In both cases, policy coordination occurs among three or more states, where their relations are based on general principles applicable to all rather than on the particularistic preferences of any one state.[25] Foremost among these principles are the indivisibility of interests, nondiscrimination, and **diffuse reciprocity**. Indivisibility of interests means that individual hardships will be met by a collective response, nondiscrimination stipulates that benefits received by one state are available to all, and diffuse reciprocity implies that all countries expect to benefit over the long run rather than every time a dispute surfaces over a particular issue.

Regardless of whether states belong to formal multilateral institutions or informal multilateral coalitions, no favoritism is shown to the powerful. Transparent procedures and uniform guidelines apply to every state without exception.

Multilateralism expedites collaboration, but it is not a cure-all for international discord. All too often, members of multilateral organizations have tried to maximize their relative gains rather than minimize their mutual losses. "Free-riding" is one problem. Thinking that they can rely on collective action to resist aggression, some states have sought to reduce their own military preparedness and bank on the defense expenditures of those powerful states with whom they are aligned. "Chain ganging" presents another problem. Knowing that they are closely linked to others, some states mobilize at the first hint of trouble and pull their allies into what otherwise might have remained a small, local conflict.

Unilateralism, bilateralism, and multilateralism are not mutually exclusive. Nor are these strategies inherently constructive or destructive. States typically mix elements of all three approaches in their foreign policies, and they occasionally use them simultaneously. Even national leaders who are deeply committed to multilateralism rarely rule out unilateral actions when their core interests are at stake. Such leaders also recognize that sometimes acting in tandem with a close partner can nudge bystanders to become engaged on a critical issue. Nevertheless, multilateralism has advantages over unilateralism and bilateralism. By taking diverse interests and viewpoints into account, multilateralism tempers great-power rivalries and increases the number of stakeholders in the maintenance of world order. This conclusion requires closer inspection.

COORDINATED CONSULTATION AND WORLD ORDER

Multilateralism can take different forms. Two common variants are concerts and collective security. As discussed in Chapters 2 and 3, the former involves regularized consultation among those at the top of the global hierarchy; the latter, full participation by all states (recall Figures 2.3 and 3.1). A concert constructed to manage the international system offers the benefit of helping control great-power rivalries that often produce polarized blocs, though at the cost of ignoring the interests of those not belonging to the elite group. Frustrated by being excluded from discussions that affect their security and well-being, small and middle powers have vociferously complained that *who* makes decisions usually determines *what* gets decided. They prefer the all-inclusive nature of collective security. While allowing every voice to be heard, the downside of collective security is its tendency to become unwieldy as membership expands. Under collective security schemes in the past, consensus building has usually proven both difficult and delayed, especially in identifying the culpable party in a serious dispute, in choosing an appropriate response, and in implementing the selected course of action to restore the international equilibrium.

Recognizing that concerts and collective security organizations have off-setting benefits and drawbacks, a third approach to multilateralism combines elements of both in a flexible modular design. As depicted in Figure 7.5, within this hybrid system, the specific countries at the center of policy deliberations would shift as different kinds of problems arise. The system would be concert-based, with some great powers taking a leadership role on certain security issues and others on a different set of issues. At the same time, this great-power concert would be anchored in a larger collective security framework, giving small and medium powers a voice in pending matters when their interests are affected or if they possess expertise in dealing with the issue in question.

Modular multilateralism is an organizational principle, not a full-bodied structure of global governance. It offers procedural guidelines for increasing international inclusiveness, not substantive solutions to specific policy problems. Like other forms of multilateralism, it functions best under certain conditions.

The first condition that holds competitive states together in a multilateral security regime is common vulnerability. Great-power concerts and collective security organizations most often arise following wars with would-be hegemons. The decline of feelings of shared risk generally loosens the bonds holding these regimes together. But with the ascendance of a danger recognized by all, the commitment to collective action grows and the likelihood that the great powers will pursue unilateral advantages declines.

A second correlate of successful multilateralism is a sense of communal duty. Effective security policy coordination requires continuous, candid communication in order to reinforce expectations of mutual obligations and joint responsibilities. During the early nineteenth century, for example, when the Concert

FIGURE 7.5 MODULAR MULTILATERALISM

Under modular multilateralism, different subgroups within a larger collectivity take the lead in policy deliberations depending on the issue at hand. As illustrated below, Great Power A would work together with States D, E, and F on one issue, while Great Powers B and C would work with States F and G on a different issue.

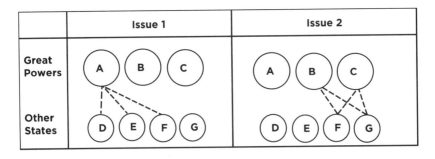

of Europe was at its zenith, a "just" equilibrium among the contending great powers meant more than an equal distribution of capabilities; it included waiving individual national interests when it was in the collective good. The great powers of that era understood that they were comanagers of international peace, which shared a commitment to the maintenance of security throughout Europe.

The third factor that strengthens multilateralism is acceptance of a code of self-restraint. Moderation and forbearance are its core values. States uphold their promises, limit the use of force, and abstain from taking advantage of concessions made by others. Respect and dignity are conferred on all, since whenever a nation has been humiliated, treated as a pariah, or denied status commensurate with its importance, a wounded sense of national pride has often triggered an aggressive response.

Finally, a dedication to cooperative security also buttresses multilateral security regimes. Armed forces can be configured in many ways. Forces whose doctrine, training, and logistics are configured for defensive rather than offensive purposes are less threatening to other countries. By embracing cooperative security, states agree to negotiate ceilings on the size and firepower of military forces and to rules governing the deployment of units and the mobilization of reserves, all of which reduce the ability of one country to concentrate its offensive forces against another. They also agree to inspections and exchanges of data on military expenditures, weapons inventories, troop maneuvers, and the like, which makes it easier to reassure others of the defensive purposes underlying their military preparations.

In summary, the key to the stability of a future marked by power deconcentration lies in the inclusiveness and transparent decision-making processes of multilateralism. Difficult to implement and demanding to maintain, multilateralism is not the answer to all of the twenty-first century's security problems, but it offers the great powers a chance to construct a world order that impedes the formation of polarized alignments and the blatant disregard of accepted norms, which has proven so destructive in the past.

LEGITIMACY AND WORLD ORDER

Self-abnegation is rare in world politics. Seldom do great powers decline an opportunity to expand their clout. The temptation to seek hegemony is hard to resist, but preponderant power usually generates opposition, even if only through **soft balancing**.[26] No state today is strong enough to discount the security concerns of other powerful states. Although America remains a strapping, prosperous nation, many international risks cannot be managed by Washington singlehandedly. Given the prohibitive costs and marginal returns from Washington acting unilaterally, or from taking a bilateral, one-on-one transactional approach to foreign policy, multilateralism offers the United States the most viable option for shoring up the world's ordering rules and institutions.

The structural shift away from American unipolarity rivets our attention on the historical preoccupation of the world's foremost states with relative status and influence. Great powers are vigorous competitors, relentlessly striving for prestige and position. Although the spread of military and economic capabilities among great powers with divergent interests creates difficulties for maintaining world order, modular multilateralism, with its emphasis on mutual responsibility and consultative decision-making, provides a procedure for great powers to tamp down disputes before they escalate to hostilities. Not all international conflict is amenable to multilateral resolution, and great-power consensus on the rules of a security regime is no guarantee of international justice, but multilateralism builds legitimacy for the normative and organizational infrastructure that undergirds world order.

Compliance with the prescriptions and prohibitions of any given system of world order can rest on coercion or consent. The shortcoming of coercion, as the eighteenth-century political philosopher Jean-Jacques Rousseau observed, is that "the strongest are still never sufficiently strong to ensure them continual mastership, unless they find means of transforming force into right, and obedience into duty."[27] Without legitimacy, a structure of world order is unlikely to be durable.

Striking a balance between power and legitimacy in an anarchic, self-help system has been called the essence of statesmanship.[28] Legitimacy refers to a widespread conviction that certain ordering rules and institutions are right and proper. When rules and institutions are established through impartial, fair procedures, they are widely perceived as authoritative. Raw power without legitimate authority elicits resistance; authority without power occasions disregard. The robustness of order hinges on how it squares power with legitimacy. When harmony is maintained, disputes tend to concern adjustments to the order rather than challenges to its fundamentals. If legitimacy wanes, however, restraints disappear, alliances polarize, and conflicts arise over the makeup of the prevailing order. Reflecting on the turbulent historical record of such polarized great-power systems, one pioneering peace researcher has concluded that they "usually eventuated in general war." Over time, they worked "not only against peace but against the security of states."[29]

KEY TERMS

balancer 154

condominiums 157

diffuse reciprocity 158

ententes 157

hypersonic weapons 147

kinetic military action 155

mixed-motive game 148

multiple independently targetable
 reentry vehicles (MIRVs) 147

nonpolarity 150

polarization 150

public goods 155

purchasing power parity (PPP) 146

scenario 146

soft balancing 161

tripolarity 149

Rethinking World Order

Life can only be understood backwards;
but it must be lived forwards.

—SØREN KIERKEGAARD,

DANISH PHILOSOPHER

Nation-states are sovereign. No higher authority possesses the right to regulate their behavior. No legal superior exists to resolve their disputes. And no guardian stands ready to defend them when they are threatened. As a result of this anarchic environment, even well-meaning national leaders engage in self-help. Uncertain about the intentions of others, they cultivate their state's power, knowing that at the end of the day they are on their own. When push comes to shove, they are responsible for protecting their country, judging whether a foreign power has violated its territorial integrity or political independence, and punishing the perpetrator of the transgression.

Ever since the Peace of Westphalia, great powers have created rules and institutions to tame the harshness of world politics, bringing a degree of predictability to international interactions. Not surprisingly, these security regimes have reflected the values and interests of the strongest states and, as military and economic power has shifted over time, so have the rules and institutions of world order.

The seeds for the contemporary liberal order were planted following the First World War and matured after the Second World War. Remarkably, what ensued has now stretched into the longest period in modern history without armed conflict between great powers. Yet achieving peace and prosperity inspired a false sense of confidence in many Western capitals, particularly in Washington when the United States attained a position of primacy after the collapse of the Soviet Union. Although lengthy unipolar periods were common in antiquity, they have been short and sporadic in the modern era. As America's unipolar moment receded with the rise of China and resurgence of Russia, and as the Trump administration has derided many of the rules and institutions of the liberal order, scholars, journalists, and policymakers understandably have begun to question whether the pillars of that order remain sturdy enough to support peace in the years ahead.

Much hinges on how China, Russia, the United States, and other great powers interact with each other. Some policy choices are certain to set a train of events in motion that will complicate efforts to renovate the current world order. Muscular unilateralism, coupled with a win-at-all-costs mentality, accelerate competition and trigger polarized alignments, which heighten tensions and makes multipolar systems prone to armed conflict.[1] In contrast, when national leaders jettison the practices of power politics for those of cooperative security, and act in an inclusive, multilateral manner, the prospects for shoring up the legitimacy of ordering rules and institutions improve.

Acting with restraint and a sense of collective responsibility can be problematic for great powers that are accustomed to imposing their will on other countries. Why relinquish a strategic advantage? Is it prudent to sacrifice self-interest for the sake of others? Can rivals be trusted not to betray you? The choices facing those who lead great powers are difficult, and the decision they reach will have significant ramifications for the global future.

....

CHANGE AND CONTINUITY IN CONTEMPORARY WORLD POLITICS

World politics is a combination of change and continuity, and it is this complex mixture that makes the future of international order so unpredictable. Change is fascinating; it excites our curiosity and fuels our imagination. Still, we must be mindful that certain aspects of world politics are deeply entrenched. As we think about the problems facing humanity, it is worth pausing to review some of the constants of great-power politics.

Table 8.1 displays those features of world politics that are relatively permanent and those that vary. Striving for military and economic capabilities is a continuity in the behavior of great powers, but how capabilities are dispersed varies because differential growth rates produce disparities in strength. Thus, while all great powers constantly pursue military might, their respective force ratios change. Stratification persists, but how the great powers are ranked in comparison to one another fluctuates over time.

As discussed in the introductory chapter, changes in the relative standing of great powers periodically beget power transitions, which sometimes result in wars between an established hegemon and a rising challenger. Each past war for global leadership has been followed by an attempt by the victor to formulate rules and institutions that tilt the playing field to its benefit. Preserving supremacy is costly, however. Every hegemon shoulders a heavy financial burden to maintain

TABLE 8.1 CONSTANCY AND VARIATION IN GREAT-POWER POLITICS

Constants	Variable Properties
Salience of power	Distribution of power
Existence of great powers	Number of great powers
Great-power pursuit of military capability	Great-power force ratios
Great-power rivalry	Intensity of competition among great powers
Stratification of the state system	Rank order of the great powers
International anarchy	Density of ordering rules and institutions

its rank, often straining to extend its dominion abroad at the expense of economic development at home. Imperial overstretch—the gap between foreign commitments and domestic resources—has always made hegemony tenuous in the modern era.[2] Sooner or later primacy has slipped from the leader's grasp as rivals have risen to challenge the status quo, culminating in a showdown aimed at establishing a new world order.

Will that be humankind's fate? Projecting the future of world order by referring to previous power transitions is not as straightforward as it seems. History doesn't speak with a single voice, and its lessons are subject to different interpretations. The past contains more than one pattern of hegemonic rise and fall, and the present may differ in many respects from what has happened previously. The growing web of financial, commercial, and cultural connections that reduce the importance of national boundaries is creating a new global agenda whose dynamics could easily pull the great powers away from past patterns. Money, goods, and people cross borders at a pace few journalists or government officials could have imagined a century ago; what's more, advances in information technology and artificial intelligence are changing how we now conceive of security and world order.

The current international system is new not only because another power transition is underway. It can be called new because there are different answers to key questions that shape how we think about world politics.

- *How are the international system's major actors defined?* Formerly they were almost exclusively sovereign, territorial states, but now nonstate actors are playing ever-larger roles in world politics.

- *What are the major actors' primary foreign policy goals?* Formerly they centered on acquiring territory and building empires, but now they focus on amassing wealth through global finance and commerce.

- *What are their principal means for pursuing those goals?* Formerly it was a reliance on military and economic might, but now a variety of cyberweapons have been added to the national security arsenal.

- *What are the major dangers facing the major actors?* Formerly the threat of military attack was the foremost danger, but now a host of non–military threats also exist, including environmental degradation, climate change, international drug trafficking, and the possibility of pandemics—deadly contagious diseases crossing national borders.

Simply put, the landscape of world politics is today quite different from previous periods of power transition. Even seemingly local events have far-reaching consequences. "The world of the digital age is like a taut web," writes one commentator. "Tweak one string and the whole network vibrates."[3] The international system is changing, reaching unprecedented heights of interconnectivity, and it should not come as a surprise that the strategies of its three leading competitors—China, Russia, and the United States—are changing as well.

CRITICAL QUESTIONS FOR WORLD ORDER IN THE TWENTY-FIRST CENTURY

Having touched on a few prominent continuities and discontinuities in modern great-power politics, we can turn to consider some of the most worrisome issues facing humanity today. Constructing ordering rules and institutions that will be accepted as legitimate is hard because the world is undergoing a fundamental transformation. Beyond the passing of American unipolarity, other momentous changes are happening. Something revolutionary, not simply new, is unfolding. To think through how these changes may affect world order, reflect on the following questions.

Has Cyberwarfare Put Sovereignty at Bay?

In the digital age, borders are not barriers. Hackers can penetrate any country. They have the capacity to conduct surveillance; steal data; disseminate disinformation; and impair power grids, air traffic control systems, self-driving vehicles, smart home devices, and anything else that is part of the so-called Internet of Things. With the expansion of information technology into almost every domain of human activity, we are entering an unprecedented era. Sovereignty is now at bay, because no government has the control that territorial states once maintained over their internal affairs. When shadowy parties of uncertain affiliation are able to undertake actions of increasing intrusiveness, warns Henry Kissinger, "the very definition of state authority may turn ambiguous."[4]

As conventionally envisioned, Westphalian nation-states were hard-shelled political units that could regulate what entered their material space.

Physical attacks against them used kinetic force to penetrate their boundaries, destroying targets and seizing territory. In contrast, today's states are porous units that have difficulty policing virtual space. Unimpeded by geography, online attacks against them penetrate their computer systems, extracting sensitive information, preventing access to networks, or compromising the integrity of an operating system by altering critical data. The Stuxnet worm, a striking example of an integrity attack, was released sometime around 2009 to sabotage Iranian nuclear centrifuges. Since meticulous forensic research is needed to attribute responsibility to the perpetrator of a cyberattack, and since the evidence is not always conclusive, deterring attacks with threats of retaliation is difficult (see Box 8.1). Equally problematic, signs of a cyberattack may not appear until long after it was launched, giving plausible deniability to the perpetrator.[5]

Box 8.1   You Decide

For more than a decade, the great powers have struggled with the question of how to deter cyberattacks. While much thought has been given to deterring nuclear and conventional military attacks, theorizing about cyberattacks remains in its infancy.

Suppose that you work for the U.S. Cyber Command and have been asked to develop a plan for deterring cyberattacks on the United States. To complete this assignment you must think theoretically, drawing upon your abstract ideas about how international actors behave in order to make concrete policy recommendations on cybersecurity. Although there is no single way to do this, thinking theoretically typically involves several steps. First, it entails hypothesizing that a relationship exists between an independent variable (X) and a dependent variable (Y), where the former represents the set of actions you recommend, and the latter depicts whether deterrence succeeds or fails.

When choosing a course of action, consider different ways that you might deter an international adversary. Strategists distinguish between two general approaches. The first, *deterrence by denial*, is based on the assumption that adversaries can be convinced to forego an attack if they are shown that their efforts would be futile. The second, *deterrence by punishment*, rests on the premise that threatening to retaliate with unacceptably high costs will convince adversaries not to attack. While it is possible to opt for some mixture of denial and punishment, let's keep this exercise simple and assume that you are tasked with choosing the single approach that you think is the most promising. If you select denial, what specific things would you recommend in order to convince a possible adversary that its cyberattack would be ineffective? If you select punishment, how would the severity of a cyberattack influence your calculations on retaliation?

The second step in thinking theoretically is to specify the conditions $(C_1, C_2, C_3, \ldots C_n)$ under which you expect the relationship between X and Y to hold. Two conditions that you may wish to consider are the types of adversaries and the types of attacks that you wish to deter. Do you expect your program of recommended actions to be equally successful on any adversary? Or will it only deter certain kinds of adversaries; for instance, terrorists, criminal organizations, or nation-states? Do you expect that your program of actions will deter all cyberattacks? Or will it only be effective against certain kinds of attack, such as those aimed at disrupting service versus those meant to destroy infrastructure?

Finally, the third step in thinking theoretically is to propose an answer as to *why* you expect the postulated relationship between X and Y to exist. This intellectual task will be the most challenging, for it requires that you offer a cogent explanation of how your policy proposal will work. Imagine that successful deterrence is the end result of some causal process. What are the intervening variables $(Z_1, Z_2, Z_3, \ldots Z_n)$ driving that process? How does the set of actions you recommend set them in motion? Medical science offers an example of how to think in these terms. When a foreign antigen enters a healthy body through vaccination, it sets in motion a causal process that evokes the specific antibody that gives immunity to the disease in question. Thus, behind the policy of preventive immunization is a theory of how inoculation (X) under certain health conditions $(C_1, C_2, C_3, \ldots C_n)$ activates those factors $(Z_1, Z_2, Z_3, \ldots Z_n)$ that ultimately give a person resistance to a particular disease (Y). Similarly, underpinning your recommendation is an implicit theory that links a program of action to various causal factors that under certain conditions yields deterrence success.

How would you put into understandable words the implicit theory behind the policy proposal that you will recommend to the president? What types of actors and forms of cyberattack will your proposal deter? What is the causal process that you believe will result in successful deterrence?

The cyberattack on Estonia during the spring of 2007 highlights the problem of tailoring an effective response to this opaque form of conflict. Following a dispute with Russia over the removal of a statue in Tallinn honoring the Soviet army's sacrifices during World War II, hackers attacked Estonian governmental, banking, and media websites. Estonia's foreign minister blamed Moscow and, as a North Atlantic Treaty Organization (NATO) member, brought the attack to the alliance's attention. Though expressing concern, the rest of the alliance declined to interpret the incident as falling under their mutual security guarantee. They were not willing to risk military hostilities in the physical world when it was unclear what constituted aggression in the virtual world.

Small and middle powers are not the only types of states that are vulnerable to cyberattacks. Great powers are vulnerable, too. A case in point is the 2016 U.S. presidential election. Russia's Internet Research Agency (IRA), based in St. Petersburg, had assembled a legion of Internet trolls to flood social media with incendiary rumors and conspiracy theories, which were amplified by thousands of **botnets** that automatically reposted the propaganda. The aim of the IRA was to drive a wedge between Americans and reduce their faith in democratic institutions. The sophisticated operation also included activities orchestrated by a group of hackers known as "Cozy Bear," who were linked to the Russian Federal Security Service (FSB), and a second group known as "Fancy Bear" that had ties to Russian military intelligence (GRU). After these hackers penetrated files belonging to the Democratic National Committee and John Podesta, the chairman of Hillary Clinton's presidential campaign, a huge number of documents and private e-mails were provided to WikiLeaks, which published information that painted an unflattering image of Clinton, provoking outrage toward her and support for Donald Trump. While political analysts still debate how much influence the dissemination of this misinformation had on the election's outcome, one thing became clear: shocking, inflammatory, and easily digested material in cyberspace tends to crowd out content that is measured, reasonable, and nuanced.[6]

By eroding the long-standing legal distinction between peace and war, inexpensive, incessant, and potentially incapacitating digital attacks provide fertile ground for the growth of a no-holds-barred cyberworld, which would allow covert assaults to cripple other states in the name of national security. As competition among the great powers increasingly takes place in cyberspace, it is imperative that a collective understanding is reached about the limits of admissible behavior. Although the great powers share common interests in protecting their sovereignty and preventing criminal and terrorist organizations from operating freely in cyberspace, they have different visions of internet governance that diverge over questions of openness. Patient, exhausting diplomacy will be needed to add cybersecurity norms and institutions to the architecture of world order.

Will Advances in Technology Weaken Normative Restraints on the Use of Force?

In a memoir written while incarcerated in Spandau Prison for complicity in war crimes and crimes against humanity, Albert Speer, minister of armaments and war production for Nazi Germany, ruminated on the allure of technological progress. "Dazzled by the possibility of technology," he wrote, "I devoted critical years of my life to serving it. But in the end my feelings about it are highly skeptical." Unleashed technology, Speer feared, would lead to "a great new war [that] will end with the destruction of human culture and civilization."[7]

For many people today, the prospect of automated warfare—a possibility created by developments in robotics and artificial intelligence—portends the danger alluded to by Speer. Intelligent autonomous weapons, which would operate without human supervision, could radically change how military force is used. Critics fear that national leaders are more likely to wage war if they do not have to put their troops in harm's way. Currently, China, Russia, and the United States are investing heavily in research on lethal autonomous systems, which range from aerial drones to terrestrial robots that could identify and engage targets using voice and facial recognition software. Computer scientists believe that in the years ahead autonomous systems will be able to collaborate on the battlefield without human input. Swarms of these small, relatively inexpensive intelligent machines, some defense analysts predict, would be able to overwhelm the large, expensive, heavily manned military platforms that the United States currently relies upon.[8]

The idea of machine-based agency raises puzzling ethical and legal questions. What happens when the sensors and software guiding a killing machine malfunction, either by chance or due to a virus? Who bears responsibility for a lethal autonomous weapon gone awry? Who should be held accountable for a fully independent drone that demolishes a building housing noncombatants? Who is culpable for a robot soldier that opens fire on individuals who are surrendering? How do we assess moral guilt and legal liability in an armed conflict fought by machines?

Another technological advance with complex implications pertains to quantum computers, which theoretically could perform computations in seconds that otherwise would take conventional computers years. Whichever great power develops a large-scale operational version of this technology will have the ability to break traditional cryptographic systems, giving that state a decisive military advantage.

Revolutionary changes in technology are likely to alter the rules for conducting world politics, wearing away normative restraints on great-power behavior. Direct, full-scale armed conflict among states has historically occurred less often when the great powers accepted binding norms that constrained the range of foreign policy choice. The advent of lethal autonomous weapons, coupled with the ability to break an adversary's cryptographic algorithms, will exert pressure for a relatively more permissive climate of normative opinion because great powers that possess these innovative technologies will be tempted to deploy them.

Reflecting on the cataclysmic wars of the twentieth century, Henry Stimson, who served as U.S. secretary of war (1911–1913, 1940–1945) and secretary of state (1929–1933), urged humanity never to forget that armed conflict debases everyone. "Under modern conditions of life, science, and technology," he asserted, "all war has become greatly brutalized, and no one who joins in it, even in self-defense, can escape becoming also in a measure brutalized."[9] A permissive normative order contains rules that give political leaders enormous latitude to do whatever they think is necessary to bolster national security. Unconstrained by firm, explicit boundaries over if and when various means of using force are acceptable, and free to renege on verbal promises and written agreements, permissive norms empower the dog-eat-dog practices of power politics. This does not bode well for world order.

Does a Nuclear Arms Race Threaten World Order?

The tensions between the United States and the Soviet Union during the Cold War never erupted into combat. One reason was the series of arms control agreements that the superpowers negotiated after the Cuban missile crisis. Prior to their face-off in October 1962, Washington and Moscow seemed trapped in an action-reaction cycle in which the two sides increased their armaments in response to one another. Beginning with the 1963 "Hot Line" agreement, which established a direct communication system between their chief executives, they reached several agreements that slowed their arms race and reduced the risk of nuclear war.

Although government secrecy prevents an exact count, estimates suggest that at the height of the Cold War the United States and the Soviet Union possessed a combined total of over 60,000 nuclear warheads. Owing to arms control treaties, nuclear stockpiles have plummeted ever since. In 2010, presidents Barack Obama and Dmitry Medvedev signed a new Strategic Arms Reduction Treaty (START) that reduced each country's strategic arsenal to 1,550 deployed warheads but did not deal with low-yield tactical nuclear warheads. If the treaty is not extended by the United States and Russia, for the first time in roughly half a century no limits will exist on the number of nuclear weapons possessed by the two countries. Meanwhile, the Trump administration has withdrawn from the 1987 Intermediate-Range Nuclear Forces (INF) Treaty, arguing that Russia was not in compliance and China was not constrained by the agreement's provisions. "Let it be an arms race," President Trump declared. "We will outmatch them at every pass and outlast them all."[10]

The American arsenal consists primarily of strategic weapons built for **counterforce targeting** and **countervalue targeting**. In keeping with the modernization program initiated by the Obama administration, each leg of the U.S. nuclear triad will be upgraded at a cost of $1.7 trillion over 30 years,[11] with plans for the B-21 long-range stealth bomber to enter into service by 2025, the first Columbia-class ballistic missile submarine by 2027, and a new intercontinental ballistic missile by 2030. Russia and China are modernizing their strategic forces, too. But under a strategy known as "escalate to de-escalate," they have also deployed various battlefield nuclear weapons, including short-range missiles, artillery, and land mines. A limited nuclear escalation during a conventional military crisis, so their thinking goes, will be persuasive enough to convince an opponent to back down but not so threatening as to provoke all-out retaliation. Some American policymakers agree that things will not inevitably spin out of control if one side in a crisis engages in a limited nuclear escalation. According to the Trump administration's 2018 *Nuclear Posture Review*, the United States requires tactical nuclear weapons to bridge the gap between conventional and full-scale nuclear war and is developing a low-yield nuclear weapon known as the W76-2 to fulfill that need.[12]

Rules and institutions to control nuclear weapons remain more than ever a vital component of world order. In an anarchic world, where self-interested governments regularly vie for advantage, many problems defy unilateral solutions. Yet if the great powers stubbornly choose to go it alone, these threats are certain to fester. So long as the consequences are bearable, acting independently may appear attractive, insofar as it appeals to national pride and bolsters a sense of exceptionalism. But when troubles worsen, the need for multilateralism grows. The question today is whether the great powers can overcome their mutual suspicions, chart a new course on arms control, and take bold action to extinguish the sparks of a dangerous new arms race.

Will Mercantilist Trade Wars Increase Political Friction?

Since military coercion can backfire—draining national budgets, producing massive casualties, and provoking international criticism—great powers have often used economic statecraft to influence other countries. Beyond offering incentives like economic aid, the arsenal of economic strategies also includes the option to implement sanctions, such as placing tariffs and quotas on imports from a targeted state, boycotting its products, refusing to sell it raw materials or manufactured goods, and freezing its financial assets. Economic sanctions have a checkered history. They are slow and often ineffective. Moreover, according to a study of some 200 cases, when they were used to punish a foreign government, military conflict became far more likely to occur between the disputants than if sanctions had not been imposed.[13]

Rather than inducing compliance, economic sanctions mainly serve a symbolic function by publicizing the target country's unacceptable behavior to foreign and domestic audiences. Nevertheless, national leaders frequently tout tariffs and import quotas as a way to protect domestic companies from foreign competition, even though protectionist barriers to imports may incite debilitating trade wars. The Smoot-Hawley Tariff Act of 1930, for example, increased U.S. tariffs significantly and, in so doing, triggered a series of retaliatory measures by former American trade partners, which contributed to the collapse of global commerce. Protectionist measures, such as those favored by Donald Trump, who has repeatedly bragged that he is "a tariff man," repudiate the post–World War II liberal economic order that was painstakingly built, step by step, through the General Agreement on Tariffs and Trade (GATT) and, later, the World Trade Organization (WTO). As discussed in Chapters 3 and 5, the rules of these institutions were predicated on four principles: (1) *reciprocity* through which countries which lowered their tariffs could expect their trading partners to do the same in exchange; (2) *nondiscrimination*, meaning that all members to the liberal trade regime had the same level of access to the markets of other member states;

(3) the *most-favored nation (MFN)* rule, maintaining that preferences granted to one state required that the same preferences were granted to all other participants so that there would exist no "favored nation" among the members; and (4) *transparency,* prohibiting secret trade regulations hidden from view from other members. The principles worked. Global trade expanded, as did the wealth of participating nations.

To be sure, the benefits of free trade were never evenly distributed; some countries' economies grew faster than others. This was especially true of the great powers, as indicated by China's boast that its aggregate national wealth would exceed that of the United States by the year 2025. In response, the Trump administration mounted a direct attack on free trade, imposing high tariffs on Chinese imports to the United States, to which China promptly responded in kind. The risks of this quarrel became apparent at the meeting of Chinese President Xi Jinping and U.S. President Donald J. Trump at the November 2018 **Group of Twenty (G20)** summit in Argentina. Xi openly declared China's intent to outstrip America in technology and displace its influence in Asia and beyond, and Trump proclaimed that he would win in a confrontation between the economic powerhouses.[14] The outcome of any economic showdown was less certain to outside observers who noted that Beijing had leverage over Washington. The American economy depends on foreign capital to sustain its enormous current account deficit. As 2019 began, U.S. debt to China was estimated at over $1.12 trillion. By dumping U.S. Treasury bills and other dollar-denominated assets, China could cause economic problems for the United States, though weakening the U.S. economy would be counterproductive since American consumption of Chinese goods is important for China's economic growth. This does not necessarily mean that commercial competition will culminate in a full-scale Sino-American war. Continuing trade between great-power adversaries is not unusual—even in the midst of hostilities.[15] Still, an unrestrained trade war between China and America would be devastating for both states, whose economies are heavily dependent on the continuation of trade between them that now exceeds $2 billion each day.[16] This is not an auspicious time for either contender for global primacy to start a military fight.

Trump's economic policies are based on **neomercantilism**—the economic nationalist theory that maintaining a **balance-of-trade surplus** by reducing imports, stimulating domestic production, and promoting exports increase a state's prosperity and power in comparison to its economic competitors. Economic nationalism fueled his insistence that the liberal economic order had facilitated China's growth while allowing America's relative standing to slip. China has "drained so much money out of our country," Trump insisted. "That's not going to happen anymore."[17] His emphasis on relative gains reveals why a world order that promises mutual economic benefits can encounter stiff resistance if one or more great powers believe that gains realized by one competitor will come at the expense of the others.

Can a Framework of World Order Be Effective Without Including Nonstate Actors?

For the past three and a half centuries, students of world politics have looked at the geostrategic landscape through a lens that accentuated the interaction of sovereign territorial states. According to one of the dominant metaphors in the field of international relations, states resemble billiard balls on a pool table. Just as knowing the location of the balls, the direction of their movement, and the force at which they strike one another allows a spectator to predict the result of each collision, knowing the geographic location, policy direction, and military force employed by one state against another helps an analyst forecast the outcomes of international exchanges. Because nation-states are the primary actors on the world stage and great powers play the leading roles, a state-centric lens highlights important phenomena. Yet it does not reveal everything.

Obscured from this view is the web of nonstate actors that connects people across the globe. More than at any time since the Peace of Westphalia, nonstate actors are exercising influence in international affairs. Greenpeace, Amnesty International, Doctors Without Borders, and many other transnational groups are bringing their expertise to bear on policy problems. World politics is increasingly shaped by networks of coordination, where government officials and members of nongovernmental organizations jointly address global and regional problems. Great powers may receive top billing, but they are not the sole performers in the drama of world politics. Ethnopolitical associations, religious movements, issue-advocacy groups, multinational corporations, terrorist organizations, and crime syndicates are also members of the cast.

If networks of non-sovereign entities now exist alongside hierarchies of sovereign states, perhaps it is warranted to think about world order in a fresh way. Recall that in the previous chapter we saw that multilateralism had advantages over unilateralism and special bilateral deals when building world order. Furthermore, a flexible, modular approach to multilateralism that gives space for small- and medium-sized countries to participate alongside the great powers on a case-by-case basis can enhance the legitimacy of a set of ordering rules and institutions. Given the growing importance of transnational networks in twenty-first-century world politics, it may be justifiable to define modular multilateralism more broadly to include those nonstate actors that have the skills and experience to contribute to managing the most pressing issues on the global agenda.

Should the Rules and Institutions of World Order Apply to Outer Space?

Shadows of the past are visible today. Although the practice of colonization has faded, the age-old desire to acquire territory continues to motivate many states, as seen by Russia's seizure of Crimea, China's conflict with neighboring states over maritime claims, and the efforts of various countries to control vast swaths of the Arctic. Beyond these terrestrial ambitions, the great powers have set their eyes on a new frontier—outer space. U.S. President Donald Trump, for example, has proposed a "Space Force" to complement America's traditional military branches. Roscosmos, the Russian space agency, is developing a new reusable piloted spacecraft and has unveiled an ambitious lunar program. Not to be left behind, China succeeded in landing a rover on the "dark side" of the moon in 2019 and plans to operate its own space station and send astronauts to the moon in the coming years.

All three great powers envision outer space as a domain that will become central to their military capabilities. Already they rely on satellites for communication, navigation, and surveillance. Protecting these vulnerable assets is essential for national security. During the Cold War, the Soviet Union tested "space mines" that could disable a satellite by spraying it with shrapnel. Today anti-satellite missiles have been developed by China, Russia, and the United States that not only can destroy satellites in low orbit but also threaten those in higher geosynchronous orbits.[18] When U.S. President Ronald Reagan proposed the Strategic Defense Initiative (SDI) in 1983, which would have put lasers and particle-beam weapons in space, many defense experts scoffed at the idea. The technology simply did not exist. However, computing power has increased exponentially since Reagan's day, and research on sensors and directed-energy weapons has also advanced considerably. What once was science fiction may soon become reality, raising new issues for maintaining peace among the great powers.

The 1967 Outer Space Treaty prohibited placing nuclear weapons in orbit around the earth, banned such weapons from being stationed deeper in space, and declared that the moon and other celestial bodies should only be used for peaceful purposes. Beyond these preliminary injunctions, little progress has been made on developing a code of conduct for spacefaring great powers. As plans are drawn up in Beijing, Moscow, and Washington to establish bases on the moon and to travel to and even populate Mars, the prospects for great-power friction multiply, and the stakes become more consequential.

Will Climate Change Overwhelm Efforts to Preserve World Order?

"What humankind makes, unmakes humankind," the journalist Norman Cousins once quipped.[19] Humanity, he lamented, has created the means for its own destruction. Nuclear war is an obvious example. Yet there is another way by which humanity could perish through its own habits. It is a hazard produced primarily by the world's great industrial powers, a self-inflicted menace that endangers everyone, everywhere. The threat derives from the relentless use of fossil fuel energy, which is causing the earth's average temperature to rise due to the emission of "greenhouse" gases—primarily carbon dioxide (CO_2) and chlorofluorocarbons (CFCs)—that trap heat emitted from the planet's surface which otherwise would escape into outer space.

Climate change is not a hypothesis about a long-term problem. It is happening now. "The twenty-two warmest years on record have occurred in the past 22 years, with the past four years the four warmest; the concentration of carbon dioxide in the atmosphere is the highest it has been in three million years."[20] The U.S. Department of Defense defines global warming as a threat to national security. The December 2015 UN Climate Change Conference in Paris urged the world's nations to reduce emissions 60 percent below 2010 levels by 2050, concurring with UN climate chief Christiana Figueres that "whatever gets done over the next ten to fifteen years, whatever gets invested in the energy system … is going to determine the energy mix that we will have for at least fifty years. It is going to determine the quality of life of this century and beyond."[21] Climate change is a global problem with fateful implications. It is not hyperbole to say that it is *the* biggest threat to world order, because it would cause significant changes in weather patterns that affect human well-being, creating new flash points over territory and resources as some regions become uninhabitable.

The scientific consensus today is that (a) the earth is warming, (b) human activity is a principal cause, (c) it is affecting the planet's climate, and (d) the impact is substantial. Where climatologists disagree is over how rapidly things are changing and whether the planet is approaching a "tipping point," where small increases in temperature could suddenly cause catastrophic effects. If the earth's surface temperature continues to rise, as it has without interruption for the past fifteen years, ice caps and glaciers will melt; sea levels will rise; low-lying coastal land, including cities and islands throughout the world, will flood; oceans will become more acidic as they absorb carbon dioxide; extreme weather events such as hurricanes, droughts, and wildfires will become more severe; and tropical diseases will spread to previously temperate regions that were formerly too cold for their insect carriers. In short, climate change will shatter economies, jeopardize health, and trigger civil strife.[22]

Climate change is a major part of a larger environmental crisis. Also injurious to human well-being are biodiversity loss and land degradation due to deforestation, soil erosion, and industrial farming. The world has entered a period of environmental instability likely to cause widespread dislocation. Unless greenhouse gases are reduced, biodiversity preserved, and land protected, the impact could be both dramatic and devastating, imperiling humans for an untold future. No great power will be immune, and only through their cooperation can humanity bring this multifaceted growing threat to world order under control.

THE QUEST FOR WORLD ORDER

It is relatively easy to patch together an international arrangement that will last for a generation, remarked British prime minister David Lloyd George following World War I. "What is difficult, however, is to draw up a peace which will not provoke a fresh struggle."[23] As the questions discussed previously indicate, deep fault lines divide the great powers. The rifts are so pronounced that any issue touching on world order can arouse controversy. Status quo powers, realizing what they stand to lose if the old order is replaced, will press for salvaging as much of it as possible. Revisionist powers, angling for something that works more to their advantage, will clamor for an overhaul. Crafting an international framework of rules and institutions that are resilient and accepted as legitimate has never been so difficult.

Although power is more dispersed today than during America's unipolar moment, the United States remains a pivotal player in global affairs, possessing the only military with truly global reach and the world's most innovative economy. However, military and economic capabilities are deficient if they cannot be converted into diplomatic influence. Respect is the cornerstone of successful diplomacy. To exert influence, reputation matters. Under the Trump administration, America's international reputation has been squandered; its once-robust network of multilateral coalitions, weakened. In his 2019 State of the Union address, Donald Trump boasted, "America is winning each and every day." But what does that mean if the methods tarnish the country's reputation? Who wants to throw in their lot with someone who cannot be trusted to keep his word or abide by his commitments? Winning through bombast and opportunism is not a viable security strategy. As former president Dwight Eisenhower made clear, "It is not the goal of the American people that the United States should be the richest nation in the graveyard of history."[24]

On January 29, 2019, Dan Coats, the director of national intelligence, testified before the U.S. Senate Intelligence Committee that skepticism was increasing throughout the world about the political model championed by the United States. In the coming years, he predicted, America will be tested by rivals "that exploit the weakening of the post-World War II international order." Challenges were growing, not diminishing. Behind the ceremonial smiles and handshakes at international gatherings, rifts of suspicion and distrust were opening. According to Coats, China and Russia were "more aligned than at any point since the mid-1950s ... taking advantage of rising doubts in some places about the liberal democratic model."

Until recently, China followed a low-profile strategy described by Deng Xiaoping, the nation's leading political figure from 1978 through 1989, as "hide your strength, bide your time." Instead of challenging the American-led world order, its leaders pursued a national security strategy of "active defense"[25] and emphasized China's "peaceful rise" to great-power status. At the Nineteenth Party Congress in 2017, however, President Xi Jinping spoke of the dawn of "a new era" in which China moves "closer to center stage" and offers an "option for other countries."[26] Under China's Belt and Road Initiative, the most ambitious infrastructure venture in history, Beijing is laying the foundation for a trade zone that spans Asia, Europe, and Africa, positioning China at its heart. Together with railways, ports, and pipelines, this new Silk Road is intended to include fiber-optic cables, satellite relay stations, and 5G mobile networks. In short, Beijing is changing geopolitical realities as "a vast, integrated Eurasian supercontinent is proving to be a salient feature of an emerging global order."[27]

China also hopes to change the rules and institutions that govern cyberspace. For decades, the Internet has followed the bottom-up, private-sector-led template favored by the United States. In contrast to this market-centric approach, President Xi is promoting "cyber-sovereignty" as an organizing principle, publicizing the benefits of top-down, national Internets closely regulated by individual governments.[28] Rather than being open and global, cyberspace would be closed and local. States would exercise jurisdiction over online operations, circumscribing access to information through censorship and restrictions on virtual private networks. The digital revolution is ushering in what has been described as "the biggest geopolitical revolution in history."[29] Because contentious great-power debate over how cyberspace should be managed is certain to intensify, cultivating shared norms for state behavior is critical for the construction of a solid framework of world order in the twenty-first century.

"All history shows," the revered realist thinker Hans J. Morgenthau theorist noted, "that nations active in international politics are consistently preparing for, actively involved in, or recovering from organized violence in the form of war."[30] This book has taken as its point of departure the efforts by great powers to build world order after the First and Second World Wars—two devastating clashes that many historians regard as a continuation of the same contest for international primacy. The framework of world order that emerged after this protracted struggle has begun to unravel. The United States, the architect of that liberal order, is suffering from deep-seated problems. Inequality in America is at its highest in almost a century, upward mobility is below that registered in most other industrial societies, and public trust in government is approaching a historic low. Throughout the world, authoritarianism is on the rise and democracy is in decline. As an eminent French statesman summarized the situation, the three main safety mechanisms of the post–World War II system "are no longer functioning: no more American power willing to be the last-resort enforcer of international order; no solid system of international governance; and, most troubling, no real concert of nations able to re-establish common ground."[31]

World order, we have argued throughout this book, is not self-sustaining; it requires for its maintenance a common vision and a concerted effort by the great powers. America and the order it forged at the end of the Second World War now faces a bewildering variety of threats. In this troubled environment, writes a distinguished U.S. diplomat, the "task will be to use what remains of the historic window of American preeminence to shape a new world order, one that accommodates new players and their ambitions while promoting our own interests."[32] The challenge is how to do this in a world dominated by three or more competing great powers that appear unwilling to work cooperatively together.

The world's future is uncertain, but it is our future. Although we cannot know exactly what it will hold, we can be sensitive how our images of the future—what we expect, what we hope for, and what we fear—all exert an influence on the present. By acting with foresight today, we sculpt the shape of tomorrow. When thinking about the future of world order it is worth remembering the advice offered by President John F. Kennedy. It would be tragic, the president once said, to believe that "we are gripped by forces we cannot control. We need not accept that view," he concluded. "No problem of human destiny is beyond human beings."[33]

KEY TERMS

balance-of-trade surplus 173

botnets 169

counterforce targeting 171

countervalue targeting 171

Group of Twenty (G20) 173

neomercantilism 173

Suggested Readings

Thousands of books, journal articles, and essays have been written on great-power politics and world order. It is easy to be overwhelmed by the sheer volume of publications on the subject. The titles that we discuss below are intended to call attention to some of the leading works, to which students may turn for supplementary information on the topics covered in this textbook. Classification follows the sequence of chapters. For reasons of space, no attempt has been made to provide exhaustive reading lists. Excluded are memoirs, government documents, and materials in foreign languages. Because we have not repeated titles, to find research on some issues it may be helpful to look at the list of references for several different chapters.

Chapter 1: Great-Power Struggles for Primacy in the Modern Era

The subject of great-power politics has drawn enormous scholarly attention. The origins of the modern world system are discussed in William Bain, ed., *Medieval Foundations of International Relations* (Abingdon: Routledge, 2017). For analyses of the Thirty Years' War and the Peace of Westphalia, see Peter H. Wilson, *The Thirty Years' War: Europe's Tragedy* (Cambridge, MA: Belknap Press, 2009); Charles W. Kegley Jr., and Gregory A. Raymond, *Exorcising the Ghost of Westphalia: Building World Order in the New Millennium* (Upper Saddle River, NJ: Prentice Hall, 2002); and Ronald G. Ash, *The Thirty Years' War, The Holy Roman Empire and Europe, 1618–1648* (New York: St. Martin's Press, 1997).

For an excellent presentation of the intellectual roots of political realism and liberalism, see Michael W. Doyle, *Ways of War and Peace* (New York: Norton, 1997). Classic realist descriptions of world politics include E. H. Carr, *The Twenty Years' Crisis*, 2nd ed. (London: Macmillan, 1946); Reinhold Niebuhr, *Moral Man and Immoral Society* (New York: Simon and Schuster, 1960); and Arnold Wolfers, *Discord and Collaboration* (Baltimore: Johns Hopkins University Press, 1962). Consult Kenneth N. Waltz's pioneering *Theory of International Politics* (Reading, MA: Addison-Wesley, 1979); and John J. Mearsheimer, *The Tragedy of Great Power Politics* (New York: Norton, 2001) for influential structural accounts. Excellent examples of data-based research inspired by liberal theorizing are Bruce Russett and John Oneal, *Triangulating Peace: Democracy, Interdependence, and International Organizations* (New York: Norton, 2001); and James Lee Ray, *Democracy and International Conflict: An Evaluation of the Democratic Peace Proposition* (Columbia: University of South Carolina Press, 1995).

To grasp how political realists interpret the role of power in world politics, you can do no better than to dive into Hans J. Morgenthau's *Politics Among Nations*, 6th ed. (New York: Knopf, 1985). For deeper probes into the concept of power, consult Joseph S. Nye, *Soft Power* (New York: PublicAffairs, 2004); John M. Rothgeb Jr., *Defining Power: Influence and Force in the Contemporary International System* (New York: St. Martin's Press, 1993); and David A. Baldwin, *Paradoxes of Power* (New York: Basil Blackwell, 1989). To explore how the very meaning of power changes over time due to technological innovations and shifting global circumstances, see Robert O. Keohane and Joseph S. Nye,

Power and Interdependence, 3rd ed. (New York: Addison Wesley-Longman, 2001); and Joseph S. Nye, *The Future of Power* (New York: PublicAffairs, 2011).

Of the many works that analyze great-power competition, the following are particularly useful: John J. Mearsheimer, *The Great Delusion: Liberal Dreams and International Realities* (New Haven, CT: Yale University Press, 2018); John A. Vasquez, *The War Puzzle Revisited* (Cambridge: Cambridge University Press, 2009); Bear F. Braumoeller, "Systemic Politics and the Origins of Great Power Conflict," *American Political Science Review* 102, no. 1 (2008): 77–93; Michael P. Colaresi, Karen Rasler, and William R. Thompson, *Strategic Rivalries in World Politics: Position, Space and Conflict Escalation* (Cambridge: Cambridge University Press, 2007); William R. Thompson, ed., *Great Power Rivalries* (Columbia: University of South Carolina Press, 1999); Benjamin Miller, *When Opponents Cooperate: Great Power Conflict and Collaboration in World Politics* (Ann Arbor: University of Michigan Press, 1995); Paul Kennedy, *The Rise and Fall of the Great Powers* (New York: Random House, 1987); Richard Ned Lebow and B. Strauss, eds., *Hegemonic Rivalry* (Boulder, CO: Westview, 1991); and Jack Levy, *War in the Modern Great Power System, 1495–1975* (Lexington: University Press of Kentucky, 1983).

David A. Lake's *Hierarchy in International Relations* (Ithaca, NY: Cornell University Press, 2009) discusses how the state system is stratified, which is elaborated upon by the contributors to Ayşe Zarakol, ed. *Hierarchies in World Politics* (Cambridge: Cambridge University Press, 2017). Researchers from several different theoretical traditions have analyzed the dynamics of structural change within the great-power pecking order. Robert Gilpin's *War and Change in World Politics* (Cambridge: Cambridge University Press, 1981) provides an excellent introduction to hegemonic stability theory. Power transition theory is explicated in Ronald L. Tammen, et al., *Power Transitions: Strategies for the 21st Century* (New York: Chatham House, 2000); and A. F. K. Organski and Jacek Kugler, *The War Ledger* (Chicago: University of Chicago Press, 1980). Charles F. Doran discusses power cycle theory in "Confronting the Principles of the Power Cycle Theory," in *Handbook of War Studies II*, Manus I. Midlarsky, ed. (Ann Arbor: University of Michigan Press, 2000): 332–368. For long-cycle theorizing, consult George Modelski and William R. Thompson, *Leading Sectors and World Powers: The Coevolution of Global Politics and Economics* (Columbia: University of South Carolina Press, 1995); Karen A. Rasler and William R. Thompson, *The Great Powers and Global Struggle, 1490–1990* (Lexington: University Press of Kentucky, 1994); William R. Thompson, *On Global War: Historical-Structural Approaches to World Politics* (Columbia: University of South Carolina Press, 1988); and George Modelski, *Long Cycles in World Politics* (London: Macmillan, 1987). Cyclical interpretations of the world economy can be found in Immanuel Wallerstein, *World-Systems Analysis* (Durham, NC: Duke University Press, 2005); Christopher Chase-Dunn, *Global Formation: Structures of the World Economy* (Oxford: Basil Blackwell, 1989); and Joshua S. Goldstein, *Long Cycles: Prosperity and War in the Modern Age* (New Haven: Yale University Press, 1988).

Hedley Bull's *The Anarchical Society: A Study of Order in World Politics*, 3rd ed. (New York: Columbia University Press, 1977) provides an excellent introduction into various restraints on great-power competition. The potential for international norms to contribute to world order is discussed in Gregory A. Raymond, "Problems and Prospects in the Study of International Norms," *Mershon International Studies Review* 41 (November): 205–245; and in Charles W. Kegley Jr. and Gregory A. Raymond, *When Trust Breaks Down: Alliance Norms and World Politics* (Columbia: University of South Carolina Press, 1990). For an evaluation of the contemporary role of international organizations in world affairs, see Julia Gray, "Life, Death, or Zombie? The Vitality of International Organizations," *International Studies Quarterly* 62, no. 1 (2018): 1–13, who concludes that most international organizations are zombies that are constrained by the limits on their authority imposed by the great powers.

A good starting point for the analysis of world order is Henry Kissinger, *World Order* (New York: Penguin, 2014). Other relevant works include Hal Brands and Charles Edel, *The Lessons of Tragedy: Statecraft and World Order* (New Haven, CT: Yale University Press, 2019); Richard Haass, *A World in Disarray: American Foreign Policy and the Crisis of the Old Order* (New York: Penguin, 2017); Charles A. Kupchan, *How Enemies Become Friends: The Sources of Stable Peace* (Princeton, NJ: Princeton University Press, 2010); Dan Caldwell and Robert E. Williams, *Seeking Security in an Insecure World* (Lanham, MD: Rowman & Littlefield, 2006); Anne-Marie Slaughter, *A New World Order* (Princeton, NJ: Princeton University Press, 2004); Charles W. Kegley Jr. and Gregory A. Raymond, *How Nations Make Peace* (New York: St. Martin's/Worth, 1999); Robert O. Keohane, *After Hegemony* (Princeton, NJ: Princeton University Press, 1984); and Alpo M. Rusi, *Dangerous Peace: New Rivalry in World Politics* (Boulder, CO: Westview, 1977). For a compilation of essays on adapting to uncertainty in international affairs, see Peter J. Katzenstein and Lucia A. Seybert, eds. *Protean Power: Exploring the Uncertain and Unexpected in World Politics* (New York: Cambridge University Press, 2018).

Chapter 2: World War I and the Versailles Settlement

The amount of scholarly material on the origins of World War I is staggering. For the diplomatic history of the period preceding the war, see F. R. Bridge and Roger Bullen, *The Great Powers and the European States System, 1814–1914*, 2nd ed. (New York: Routledge, 2005); A. J. P. Taylor, *The Struggle for Mastery in Europe, 1848–1918* (Oxford: Clarendon, 1954); and William L. Langer, *European Alliances and Alignments, 1871–1890* (New York: Knopf, 1950). Among the most noteworthy of the various accounts of the war's outbreak are Jörn Leonhard, *Pandora's Box: A History of the First World War*, trans. Patrick Camiller (Cambridge, MA: Belknap Press, 2018); Niall Ferguson, *The Pity of War: Explaining World War I* (London: Macmillan, 1999); James Joll, *The Origins of the First World War* (London: Longman, 1984); Fritz Fischer, *Germany's War Aims in the First World War* (New York: Norton, 1967); Barbara W. Tuchman, *The Guns of August* (New York: Macmillan, 1962); Luigi Albertini, *The Origins of the War of 1914*, trans. by Isabella M. Massey, 3 vols. (London: Oxford University Press, 1952–1957); Sidney B. Fay, *The Origins of the World War*, 2nd ed. (New York: Macmillan, 1930); and G. Lowes Dickinson, *The International Anarchy, 1904–1914* (New York: Century, 1926). On the aftermath of the war, see especially Robert Gerwart, *The Vanquished: Why the First World War Failed to End* (New York: Farrar, Straus and Giroux, 2016); Adam Tooze, *The Deluge: The Great War, America and the Remaking of the Global Order, 1916–1931* (New York: Penguin/Random House, 2014); H. E. Goemans, *War and Punishment: The Causes of War Termination and the First World War* (Princeton, NJ: Princeton University Press, 2001); and Graham Ross, *The Great Powers and the Decline of the European States System, 1914–1945* (London: Longman, 1983).

A rich literature also exists on the concept of a balance of power. The most valuable works include Richard Little, *The Balance of Power in International Relations: Metaphors, Myths and Models* (Cambridge: Cambridge University Press, 2007); John A. Vasquez and Colin Elman, eds., *Realism and the Balancing of Power: A New Debate* (Upper Saddle River, NJ: Prentice Hall, 2003); F. H. Hinsley, *Power and the Pursuit of Peace: Theory and Practice in the History of Relations Between States* (Cambridge: Cambridge University Press, 1963); Inis L. Claude Jr., *Power and International Relations* (New York: Random House, 1962); Ludwig Dehio, *The Precarious Balance* (New York: Knopf, 1962); and Edward V. Gulick, *Europe's Classical Balance of Power* (Ithaca, NY: Cornell University Press, 1955).

Overviews of the peace settlement can be found in Margaret MacMillan, *Paris 1919: Six Months that Changed the World* (New York: Random House, 2007); Frank S. Marston, *The Peace Conference of 1919* (London: Oxford University Press, 1944); Paul Birdsall, *Versailles Twenty Years After* (Hamden, CT: Archon, 1941); and Harold Nicolson, *Peacemaking, 1919* (New York: Harcourt, Brace, 1939). An authoritative treatment of the League of Nations is Francis P. Walters, *A History of the League of Nations*, 2 vols. (London: Oxford University Press, 1952). Other useful treatments are found in M. Patrick Cottrell, *League of Nations: Enduring Legacies of the First Experiment at World Organization* (London: Routledge, 2018); F. S. Northedge, *The League of Nations: Its Life and Times, 1920–1946* (Leicester: Leicester University Press, 1986); George Scott, *The Rise and Fall of the League of Nations* (New York: Macmillan, 1973); and Byron Dexter, *The Years of Opportunity: The League of Nations, 1920–1926* (New York: Viking, 1967). A handy anthology of readings on collective security is provided by Marina S. Finkelstein and Lawrence S. Finkelstein, eds., *Collective Security* (San Francisco: Chandler, 1966). Collective security is unfavorably compared to balance-of-power systems in Hans J. Morgenthau, *Politics Among Nations: The Struggle for Power and Peace*, 3rd ed. (New York: Alfred A. Knopf, 1966).

Revealing analyses of political idealism and the Wilsonian approach to statecraft include Thomas J. Knock, *To End All Wars: Woodrow Wilson and the Quest for a New World Order* (New York: Oxford University Press, 1992); Frank Ninkovich, *The Wilsonian Century* (Chicago: University of Chicago Press, 1999); Alexander L. George and Juliette L. George, *Woodrow Wilson and Colonel House* (New York: John Day, 1956); Thomas Bailey, *Woodrow Wilson and the Lost Peace* (New York: Macmillan, 1944); and E. H. Carr, *The Twenty-Years' Crisis, 1919–1939* (London: Macmillan, 1939). On the outlawry of war movement and the 1928 General Pact for the Renunciation of War, see Oona A. Hathaway and Scott J. Shapiro, *The Internationalists: How a Radical Plan to Outlaw War Remade the World* (New York: Simon & Schuster, 2017).

Chapter 3: World War II and the Birth of the Liberal Order

There are innumerable accounts of the Second World War. Good overviews of the conflict's origins and aftermath are provided by Gerhard Weinberg, *A World at Arms: A Global History of World War II*, 2nd ed. (Cambridge: Cambridge University Press, 2005); Donald L. Miller, *The Story of World War II*, rev. ed. of original by Henry Steele Commager (New York: Simon & Schuster, 2001); P. M. H. Bell, *The Origins of the Second World War in Europe* (London: Longman, 1986); Jonathan Haslam, *The Soviet Union and the Struggle for Collective Security in Europe, 1933–1939* (London: Palgrave Macmillan, 1984); Willard D. Range, *Franklin D. Roosevelt's World Order* (Athens: University of Georgia Press, 1959); and Herbert Feis, *Churchill, Roosevelt and Stalin: The War They Waged and the Peace They Sought* (Princeton, NJ: Princeton University Press, 1957). Orthodox interpretations of the war's causes, which emphasize Hitler's drive for European domination, are provided by Tim Bouverie, *Appeasement: Chamberlain, Hitler, Churchill, and the Road to War* (New York: Tim Duggan, 2019); Christopher R. Browning, "Giving In to Hitler,"

New York Review of Books 66, no. 14 (2019): 45–49; Walther Hofer, *War Premeditated, 1930* (London: Thames and Hudson, 1955); Lewis B. Namier, *Diplomatic Prelude, 1938–1939* (London: Macmillan, 1950); and John W. Wheeler-Bennett, *Munich, Prologue to Tragedy* (London: Macmillan, 1948). A highly provocative revisionist interpretation is presented by A. J. P. Taylor, *The Origins of the Second World War* (New York: Atheneum, 1961), which portrays Hitler as an opportunist who sought to dismantle the Versailles settlement rather than conquer Europe. Hajo Holborn, in *The Political Collapse of Europe* (New York: Alfred A. Knopf, 1951), places the events that occurred in the European theater of war within a sweeping narrative of that continent's modern diplomatic history, and Andrew Roberts, in *The Storm of War: A New History of the Second World War* (New York: HarperCollins, 2012), offers a series of interesting counterfactuals that suggest how changes in the war's conduct might have altered the outcome.

Not surprisingly, Neville Chamberlain's appeasement policy toward Nazi Germany has attracted considerable scholarly attention. Noteworthy books on this topic include Larry William Fuchser, *Neville Chamberlain and Appeasement: A Study in the Politics of History* (New York: Norton, 1982); Telford Taylor, *Munich: The Price of Tragedy* (New York, 1979); Keith Middlemas, *The Strategy of Appeasement: The British Government and Germany, 1937–1939* (Chicago: Quadrangle Books, 1972); A. L. Rowse, *Appeasement: A Study of Political Decline, 1933–1939* (New York: Norton, 1961); Samuel Hoare, *Nine Troubled Years* (London: Collins, 1954); John W. Wheeler-Bennett, *Munich: Prologue to Tragedy* (New York: Macmillan, 1948); and Keith Feiling, *Life of Neville Chamberlain* (London: Macmillan, 1946). For a useful presentation of the French perspective, see Rene Albrecht-Carrié, *France, Europe, and the Two World Wars* (New York: Harper, 1961).

Of the many studies of Hitler's behavior, the most prominent are Ian Kershaw, *Hitler: A Biography* (New York: Norton, 2008); Klaus Hidebrand, *The Foreign Policy of the Third Reich*, trans. Anthony Fothergill (Berkeley: University of California Press, 1973); Alan Bullock, *Hitler: A Study in Tyranny*, rev. ed. (New York: Harper and Row, 1962); and Hugh Trevor-Roper, *The Last Days of Hitler*, 6th ed. (Chicago: University of Chicago Press, 1987). Hitler's skill at manipulating other great powers is discussed in William J. Newman, *The Balance of Power in the Interwar Years, 1919–1939* (New York: Random House, 1968).

For analyses of the onset and termination of fighting in Pacific theater of the war, see John E. Dower, *Embracing Defeat: Japan in the Wake of World War II* (New York: Norton, 2000); Leon V. Sigal, *Fighting to a Finish: The Politics of War Termination in the United States and Japan, 1945* (Ithaca, NY: Cornell University Press, 1988); Jonathan G. Utley, *Going to War with Japan, 1937–1941* (Knoxville: University of Tennessee Press, 1985); John Toland, *The Rising Sun: The Decline and Fall of the Japanese Empire, 1936–1945* (New York: Random House, 1970); Dorothy Borg, *The United States and the Far Eastern Crisis of 1933–1938* (Cambridge, MA: Harvard University Press, 1964); William L. Neumann, *America Encounters Japan: From Perry to MacArthur* (Baltimore: Johns Hopkins University Press, 1963); Paul W. Schroeder, *The Axis Alliance and Japanese-American Relations* (Ithaca, NY: Cornell University Press, 1958); and William L. Langer and S. Everett Gleason, *The Undeclared War, 1940–1941* (New York: Harper and Bros, 1953). Robert J. C. Butow authors a revealing study of the influence of the atomic bomb on Japan's acceptance of the allies' insistence on unconditional surrender in his *Japan's Decision to Surrender* (Stanford: Stanford University Press, 1954). Gar Alperovitz's *Atomic Diplomacy: Hiroshima to Potsdam* (New York: Simon & Schuster, 1965) argues that the American use of the atomic bomb had less to do with inducing the Japanese to surrender than to exert pressure on Russia. For a thorough treatment of this issue, see Martin J. Sherwin, *A World Destroyed: The Atomic Bomb and the Grand Alliance* (New York: Alfred A. Knopf, 1975).

For authoritative treatments of economic institutions established after the war, see Donald Maxwell, *John Maynard Keynes and International Relations: Economic Paths to War and Peace* (Oxford: Oxford University Press, 2006); Douglas Irwin, *Against the Tide: An Intellectual History of Free Trade* (Princeton, NJ: Princeton University Press, 1997); Harold James, *International Monetary Cooperation since Bretton Woods* (Oxford: IMF and Oxford University Press, 1996); Barry Eichengreen, *Golden Fetters: The Gold Standard and the Great Depression, 1919–1939* (New York: Oxford University Press, 1992); David E. Kaiser, *Economic Diplomacy and the Origins of the Second World War: Germany, Britain, France and Eastern Europe, 1930–1939* (Princeton, NJ: Princeton University Press, 1980); and Charles P. Kindleberger, *The World in Depression, 1929–1939* (Berkeley: University of California Press, 1973).

Informative works on the birth of the United Nations include Laurence C. Peters, *The United Nations: History and Core Ideas* (New York: Palgrave Macmillan, 2015); Paul Kennedy, *The Parliament of Man: The Past, Present, and Future of the United Nations* (New York: Random House, 2006); and Inis L. Claude Jr., *Swords into Plowshares: The Problems and Progress of International Organization*, 3rd ed. (New York: Random House, 1964).

Chapter 4: The Cold War and Its Consequences

The literature addressing the origins, conduct, and conclusion of the Cold War is extensive. For analyses of the Cold War's origins, consult John Lewis Gaddis, *We Now Know: Rethinking Cold War History* (New York: Oxford University Press, 1997); Deborah W. Larson, *Origins of Containment: A Psychological Explanation* (Princeton, NJ: Princeton University Press, 1985); Thomas G. Paterson, *On Every Front: The Making of the Cold War* (New York: Norton, 1978); John Lewis Gaddis, *The United States and the Cold War, 1941–1947* (New York: Columbia University Press, 1972); Melvyn P. Leffler's acclaimed *For the Soul of Mankind: The United States, the Soviet Union and the Cold War* (New York: Hill and Wang, 2007) and *A Preponderance of Power: National Security, the Truman Administration and the Cold War* (Palo Alto, CA: Stanford University Press, 1993); Daniel Yergin, *Shattered Peace: The Origins of the Cold War and the National Security State* (Boston: Houghton Mifflin, 1977); and Hope M. Harrison, *After the Berlin Wall: Memory and the Making of the New Germany, 1989 to the Present* (Cambridge: Cambridge University Press, 2019).

To probe more deeply the conduct of the Cold War, examine Odd Arne Westad, *The Cold War: A World History* (New York: Basic Books, 2019); Benn Steil, *The Marshall Plan: Dawn of the Cold War* (New York: Simon and Schuster, 2019); John Lewis Gaddis, *Strategies of Containment: A Critical Appraisal of American National Security Policy During the Cold War*, rev. ed. (New York: Oxford University Press, 2005); Brian Crozier, Drew Middleton, and Jeremy Murray-Brown, *This War Called Peace* (New York: Universe Books, 1985); Melvyn P. Leffler, ed., *The Cambridge History of the Cold War* (Cambridge: Cambridge University Press, 2009); Norman M. Naimark, *Stalin and the Fate of Europe* (Cambridge, MA: Belknap Press, 2019); Henry A. Kissinger, *Diplomacy* (New York: Simon and Schuster, 1994); J. David Singer, "Peace in the Global System," in *The Long Postwar Peace*, ed. Charles W. Kegley Jr. (New York: HarperCollins, 1991): 56–84; and Michael Brecher and Jonathan Wilkenfeld, "International Crises and

Global Instability," in *The Long Postwar Peace*, ed. Charles W. Kegley Jr. (New York: HarperCollins, 1991): 85–104.

On how the Cold War ended, see Richard K. Herrmann and Richard N. Lebow, eds., *Ending the Cold War: Interpretations, Causation, and the Study of International Relations* (London: Palgrave Macmillan, 2004); Raymond L. Garthoff, *The Great Transition: American-Soviet Relations and the End of the Cold War* (Washington, DC: Brookings Institution Press, 1994); John Gerald Ruggie, *Winning the Peace* (New York: Columbia University Press, 1996); Charles W. Kegley Jr., "How Did the Cold War Die? Principles for an Autopsy," *Mershon International Studies Review* 38 (1994): 11–41; Thomas Risse-Kappan, "Did 'Peace Through Strength' End the Cold War?" *International Security* 16 (1991): 162–188; Charles W. Kegley and Gregory A. Raymond, *The Global Future* (Boston: Wadsworth, 2014), 17–20; Fred Charles Iklé, *Annihilation from Within* (New York: Columbia University Press, 2007); and Dan Reiter, *How Wars End* (Princeton, NJ: Princeton University Press, 2009).

For reflections on the Cold War's "long peace," see John Lewis Gaddis, *The Long Peace: Inquiries into the History of the Cold War* (New York: Oxford University Press, 1987); and Frank C. Zagare, "Explaining the Long Peace," *International Studies Review* 20 (2018): 422–437. Several works look at the Cold War through the lens of clashing empires. For a valuable analysis of the concept of empire, see Michael W. Doyle, *Empires* (Ithaca, NY: Cornell University Press, 1986). Applications to the Cold War include Morris J. Blachman and Donald J. Puchala, "When Empires Meet: The Long Peace in Long-Term Perspective," in *The Long Postwar Peace*, ed. Charles W. Kegley Jr. (New York: HarperCollins, 1991): 177–201; Andrew J. Bacevich, ed., *The Imperial Tense: Prospects and Problems of American Empire* (Chicago: Ivan R. Dee/Roman and Littlefield, 2003); William Appleman Williams, *Empire as A Way of Life* (New York: Oxford University Press, 1980); Lloyd C. Gardner, *Imperial America* (New York: Harcourt Brace Jovanovich, 1976); and Chalmers Johnson, *The Sorrows of Empire* (New York: Metropolitan Books/ Henry Holt, 2004).

To review interpretations of the consequences of the Cold War, see John Mueller, "What Was the Cold War About? Evidence from Its Ending," *Political Science Quarterly* 119, no. 4 (Winter 2004–2005): 609–631; Anatol Rapaport, *Peace: An Idea Whose Time Has Come* (Ann Arbor: University of Michigan Press, 1992); Richard N. Haass, *The Opportunity: America's Moment to Alter History's Course* (New York: Public Affairs Press, 2005); Francis Fukuyama, *The End of History and the Last Man* (New York: Free Press, 1992); Charles W. Kegley Jr., "The Neoidealist Moment in International Relations? Realist Myths and the New International Realities," *International Studies Quarterly* 37, no. 2 (1993): 131–146; Kenneth N. Waltz, "Structural Realism after the Cold War," *International Security* 25, no. 1 (2000): 5–41; and Robert Kagan's *Of Paradise and Power* (New York: Alfred A. Knopf, 2003). Useful discussions of whether the peaceful end of the Cold War was squandered are provided in Stephen F. Cohen's *Soviet Fates and Lost Alternatives: From Stalinism to the New Cold War* (New York: Columbia University Press, 2009); and Marshall I. Goldman's *Lost Opportunity* (New York: Norton, 1996).

Chapter 5: America's Unipolar Moment

Among the best analyses of post-Cold War unipolarity are William J. Burns, *The Back Channel* (New York: Random House, 2019); Hal Brands, *Making the Unipolar Moment:*

U.S. Foreign Policy and the Rise of the Post–Cold War Order (Ithaca, NY: Cornell University Press, 2016); Nuno P. Monteiro, *Theory of Unipolar Politics* (New York: Cambridge University Press, 2014); Birthe Hansen, *Unipolarity and World Politics: A Theory and its Implications* (New York: Routledge, 2011); and Thomas S. Mowle and David H. Sacko, *The Unipolar World: An Unbalanced Future* (New York: Palgrave Macmillan, 2007). For contrasting realist and liberal institutionalist interpretations of this period, see John J. Mearsheimer, *The Great Delusion: Liberal Dreams and International Realities* (New Haven, CT: Yale University Press, 2018); and G. John Ikenberry, *Liberal Leviathan: The Origins, Crisis, and Transformation of the American World Order* (Princeton, NJ: Princeton University Press, 2011).

Much of the literature on America's unipolar moment wrestles with the question of whether the United States was an empire. Examples of works that take the affirmative view include Jim Garrison, *America as Empire* (San Francisco: Berrett-Koehler, 2004); and Andrew J. Bacevich, *American Empire* (Cambridge, MA: Harvard University Press, 2002). Other observers are less certain. Geir Lundestad, in *The American "Empire"* (Oslo: Norwegian University Press, 1990), counters that America acted as an empire by invitation rather than coercion; Niall Ferguson, in *Colossus: The Price of America's Empire* (New York: Penguin, 2004), suggests that the United States in this period is best seen as a "liberal" empire; and William E. Odom and Robert Dujarric, in *America's Inadvertent Empire* (New Haven, CT: Yale University Press, 2004), propose that the United States was unlike an empire in the classical sense insofar as deferring to U.S. global leadership was voluntary and economically advantageous.

Scholars also disagree over how the United States fared under unipolarity and whether it will remain at the pinnacle of world power. Several analysts have charged that the United States recklessly believed that it could use its preeminent military power to bend others to its will. See Nancy Soderberg, *The Superpower Myth: The Use and Misuse of American Might* (New York: John Wiley, 2005); Robert Jay Lifton, *The Superpower Syndrome* (New York: Nation Books, 2003); and Ronald Steel, *Temptations of a Superpower* (Cambridge, MA: Harvard University Press, 1995). Stephen M. Walt's *The Hell of Good Intentions: America's Foreign Policy Elite and the Decline of U.S. Primacy* (New York: Farrar, Straus and Giroux, 2018) argues that the United States frittered away its global standing. Michael Beckley, in his *Unrivaled: Why America Will Remain the World's Sole Superpower* (Ithaca, NY: Cornell University Press, 2018), contends that America has maintained its comparative advantages over other great powers and its primacy will continue. Regardless of how the United States fared, some commentators hold that American primacy benefited the wider international community. See, for instance, Michael Mandelbaum, *The Case for Goliath: How America Acts as the World's Government in the 21st Century* (New York: PublicAffairs, 2005); and Robert J. Lieber, *The American Era* (New York: Cambridge University Press, 2005).

There is a large body of work on the Persian Gulf War. For an informative compilation of materials, see Micah L. Sifry and Christopher Cerf, *The Gulf War Reader: History, Documents, Opinions* (New York: New York Times Books, 1991). Michael R. Gordon and Bernard E. Trainor provide a clear account of the conflict in *The General's War: The Inside Story of the Conflict in the Gulf* (Boston: Little, Brown, 1995). The difficulties of using the threat of military force as an instrument for modifying the behavior of leaders like Saddam Hussein are discussed in Alexander L. George, *Forceful Persuasion: Coercive Diplomacy as an Alternative to War* (Washington, DC: United States Institute of Peace Press, 1991).

Journalist Bob Woodward traces the impact of the 9/11 terrorist attacks on decisions that led to the war in Afghanistan and second war with Iraq in *Bush at War* (New York: Simon & Schuster, 2002) and *Plan of Attack* (New York: Simon & Schuster, 2004). In *America Alone: The Neoconservatives and the Global Order* (Cambridge: Cambridge University Press, 2004), Stefan Halper and Jonathan Clarke examine the influence of neoconservative thought on the U.S. foreign policy decision-making process. Useful descriptions of the Iraq war are given in John Keegan, *The Iraq War* (New York: Vintage, 2005); Williamson Murray and Robert H. Scales Jr., *The Iraq War: A Military History* (Cambridge, MA: Belknap Press, 2003); and Thomas E. Ricks, *The Gamble: General David Petraeus and the American Military Adventure in Iraq, 2006–2008* (New York: Penguin, 2009). The ramifications of the war are analyzed in Charles W. Kegley Jr. and Gregory A. Raymond, *After Iraq: The Imperiled American Imperium* (New York: Oxford University Press, 2007).

Important insights into the debate within the Clinton administration over democratization and NATO expansion can be gleaned from James M. Goldgeier, *Not Whether but When: The U.S. Decision to Enlarge NATO* (Washington, DC: Brookings Institution Press, 1999). For background on democratic peace theory and the problems of establishing democratic rule, consult Bruce M. Russett, *Grasping the Democratic Peace: Principles for a Post-Cold War World* (Princeton, NJ: Princeton University Press, 1993); and Juan Linz and Alfred Stepan, *Problems of Democratic Transition and Consolidation: Southern Europe, South America, and Post-Communist Europe* (Baltimore: Johns Hopkins University Press, 1996). For distinctions among differing levels of democratic governance and their political impact, see Arend Lijphart, *Patterns of Democracy: Government Forms and Performance in Thirty-Six Countries* (New Haven, CT: Yale University Press, 1999).

For discussions of humanitarian intervention and the wars in the Balkans, see Samantha Power, *A Problem from Hell: America and the Age of Genocide* (New York: Basic Books, 2002); Alton Frye, *Humanitarian Intervention: Crafting a Workable Doctrine* (New York: Council on Foreign Relations, 2000); Tim Judah, *Kosovo: War and Revenge* (New Haven, CT: Yale University Press, 2000); Richard Holbrooke, *To End a War* (New York: Modern Library, 1999); and David Carmet and Patrick James, *Peace in the Midst of Wars: Preventing and Managing International Ethnic Conflicts* (Columbia: University of South Carolina Press, 1998).

To place the conduct of the wars in the Balkans, Afghanistan, and Iraq in a broader historical context, see Robert A. Pape, *Bombing to Win: Air Power and Coercion in War* (Ithaca, NY: Cornell University Press, 1996); Christopher M. Gacek, *The Logic of Force: The Dilemma of Limited War in American Foreign Policy* (New York: Columbia University Press, 1994); Bruce Berkowitz, *The New Face of War: How War Will Be Fought in the 21st Century* (New York: Free Press, 2003); and Max Boot, *The Savage Wars of Peace: Small Wars and the Rise of American Power* (New York: Basic Books, 2002).

The roots of the 2008 financial crisis are explained in Quinn Slobodian, *Globalists: The End of Empire and the Birth of Neoliberalism* (Cambridge, MA: Harvard University Press, 2018); and Adam Tooze, *Crashed: How a Decade of Financial Crises Changed the World* (New York: Viking, 2018). A good introduction to the impact of the crisis on U.S. foreign policy is Michael Mandelbaum, *The Frugal Superpower: America's Global Leadership in a Cash-Strapped Era* (New York: PublicAffairs, 2010). Several books on the foreign policy of Barack Obama touch on how overextension and resource constraints shaped his strategic calculations. For general guidance on foreign policy decision-making in the Obama administration, see Charlie Savage, *Power Wars: Inside Obama's Post-9/11*

Presidency (New York: Little, Brown, 2015); Martin S. Indyk, Kenneth G. Lieberthan, and Michael E. O'Hanlon, *Bending History: Barack Obama's Foreign Policy* (Washington, DC: Brookings Institution Press, 2012); James Mann, *The Obamians: The Struggle Inside the White House to Redefine American Power* (New York: Viking, 2012); and Bob Woodward, *Obama's Wars* (New York: Simon & Schuster, 2010).

Chapter 6: The Unraveling Liberal Order

Different strands of conservative political thought have existed in the United States since the end of the Second World War. Jeane J. Kirkpatrick summarizes some of the bedrock assumptions of conservative approaches to foreign policy in *Defining a Conservative Foreign Policy* (Washington, DC: The Heritage Foundation, 1993), and Colin Dueck provides a useful overview of the impact of conservative theorizing on the Republican Party in *Hard Line: The Republican Party and U.S. Foreign Policy since World War II* (Princeton, NJ: Princeton University Press, 2010). Recent examples of conservative internationalism include Charlie Laderman, "Conservative Internationalism: An Overview," *Orbis* 62, no. 1 (2018): 6–21; Paul D. Miller, *American Power and Liberal Order: A Conservative Internationalist Grand Strategy* (Washington, DC: Georgetown University Press, 2016); and Henry Nau, *Conservative Internationalism* (Princeton, NJ: Princeton University Press, 2013). A neoconservative variant of this approach is described in William Kristol and Robert Kagan, "Toward a Neo-Reaganite Foreign Policy," *Foreign Affairs* 75, no. 4 (1996): 18–32; for a critique, see Kim R. Holmes and John Hillen, "Misreading Reagans' Legacy: A Truly Conservative Foreign Policy," *Foreign Affairs* 75, no. 5 (1996): 162–169. For an example of conservative realism, see Winston Lord, *Kissinger on Kissinger: Reflections on Diplomacy, Grand Strategy, and Leadership* (New York: All Points Books, 2019); also see Henry Kissinger, *White House Years* (Boston: Little, Brown, 1979). Among the noteworthy examples of proponents of conservative nationalism, see Jeremy A. Rabkin, *The Case for Sovereignty: Why the World Should Welcome American Independence* (Washington, DC: AEI Press, 2004); and Julian Ku and John Yoo, *Taming Globalization: International Law, the US Constitution, and the New World Order* (New York: Oxford University Press, 2012). A libertarian variant of this outlook is presented in Ted Carpenter, *Smart Power: Toward a Prudent Foreign Policy* (Washington, DC: Cato Institute, 2008).

The controversy over whether Donald Trump's actions on the world stage represent a conservative approach to foreign policy have spawned a welter of polemics, both supportive and critical of his behavior. Valuable studies of Trump's foreign policy include Ivo H. Daalder and James M. Lindsay, *The Empty Throne: America's Abdication of Global Leadership* (New York: PublicAffairs, 2018); Robert Kagan, *The Jungle Grows Back: America and Our Imperial World* (New York: Alfred A. Knopf, 2018); Hal Brands, *American Grand Strategy in the Age of Trump* (Washington, DC: Brookings Institution Press, 2018); and Robert Jervis, Francis J. Gavin, Joshua Rovner, and Diane Labrosse, eds. *Chaos in the Liberal Order: The Trump Presidency and International Politics in the Twenty-First Century* (New York: Columbia University Press, 2018).

Sobering accounts of Trump's impact on American democracy include Steven Levitsky and Daniel Ziblatt, *How Democracies Die* (New York: Crown, 2018); and Tom Ginzburg and Aziz Z. Huq, *How to Save a Constitutional Democracy* (Chicago: University of Chicago Press, 2018). Without American leadership in defending democratic ideals, argues Larry Diamond in *Ill Winds: Saving Democracy from Russian Rage, Chinese*

Ambition, and American Complacency (New York: Penguin, 2019), the twenty-first century could become dominated by autocratic regimes. The philosophical roots of modern populism and the rise of illiberal regimes are explored in Timothy Snyder, *The Road to Unfreedom: Russia, Europe, America* (New York: Tim Duggan, 2018). An excellent portrayal of contemporary demagoguery is given in Michiko Kakutani's *The Death of Truth: Notes on Falsehood in the Age of Trump* (New York: Tim Duggan, 2018). Kathleen Hall Jamieson and Doron Taussig provide an incisive analysis of Trump's rhetorical strategy in "Disruption, Demonization, Deliverance, and Norm Destruction," *Political Science Quarterly* 132, no. 4 (2017): 619–650. For an argument that Trump's election was essential for reversing America's decline, see Victor Davis Hanson, *The Case for Trump* (New York: Basic Books, 2019).

Victor Bulmer-Thomas, *Empire in Retreat: The Past, Present, and Future of the United States* (New Haven, CT: Yale University Press, 2019); David C. Hendrickson, *Republic in Peril: American Empire and the Liberal Tradition* (New York: Oxford University Press, 2019); and Ronan Farrow, *War on Peace: The End of Diplomacy and the Decline of American Influence* (New York: Norton, 2018) examine the weakening of U.S. diplomatic institutions as more emphasis is given to the military tools of foreign policy. Michael V. Hayden assesses the Trump administration's impact on the American intelligence community in his *The Assault on Intelligence: American National Security in an Age of Lies* (New York: Penguin, 2018). For a sharp critique of the U.S. foreign policy community in the immediate post-Cold War period, see Stephen M. Walt, *The Hell of Good Intentions: America's Foreign Policy Elite and the Decline of U.S. Primacy* (New York: Farrar, Straus and Giroux, 2018).

There is no shortage of opinions regarding the consequences of the Trump administration's foreign policy. For a sample of appraisals, see Randall Schweller, "Three Cheers for Trump's Foreign Policy," *Foreign Affairs* 97, no. 5 (2018): 133–143; Kori Schake, "Back to Basics: How to Make Right What Trump Gets Wrong," *Foreign Affairs* 98, no. 3 (2019): 36–43; Gideon Rose, "The Fourth Founding: The United States and the Liberal Order," *Foreign Affairs* 98, no. 1 (2019): 10–21; Richard Haass, "How World Order Ends," *Foreign Affairs* 98, no. 1 (2019): 22–30; Dov S. Zakheim, "Trump's Perilous Path," *National Interest*, no. 155 (2018): 13–21; Rebecca Friedman Lissner and Mira Rapp-Hooper, "The Day after Trump: American Strategy for a New International Order," *Washington Quarterly* 41, no. 1 (2018): 7–25; and Jake Sullivan, "The World After Trump: How the System Can Endure," *Foreign Affairs* 97, no. 2 (2018): 10–19.

Chapter 7: The Range of Great-Power Choice

For insights into the costs and benefits of unilateralist strategies, consult Joseph S. Nye Jr., *The Paradox of American Power: Why the World's Only Superpower Can't Go It Alone* (Oxford: Oxford University Press, 2002); Lester C. Thurow, *Head to Head* (New York: William Morrow, 1992); Charles A. Kupchan, *The End of the American Era* (New York: Knopf, 2002); Thomas P. M. Barnett, *The Pentagon's New Map: War and Peace in the Twenty-First Century* (New York: G. P. Putnam's Sons, 2004); Robert J. Art, *A Grand Strategy for America* (Ithaca, NY: Cornell University Press, 2003); Frederick Cooper, *Empires in World History: Power and the Politics of Difference* (Princeton, NJ: Princeton University Press, 2010). To dig deeper into the dynamics of bilateralism, consult William H. Hill, *No Place for Russia: European Security Institutions Since 1989*

(New York: Columbia University Press, 2018); and Alexander Thompson and Daniel Verdier, "Multilateralism, Bilateralism, and Regime Design," *International Studies Quarterly* 58, no. 1 (2014): 15–28. On the limits and potential of multilateral strategies, explore Jeffrey D. Sachs, *A New Foreign Policy: Beyond American Exceptionalism* (New York: Columbia University Press, 2018); Michael J. Mozart, "The Once and Future Order: What Comes After Hegemony?" *Foreign Affairs* 96, no. 1 (2017): 25–32; Thomas G. Weiss and Ramesh Thakur, *Global Governance and the UN: An Unfinished Journey* (Bloomington: Indiana University Press, 2010); G. John Ikenberry, *After Victory: Institutions, Strategic Restraint and the Building of Order After Major Wars* (Princeton, NJ: Princeton University Press, 2001); and John Gerald Ruggie, *Winning the Peace: America and World Order in the New Era* (New York: Columbia University Press, 1996).

The influence of Wilsonian liberal idealism on modern American conceptions of world order is covered in Robert S. McNamara and James G. Blight, *Wilson's Ghost* (New York: Public Affairs Press, 2001); and David Steigerwald, *Wilsonian Idealism in America* (Ithaca, NY: Cornell University Press, 1994). To picture the dangers posed by the rise of autocratic states to the preservation of the liberal international order, see Wendy Brown, *In the Ruins of Neoliberalism: The Rise of Antidemocratic Politics in the West* (New York: Columbia University Press, 2019). For an account of the reasons why realist theories of balancing are under assault, see Steven E. Lowell, "A Granular Theory of Balancing," *International Studies Quarterly* 62, no. 3 (2018): 593–605. For different interpretations of whether the United States ought to continue its globalist foreign policy, see Stephen G. Brooks and William C. Wohlforth, *America Abroad: The United States' Global Role in the 21st Century* (New York: Oxford University Press, 2016); Barry R. Posen, *Restraint: A New Foundation for U.S. Grand Strategy* (Ithaca, NY: Cornell University Press, 2015); Andrew Bacevich, *The New American Militarism: How Americans Are Seduced by War* (New York: Oxford University Press, 2013); and Eric A. Nordlinger, *Isolationism Reconfigured: American Foreign Policy for a New Century* (Princeton, NJ: Princeton University Press, 1995).

A growing number of books delve into the impact of the rise of Chinese power on world order. Among the most useful are Peter Frankopan, *The New Silk Roads* (New York: Knopf, 2019); David Shambaugh, *China's Future* (Cambridge: Polity Press, 2016); William J. Norris, *Chinese Economic Statecraft: Commercial Actors, Grand Strategy, and State Control* (Ithaca, NY: Cornell University Press, 2016); Thomas J. Christensen, *The China Challenge: Shaping the Choices of a Rising Power* (New York: Norton, 2015); Aron L. Friedberg, *A Contest for Supremacy: China, America, and the Struggle for Mastery in Asia* (New York: Norton, 2011); Rosemary Foot and Andrew Walter, *China, the United States, and Global Order* (Cambridge: Cambridge University Press, 2010); Yong Deng, *China's Struggle for Status: The Realignment of International Relations* (Cambridge: Cambridge University Press, 2008); and Robert S. Ross and Zhu Feng, *China's Ascent: Power, Security, and the Future of International Politics* (Ithaca, NY: Cornell University Press, 2008). David C. Kang, *American Grand Strategy and East Asian Security in the Twenty-First Century* (New York: Cambridge University Press, 2017), examines how East Asian states see the rise of China and American efforts to create a counterbalancing coalition. For other interpretations of China's rise and its prospects for achieving hegemony, see Bentley B. Allan, Srdjan Vucetic, and Ted Hopf, "The Distribution of Identity and the Future of International Order: China's Hegemonic Prospects," *International Organization* 72, no. 4 (2018): 839–869; Stephan G. Brooks and William C. Wohlforth, "The Rise and

Fall of Great Powers in the 21st Century," *International Security* 40, no. 3 (2016): 7–53; and Fareed Zakaria, "The New China Scare," *Foreign Affairs* 99, no. 1 (2020): 52–69.

A useful comparison of Chinese and Russian foreign policies is given in Deborah Welch Larson and Alexei Shevchenko, *The Quest for Status: Chinese and Russian Foreign Policy* (New Haven, CT: Yale University Press, 2019). The trajectory of Russian foreign policy under Vladimir Putin is examined in George S. Beebe, *The Russia Trap* (New York: Thomas Dunne Books, 2019); Angela E. Stent, *Putin's World: Russia Against the West and with the Rest* (New York: Twelve, 2019); Roger E. Kanet, ed., *Routledge Handbook of Russian Security* (New York: Routledge, 2019); Stephen F. Cohen, *War with Russia?: From Putin & Ukraine to Trump & Russiagate* (New York: Hot Books, 2019); Lilia A. Arakelyan, *Russian Foreign Policy: National Interest and Regional Integration* (New York: Routledge, 2018); Dimitri Trenin, *Should We Fear Russia?* (Malden, MA: Polity, 2016); and Jeffrey Mankoff, *Russian Foreign Policy: The Return of Great Power Politics*, 2nd ed. (Lanham, MD: Rowman & Littlefield, 2012).

For assessments of Russo-Chinese relations, see Dmitri Trenin, *From Great Europe to Greater Asia? The Sino-Russian Entente* (Moscow: Carnegie Endowment for International Peace, 2015); and Bobo Lo, *Axis of Convenience: Moscow, Beijing, and the New Geopolitics* (Washington, DC: Brookings Institution Press, 2008). To evaluate the challenge tripolarity poses to world order, see Randell L. Schweller, *Deadly Imbalances: Tripolarity and Hitler's Strategy of World Conquest* (New York: Columbia University Press, 1998); and Joshua S. Goldstein and John A. Freeman, *Three-Way Street: Strategic Reciprocity in World Politics* (Chicago: University of Chicago Press, 1990). Relations with other rising powers are discussed in Will Doig, *High-Speed Empire: Chinese Expansion and the Future of Southeast Asia* (New York: Columbia University Global Reports, 2018); Cameron G. Thies and Mark David Nieman, *Rising Powers and Foreign Policy Revisionism: Understanding BRICS Identity and Behavior through Time* (Ann Arbor: University of Michigan Press, 2017); and Elbridge A. Colby and A. Wess Mitchell, "The Age of Great-Power Competition," *Foreign Affairs* 99, no. 1 (2020): 118–130.

To grasp the continuing threat of nuclear weapons and the need for multilateral crisis management, see Stephen J. Cimbala, *Getting Nuclear Weapons Right: Managing Danger and Avoiding Disaster* (Boulder, CO: Lynne Rienner, 2018).

Chapter 8: Rethinking World Order

The number of new books and scholarly articles addressing the drama of great-power competition seems to grow daily. Valuable works on the future of world order include Michael Mandelbaum, *The Rise and Fall of Peace on Earth* (New York: Oxford University Press, 2019); Victor Bulmer-Thomas, *Empire in Retreat: The Past, Present, and Future of the United States* (New Haven, CT: Yale University Press, 2019); David C. Hendrickson, *Republic in Peril: American Empire and the Liberal Tradition* (New York: Oxford University Press, 2019); J. C. Sharman, *Empires of the Weak: The Real Story of European Expansion and the Creation of the New World Order* (Princeton, NJ: Princeton University Press, 2019); Bruno Macaes, *Belt and Road: A Chinese World Order* (London: Hurst, 2019); Parag Khanna, *The Future Is Asian* (New York: Simon & Schuster, 2019); Andrew J. Bacevich, *Twilight of the American Century* (South Bend, IN: Notre Dame University Press, 2018); Anand Giridharadas, *Winners Take All: The Elite Charade of Changing the World* (New York: Knopf Doubleday Academic, 2018); Christopher Coker, *Improbable War: China, the United States and the Logic of Great Power Conflict* (Oxford: Oxford University Press,

2015); and Niall Ferguson, *The War of the World: Twentieth-Century Conflict and the Decline of the West* (New York: Penguin Press, 2006). For an insightful analysis of how declining great powers recover their former position, see Paul K. McDonald and Joseph M. Parent, *Twilight of the Titans: Great Power Decline and Retrenchment* (Ithaca, NY: Cornell University Press, 2018). The importance of leadership in the rise and fall of great powers is examined in Yan Xuetong, *Leadership and the Rise of Great Powers* (Princeton, NJ: Princeton University Press, 2019).

For discussions of networks and their application to world politics, see Anne-Marie Slaughter, *The Chessboard and the Web: Strategies of Connection in a Networked World* (New Haven, CT: Yale University Press, 2017); Joshua Cooper Ramo, *The Seventh Sense: Power, Fortune, and Survival in the Age of Networks* (New York: Little, Brown, 2016); Zeev Maoz, *Networks of Nations: The Evolution, Structure, and Impact of International Networks, 1816–2001* (Cambridge: Cambridge University Press, 2011); Manuel Castells, *The Rise of the Network Society*, 2nd ed. (Oxford: Blackwell, 2010); and Miles Kahler, ed., *Networked Politics: Agency, Power, and Governance* (Ithaca, NY: Cornell University Press, 2009).

On the threat of cyberwarfare and artificial intelligence to world order, see Christian Brose, "The New Revolution in Military Affairs," *Foreign Affairs* 98, no. 3 (2019): 122–134; Kai-Fu Lee, *AI Superpowers: China, Silicon Valley and the New World Order* (New York: Houghton Mifflin Harcourt, 2019); Lucas Kello, *The Virtual Weapon and International Order* (New Haven, CT: Yale University Press, 2018); David E. Sanger, *The Perfect Weapon: War, Sabotage and Fear in the Cyber Age* (New York: Crown, 2018); Dina Temple-Raston, "Hacked to Bits," *New York Review of Books* 65, no. 15 (2018): 26–28; Joseph S. Nye Jr., "Deterrence and Dissuasion in Cyberspace," *International Security* 41, no. 3 (2017): 44–71; Adam Segal, *The Hacked World Order*, 2nd ed. (New York: PublicAffairs, 2017); and P. W. Singer and Allan Friedman, *Cybersecurity and Cyberwar* (New York: Oxford University Press, 2014). On the prospects for a new arms race and the next generation of warfare, see Lawrence Freeman, *The Future of War: A History* (New York: PublicAffairs, 2018); and Robert H. Latiff, *Future War: Preparing for the New Global Battlefield* (New York: Knopf Doubleday Academic, 2018). For a discussion of the issues surrounding moral decision-making by robots, see Wendell Wallach and Colin Allen, *Moral Machines: Teaching Robots Right from Wrong* (New York: Oxford University Press, 2010).

For interpretations of great-power tactics to manufacture fake news and construct false views of reality for propaganda purposes, through manipulation of public attitudes from such cybermedia as YouTube, social media platforms, Instagram trailers, Twitter, branded merchandise, reality television memes, computer games, search spikes, and other tools to shape perceived definitions of reality and influence both domestic opinion and a wider international audience, see An Xiao Mina, *Memes to Movements* (Boston: Beacon Press, 2019). To evaluate the future prospects for the survival of democracies in an age of illiberalism, see James Miller, *Can Democracy Work? A Short History of a Radical Idea, from Ancient Athens to Our World* (New York: Farrar, Straus and Giroux, 2019); and Dan Edelstein, *On the Spirit of Rights* (Chicago: University of Chicago Press, 2019).

To monitor the national and international threats posed by climate change and global warming to world order, we recommend consulting the annual IPCC *Assessment Report of the International Panel on Climate Change* (Cambridge: Cambridge University Press), the United Nations Environment Programme (UNEP), and the forecasts of the International Energy Agency. An alarming overview of the threats to world order caused by climate change and environmental deterioration is provided by Thomas L. Friedman, *Hot, Flat and Crowded* (New York: Farrar, Straus and Giroux, 2008). For insight and evidence regarding the impact of global warming on insufficient food supplies, see Lester B. Brown, *Full Planet, Empty Plates: The New Geopolitics of Food Scarcity* (New York: Norton, 2012). On the prospects for international institutions to introduce greater regulation of the practices contributing to climate change, inspect Bentley B. Allan, "Second Only to Nuclear War: Science and the Making of Existential Threat in Global Climate Governance," *International Studies Quarterly* 61, no. 4 (2017): 809–820. For assessments of the threats posed to world order and human survival, see David Wallace-Wells, *The Uninhabitable Earth: Life after Warming* (New York: Tim Duggan, 2019); Bill McKibben, *Falter: Has the Human Game Begun to Play Itself Out?* (New York: Henry Holt, 2019); and Nathaniel Rich, *Losing Earth: A Recent History* (New York: MCD/Farrar, Straus and Giroux, 2019).

Glossary

A

absolute gains: Conditions in which all participants in exchanges benefit

anarchy: The absence of a higher authority with the legitimacy and coercive capacity to make and enforce rules that place restrictions on states' international behavior

appeasement: A policy that seeks to deter a potential aggressor by making significant concessions to its demands

arbitration: A conflict-resolution procedure in which an impartial third party selected by the contending parties is authorized to make a binding decision on the issues over which the disputants are disagreeing

arms control: An effort to control arms buildups by setting limits on the number and types of weapons that states are permitted to develop or deploy

arms race: An action-reaction process in which rival states rapidly increase their military capabilities in response to one another

asymmetric war: Armed conflicts between belligerents of vastly unequal military strength in which the weaker side is often a nonstate actor that relies on unconventional tactics

autarchy: A closed, self-sufficient economic system that abstains from international trade

B

balance-of-power theory: The theory that national survival in an anarchic world is most likely when military power is distributed in such a way as to prevent a single hegemon from dominating the international system

balance-of-trade surplus: A calculation based on the value of goods and services imported and exported, wherein a surplus occurs when a country sells more abroad than it buys from foreign producers

balancer: An influential state that throws its support in decisive fashion to the weaker side of the balance of power

bandwagoning: The tendency of weaker states to align with the strongest power

beggar-thy-neighbor policies: The attempt to promote trade surpluses through policies that cause other states to suffer trade deficits

bilateral: An activity or agreement that involves two states

bipolar: An international system containing two dominant power centers

botnets: Networks of computers that have been compromised by an outside party for the purpose of conducting malicious activity on the Internet

C

coercive diplomacy: The use of threats or limited, exemplary shows of force to persuade an adversary to stop or undo an aggressive action

collective security: A security regime based on the principle that an act of aggression by any state will be met by a collective response from the rest

communitarianism: An ethical theory that places the ultimate source of moral value in political communities

compellence: A threat of force aimed at making an adversary grant some concession against its will

condominiums: The implementation by great powers of joint control over a territory

containment: A strategy aimed at preventing an adversary from threatening to use force against neighboring states to increase its territory or sphere of influence

convergence theory: The proposition that the Cold War rivalry between the Soviet Union and the United States had the unintended consequence of both countries becoming increasingly like each other in governance and economic systems

cosmopolitanism: An ethical theory that places the ultimate source of human value in individuals, thereby viewing all members of humanity as equals and rejecting parochial attachments and prejudices

counterforce targeting: Aiming nuclear weapons at the military capabilities of an opponent

countervalue targeting: Aiming nuclear weapons against an opponent's most valued nonmilitary resources, such as the people and businesses located in urban areas (sometimes known as countercity targeting)

coup d'état: A sudden, illegal, and forcible seizure of government power by an opposition group

D

demilitarizing: The removal of armed forces from a geographic area

democratic peace theory: The contention that democratically governed states are prone to settle conflicts among themselves through peaceful means rather than resorting to war

détente: The relaxation of tensions between adversaries

diffuse reciprocity: Situations where equivalent benefits are not presumed by each party in any single exchange but are expected to balance out over the course of a series of ongoing exchanges

domino theory: A metaphor popular during the Cold War, which predicted that if one state fell to communism, adjacent states would also fall in a chain reaction

E

economic sanctions: Governmental actions designed to change an adversary's policies by inflicting deprivation on that state through the limitation or termination of economic exchanges

ententes: Informal agreements between states based on a shared understanding that they have complementary strategic interests and national security goals

F

failing states: Corrupt, mismanaged governments that are incapable of controlling their country's territory and are unable to meet their citizens' basic human needs

fixed exchange rates: A system under which states establish the parity of their currencies and commit to keeping fluctuations in their exchange rates within narrow limits

free-riding: The behavior of states that benefit from the gains of international cooperation but do not pay their fair share for the resources or services that they receive

G

genocide: The deliberate attempt to exterminate an ethnic or religious group

globalization: The growth of trade, telecommunications, and other integrative processes that are widening, deepening, and accelerating the interconnectedness among societies throughout the world and thereby reducing the capacity of national governments to exert control over conditions within their countries

grand strategy: A master plan that identifies the goals that must be achieved to produce security, describes the actions required for attaining these goals, and specifies how resources will be employed to support those actions

Group of Twenty (G20): An informal forum that promotes discussions among the world's major economic powers

H

hegemonic stability theory: A school of thought postulating that peace and economic stability depend on the existence of an overwhelmingly powerful state willing and able to use its strength to regulate international relations

hegemony: The achievement by a great power of unrivaled leadership over, and substantial control over, all people and states within a specified territory

hierarchy: A distribution of power arranged into rankings, with each rank or class of actors subordinate to those above it

human rights: The social and political entitlements recognized by international law as inalienable and valid for all individuals by virtue of their humanity

humanitarian intervention: The use of force by foreign states or international organizations to protect endangered people from gross violations of their human rights

hypersonic weapons: Weapons capable of reaching speeds of Mach 5 or greater, which is equivalent to at least five times the speed of sound

I

imperial overstretch: The propensity for hegemons to lose strength when they incur excessive expenses for retaining their position of superiority, draining the resources that made them powerful enough to play an imperial role on the world stage in the first place

intergovernmental organizations: Organizations composed of states that work on issues of common interest

irredentism: The desire by one state to reclaim territory that it historically controlled but lost to another state in the aftermath of a war

isolationist policy: A policy of abstaining from military alliances, avoiding foreign economic involvements, and withdrawing from other international activities that can pull a country into conflicts that it seeks to avoid

K

kinetic military action: The use of lethal military force, usually used to draw a contrast with offensive operations conducted in cyberspace

L

levels of analysis: Alternative perspectives on world politics that may focus on the personal characteristics of decision makers, the attributes of states' societies and governing institutions, or the structure of the international system as factors influencing choices about war and peace

limited war: A war in which the territory involved, weapons employed, or objectives pursued are restrained

linkage: The strategy that U.S. cooperation with the Soviet Union in one policy area would be contingent on acceptable Soviet conduct in other areas

long peace: A prolonged period of great-power relations during which no great power went to war with another great power

M

mirror images: The propensity for each party in a conflict to see the adversary as the adversary sees it

mixed-motive game: A strategic situation where interacting parties have both complementary and competitive interests and in which the sum of the payoffs varies according to the choices they make

multilateral: An activity or agreement that involves more than two states

multiple independently targetable reentry vehicles (MIRVs): A technological innovation permitting many nuclear warheads to be delivered from a single missile

multipolar: An international system containing three or more dominant power centers

mutual assured destruction (MAD): A strategy of nuclear deterrence accepted by the United States and the Soviet Union during the Cold War in which both countries possessed the ability to survive a first strike and launch a devastating retaliatory attack so that neither side would survive a nuclear exchange

N

nationalism: The belief that political loyalty lies within a body of people who share ethnicity, linguistic, or cultural affinity and perceive themselves to be members of the same group

nation-states: Organized political entities that have a government, a well-defined territory, and permanent population whose people identifies with that polity

neomercantilism: A recent revival of an eighteenth-century school of thought claiming that states can increase their economic growth by restricting imports, subsidizing strategic industries, and expanding exports

neutralization: A guarantee by the great powers to uphold the independence and territorial integrity of a particular state on the condition that it remains impartial in disputes among the contending great powers

nongovernmental organizations: Nonprofit, voluntary groups of private citizens that work together to advance common interests on environmental, health, humanitarian, or other issues

nonpolarity: An international system that contains no dominant power centers

nontariff barriers: Government restrictions on imports from abroad not involving a tax or duty that increase the cost of importing goods into a country

P

polarity: The degree to which military and economic capabilities are concentrated among the major powers in the international system

polarization: The degree to which states cluster in alliances around the most powerful members of the international system

positive-sum game: A win-win situation where the sum of payoffs to each party to an exchange is positive

power: The ability to make an actor do something it would not otherwise do or to prevent that actor from undertaking an unacceptable action that it otherwise prefers

power transition theory: The contention that war is most likely when a dominant great power is threatened by a dissatisfied challenger's rapid growth in capabilities, which reduces the previous disparity in their relative power and is perceived to diminish the dominant power's security

preemption: Under international law, a military first strike that seeks to thwart immediately a forthcoming attack (sometimes used in nuclear strategy to refer to a military first strike that attempts to eliminate the capacity of the target to retaliate)

preventive war: Military action undertaken to preclude an adversary from acquiring the capability to attack sometime in the future

protectionism: An economic policy of creating barriers to foreign trade, such as tariffs and quotas, that protect local industries from competition

public goods: Benefits that everyone shares regardless of their individual contributions and from which no one can be excluded selectively

purchasing power parity (PPP): A model for calculating the relative purchasing power of different countries' currencies for an equal basket of commodities

R

rapprochement: An agreement by former enemies to reestablish normal relations based on the expectation that regular, orderly diplomatic exchanges will reduce the likelihood that they will experience threatening confrontations in the future

realpolitik: A doctrine prescribing that countries do whatever is expedient to advance their self-interests defined in terms of maximizing national power

regime: A set of principles, norms, and decision-making procedures governing international behavior within a specified issue area

regional trade agreements (RTAs): Agreements that reduce trade barriers among the countries of a particular geographic region

relative gains: A measure of how much one side in an agreement or exchange benefits in comparison with the other side

reparations: Compensation paid by a defeated state for damages or expenditures sustained by the victor during war-time hostilities

rollback: The U.S. strategy of liberating countries that were under the control of the Soviet Union after World War II

S

scenario: A narrative description that shows how some hypothetical future state of affairs might evolve out of the present one

second-strike capability: The ability to retaliate with nuclear weapons after absorbing a nuclear first-strike attack

security dilemma: The propensity of armaments undertaken by one state for ostensibly defensive purposes to threaten other states, which arm in reaction, with the result that the security of all states declines as their arms increase

security regime: Rules and norms to which great powers agree to abide by for the peaceful management of threats to global security

self-determination: The right of nationalities to create an independent sovereign state and choose the governmental authority that will rule them

self-fulfilling prophecies: The tendency for one's expectations to evoke behavior that helps make the expectations become true

self-help: The principle that in an anarchy states must rely on themselves to protect their security

soft balancing: Restraining the behavior of a more powerful state through such actions as denying it aerial and maritime transit privileges and obstructing its policies in international organizations rather than resorting to arms buildups and formal military alliances to counterbalance its power

soft power: The ability of a state to exercise influence in world politics through the attractiveness of its culture, political ideals, leadership, and policies

sovereignty: Under international law, the principle that no higher authority is above the state

spheres of influence: Geographic regions dominated by a great power

summit conference: Personal diplomatic negotiations between national leaders

T

tariff: A tax imposed by governments on imported goods

terrorism: The premeditated use or threat of violence perpetrated against noncombatants, usually intended to induce fear in a wider audience

triad: The combination of intercontinental ballistic missiles (ICBMs), submarine-launched ballistic missiles (SLBMs), and long-range bombers in a second-strike nuclear force

tripolarity: An international system that contains three dominant power centers

U

ultimatum: A demand containing a time limit for acquiescence and a threat of punishment for noncompliance

unipolar: An international system that contains one dominant power center

Z

zero-sum game: An exchange between interacting parties in which what one side wins, the other side loses

Notes

Chapter 1

1. See *National Security Strategy of the United States of America* (Washington, DC: Government Printing Office, 2017), 25.
2. Robert B. Strassler, ed., *The Landmark Thucydides: A Comprehensive Guide to the Peloponnesian War* (New York: Free Press, 1996), 352.
3. Concentrating on the so-called high politics of the most powerful states does not provide a complete picture of how the world works, but it provides important insights into how the rules of permissible aims and methods for conducting international relations are established, maintained, and revised. For a discussion of the differences between the behavior of great and non–great powers in the realm of high politics, see William B. Moul, "Balances without Great Powers: Some Evidence on War and Peace in the Americas, 1816–1989," *International Interactions* 39, no. 1 (2013): 30–53; and Daina Chiba, Carla Martinez Machain, and William Reed, "Major Powers and Militarized Conflict," *Journal of Conflict Resolution* 58, no. 6 (2014): 976–1002.
4. The relationship between international standing and the distribution of resources is suggested by Richard Rosecrance, *International Relations: Peace or War?* (New York: McGraw-Hill, 1973), 108–109.
5. David A. Baldwin, *Paradoxes of Power* (New York: Basil Blackwell, 1989), 26. On the problems of measuring power, see Michael Beckley, "The Power of Nations: Measuring What Matters," *International Security* 43, no. 2 (2018): 7–44.
6. Joseph S. Nye Jr., *Soft Power* (New York: Public Affairs Press, 2004).
7. For empirical evidence, see Renato Corbetta and William J. Dixon, "Multilateralism, Major Powers, and Militarized Disputes," *Political Research Quarterly* 49, no. 4 (2004): 5–14; Paul K. Huth, "Major Power Intervention in International Crises, 1918–1988," *Journal of Conflict Resolution* 42, no. 6 (1998): 744–770; Randolph M. Siverson and Harvey Starr, "Opportunity, Willingness, and the Diffusion of War," *American Political Science* Review 84, no. 1 (1990): 47–67; Yoshinobu Yamamoto and Stuart A. Bremer, "Wider Wars and Restless Nights: Major Power Intervention in Ongoing Wars," in *The Correlates of War II: Testing Some Realpolitik Models*, ed. J. David Singer (New York: Free Press, 1980), 199–229.
8. K. J. Holsti, *International Politics*, 4th ed. (Englewood Cliffs, NJ: Prentice-Hall, 1983), 114–159. In asymmetric wars between 1800 and 2003—armed conflicts where the disparity in power between the belligerent parties was 10:1—the weaker side prevailed 28.5 percent of the time. Ivan Arreguín-Toft, *How the Weak Win Wars: A Theory of Asymmetric Conflict* (Cambridge: Cambridge University Press, 2005), 3.
9. See Jeremy Black, *The Rise of the European Powers, 1679–1793* (London: Edward Arnold, 1990), 1–2, 198–199. The roster presented here is based on Jack S. Levy, *War in the Modern Great Power System, 1495–1975* (Lexington: University Press of Kentucky, 1983); and the "State System Membership List, v2016," Correlates of War Project, accessed September 18, 2019, http://www.correlatesofwar.org/data-sets/state-system-membership.

10. Thomas S. Mowle and David H. Sacko, *The Unipolar World: An Unbalanced Future* (New York: Palgrave Macmillan, 2007): 8.

11. Paul Kennedy, *The Rise and Fall of the Great Powers* (New York: Random House, 1987): xvi.

12. Dwight D. Eisenhower, quoted in Carl Sagan, *Billions and Billions: Thoughts on Life and Death at the Brink of the Millennium* (New York: Random House, 1997): 238. Also see Daniel W. Drezner, "Military Primacy Doesn't Pay (Nearly as Much as You Think)," *International Security* 38, no. 1 (2013): 52–79.

13. The depiction of the relationship between the declining defender and rising challenger is based on Ronald L. Tammer et al., *Power Transitions: Strategies for the 21st Century* (New York: Chatham House, 2000): 21–22.

14. A. F. K. Organski, *World Politics*, 2nd ed. (New York: Knopf, 1968). Also see Sam R. Bell and Jesse C. Johnson, "Shifting Power, Commitment Problems, and Preventive War," *International Studies Quarterly* 59, no. 1 (2015): 124–132; Alexandre Debs and Nuno P. Monteiro, "Known Unknowns: Power Shifts, Uncertainty, and War," *International Organization* 68, no. 1 (2014): 1–31; Robert Gilpin, *War and Change in World Politics* (Cambridge: Cambridge University Press, 1981): 93; and Susan G. Sample, "Power, Wealth, and Satisfaction: When Do Power Transitions Lead to Conflict?" *Journal of Conflict Resolution* 62, no. 9 (2018): 1905–1931. On the impact of abrupt shifts in the distribution of power among leading states on domestic politics, see Seva Gunitsky, "From Shocks to Waves: Hegemonic Transitions and Democratization in the Twentieth Century," *International Organization* 68, no. 3 (2014): 561–597.

15. See Charles F. Doran, "Confronting the Principles of the Power Cycle: Changing Systems Structure, Expectations, and War," in *Handbook of War Studies II*, ed. Manus I. Midlarsky (Ann Arbor: University of Michigan Press, 2000): 332–368; Woosang Kim, "Power Transitions and Great Power War from Westphalia to Waterloo," *World Politics* 45, no. 1 (1992): 157; and Brock F. Tessman and Steve Chan, "Power Cycles, Risk Propensity and Great Power Deterrence," *Journal of Conflict Resolution* 48, no. 2 (2004): 131.

16. For a summary of these research findings, see Daniel S. Geller and J. David Singer, *Nations at War: A Scientific Study of International Conflict* (New York: Cambridge University Press, 1998): 139, 194.

17. Hedley Bull, *The Anarchical Society: A Study of Order in World Politics*, 2nd ed. (New York: Columbia University Press, 1977): 5, 13.

18. Henry Kissinger, *World Order* (New York: Penguin, 2014): 9.

19. Gregory A. Raymond, "Democracies, Disputes, and Third-Party Intermediaries," *Journal of Conflict Resolution* 38, no. 1 (1994): 24–42.

20. John J. Mearsheimer, *The Tragedy of Great Power Politics* (New York: Norton, 2001), 32–36.

21. Jean-Jacques Rousseau, "The State of War," in *World Politics*, 2nd ed., ed. Arend Lijphard (Boston: Allyn and Bacon, 1971): 56.

22. See Charles L. Glasser, "The Security Dilemma Revisited," *World Politics* 50, no. 1 (1997): 171–201; John H. Herz, "Idealist Internationalism and the Security Dilemma," *World Politics* 2, no. 2 (1950): 157–180; Robert Jervis, "Cooperation Under the Security Dilemma," *World Politics* 30, no. 2 (1978): 167–214; and Jack Snyder, "The Security Dilemma in Alliance Politics," *World Politics* 36, no. 4 (1984): 461–495.

23. Russell J. Leng, *Interstate Crisis Behavior, 1816–1980: Realism versus Reciprocity* (Cambridge: Cambridge University Press, 1993): 194.

24. Reinhold Niebuhr, *The Structure of Nations and Empires: A Study of the Recurring Patterns and Problems of the Political Order in Relation to the Unique Problems of the Nuclear Age* (New York: Charles Scribner's Sons, 1959): 7.

Chapter 2

1. I. S. Bloch, *The Future of War in its Technical, Economic and Political Relations*, trans. R. C. Long (Boston: Ginn, 1902).

2. Norman Angell, *The Great Illusion: A Study of the Relationship of Military Power in Nations to their Economic and Social Advantage* (London: William Heineman, 1910).

3. Andrew Carnegie, quoted in Arthur Eyffinger, *The Peace Palace* (The Hague: Carnegie Foundation, 1988): 110.

4. See John G. Stoessinger, *Why Nations Go to War*, 8th ed. (Boston: Bedford/St. Martin's, 2001): 20; Barbara W. Tuchman, *The Guns of August* (New York: Dell/Macmillan, 1962): 93; and Samuel R. Williamson Jr., "The Origins of World War I," in *The Origin and Prevention of Major Wars*, eds. Robert I. Rotberg and Theodore K. Rabb (New York: Cambridge University Press, 1988): 230.

5. John H. Maurer, "Arms Control and the Anglo-German Naval Race before World War I: Lessons for Today?" *Political Science Quarterly* 112, no. 2 (1997): 290.

6. Ray Stannard Baker and William E. Dodd, eds., *The Public Papers of Woodrow Wilson*, vol. 1. (New York: Harper & Bros., 1927): 342.

7. Woodrow Wilson, quoted in Herbert Hoover, *The Ordeal of Woodrow Wilson* (New York: Mc-Graw-Hill, 1958): 27. Some theorists contend that keeping the peace is not the primary aim of a balance of power; its purpose is preserving the system of independent states by thwarting aspiring hegemons. According to this line of reasoning, war can be used as an instrument for achieving that goal.

8. Georges Clemenceau, quoted in Frederic C. Lane, Eric F. Goldman, and Erling M. Hunt, *The World's History*, 3rd ed. (New York: Harcourt, Brace, 1959): 571.

9. Georges Clemenceau, quoted in David Milne, *Worldmaking: The Art and Science of American Diplomacy* (New York: Farrar, Straus and Giroux, 2015): 115.

10. Gordon A. Craig and Alexander L. George, *Force and Statecraft: Diplomatic Problems of Our Time*, 3rd ed. (New York: Oxford University Press, 1995): 45.

11. *The Public Papers of the Presidents of the United States: Herbert Hoover, 1929* (Washington, DC: Government Printing Office, 1974): 372.

12. Emer de Vattel, *The Law of Nations* (Indianapolis: Liberty Fund, 2008): 496.

13. Robert Lansing, *The Peace Negotiations: A Personal Narrative* (Boston: Houghton Mifflin, 1921): 272.

Chapter 3

1. Neville Chamberlain, quoted in Donald Kagan, *On the Origins of War* (New York: Doubleday, 1995): 402.

2. Neville Chamberlain, quoted in Martin Gilbert, *The Roots of Appeasement* (New York: Plume, 1966): 170.

3. Winston S. Churchill, *The Gathering Storm*, vol. 1 of *The Second World War* (Boston: Houghton Mifflin, 1948): iv.

4. Adolf Hitler, quoted in Gordon A. Craig and Alexander L. George, *Force and Statecraft: Diplomatic Problems of Our Time*, 2nd ed. (New York: Oxford University Press, 1990): 99.

5. Samuel I. Rosenman, ed., *Public Papers and Addresses of Franklin D. Roosevelt* (New York: Harper Brothers, 1943): 558.

6. James F. Byrnes, quoted in Daniel Yergin, *Shattered Peace* (Boston: Houghton Mifflin, 1977): 67.

7. Joseph Stalin, quoted in Milovan Djilas, *Conversations with Stalin*, trans. Michael B. Petrovich (New York: Harcourt, Brace & World, 1962): 66, 73.

8. Winston S. Churchill, *The Grand Alliance*, vol. 3 of *The Second World War* (Boston: Houghton Mifflin, 1950), 370. Occasionally Churchill expressed a more positive assessment of Stalin. For instance, after a long drinking session with Stalin during his August 1942 visit to Moscow, Churchill commented that it was a "pleasure" to work with such a "great man." For a description of their meeting, see http://www.bbc.com/news/uk-22623251.

9. Winston S. Churchill, quoted in Adam B. Ulam, *The Rivals: America and Russia since World War II* (New York: Penguin, 1971): 55.

10. Some scholars argue that a brief period of unipolarity existed at the end of the war. Whereas the Soviet Union suffered devastating human and material losses during the war, American territory was relatively unscathed. Economically, the United States accounted for roughly half of international production. Militarily, it held a monopoly on nuclear weapons, had unrivaled strategic air power, and possessed naval forces with global reach. By this account, bipolarity did not emerge until a few years later, when the Soviet Union began to recover economically and acquired nuclear weapons.

11. Cordell Hull, *Memoirs*, vol. 2 (New York: Macmillan, 1948): 1314.

12. Samuel I. Roseman, ed., *Public Papers and Addresses of Franklin D. Roosevelt, 1944–45*, (New York: Harper & Brothers, 1950): 586.

13. Adolf Hitler, quoted in Alan Bullock, *Hitler: A Study in Tyranny* (New York: Harper and Row, 1962): 772–773.

14. Joseph Stalin, quoted in Vladislav M. Zubok, *A Failed Empire: The Soviet Union in the Cold War from Stalin to Gorbachev* (Chapel Hill: University of North Carolina Press, 2007): 33.

15. Dwight Eisenhower, quoted in Andrew J. Rotter, "Atomic Bomb: Wartime Endgame and Cold War Catalyst," in Dennis Merrill and Thomas G. Patterson, eds., *Major Problems in American Foreign Relations*, vol. 2, 7th ed. (Boston: Wadsworth, 2010): 214.

16. Joseph Stalin, quoted in David Holloway, *Stalin and the Bomb: The Soviet Union and Atomic Energy, 1939–1956* (New Haven, CT: Yale University Press, 1994): 171.

17. Joseph Stalin, quoted in Ronald Grigor Suny, *The Soviet Experiment* (New York: Oxford University Press, 1998): 345.

Chapter 4

1. Maxim Litvinov, quoted in Hugh Phillips, "Maxim M. Litvinov and Soviet-American Relations, 1918–1946," *Kennan Institute Occasional Paper #263* (Washington, DC: Woodrow Wilson International Center, 1996): 11.

2. J. V. Stalin, "Pre-Election Speech of February 9, 1946," in *Speeches Delivered at Meetings of Voters of the Stalin Electoral District* (Moscow: Foreign Languages Publishing House, 1950): 41.

3. Maxim Litvinov, quoted in Geoffrey Roberts, "Litvinov's Lost Peace, 1941–1946," *Journal of Cold War Studies* 4, no. 2 (2002): 25.

4. Harry Hopkins, quoted in Arthur A. Kerch Jr., *Ideas, Ideals and American Diplomacy* (New York: Appleton-Century-Crofts, 1966): 171.

5. Harry S. Truman, *Memoirs*, Vol. I (Garden City, NJ: Doubleday, 1955).

6. James F. Byrnes, quoted in Thomas G. Paterson, *On Every Front: The Making of the Cold War* (New York: Norton, 1978): 314.

7. Trygve Lie, quoted in Frederick L. Schuman, *International Politics*, 7th ed. (New York: McGraw-Hill, 1958): 235.

8. V. I. Lenin, *Collected Works*, vol. 8 (New York: International Publishers, 1929): 296.

9. Anne Applebaum, "How the Communists Inexorably Changed Life," *New York Review of Books*, November 22, 2012: 37.

10. Urie Bronfenbrenner, "The Mirror Image in Soviet-American Relations," *Journal of Social Issues* 27, no. 1 (1971): 46–51.

11. W. Averell Harriman, quoted in Harry S. Truman, *Memoirs*, vol. 1 (Garden City, NY: Doubleday, 1955): 71.

12. Andrei Zhdanov, *The International Situation* (Moscow: Foreign Languages Publishing House, 1947).

13. George F. Kennan, *Memoirs* (Boston: Little Brown, 1967): 683–684.

14. Strictly speaking, the United States was a tacit partner in the Central Treaty Organization (CENTO). Although Washington did not formally join the organization, it sent an observer delegation to CENTO council meetings and sat on its military and economic committees.

15. Edward Barrett, quoted in John G. Stoessinger, *Why Nations Go to War*, 8th ed. (Boston: Bedford/St. Martin's, 2001): 59.

16. Ronald Reagan, quoted in Stephen F. Cohen, *Soviet Fates and Lost Alternatives* (New York: Columbia University Press, 2009): 160.

17. Patrick Glynn, "Letter to the Editor," *Foreign Policy* 90 (1993): 172.

18. See, for example, Jack F. Matlock Jr., *Reagan and Gorbachev: How the Cold War Ended* (New York: Random House, 2004); James A. Baker III, *The Politics of Diplomacy* (New York: Putnam, 1995); and Georgi Arbatov, *The System: An Insider's Life in Soviet Politics* (New York: Random House, 1992).

19. Anatoly Dobrynin, quoted in Peter Beinart, "Ronald Reagan," *Foreign Policy* 180 (2010): 31.

20. Marshall I. Goldman, *What Went Wrong with Perestroika?* (New York: W. W. Norton, 1991): 107.

21. Carl Sagan, "Between Enemies," *Bulletin of the Atomic Scientists* 48 (1992): 24.

22. See Harold D. Lasswell, "The Garrison State Hypothesis Today," in Samuel P. Huntington, ed. *Changing Patterns of Military Politics* (New York: Free Press, 1962): 641–644; Richard J. Barnet, *The Economy of Death* (New York: Atheneum, 1969); and Steven J. Rosen, ed., *Testing the Theory of the Military Industrial Complex* (Lexington, MA: D. C. Heath, 1973). On convergence theory, see Zbigniew Brzezinski and Samuel P. Huntington, *Political Power: USA/USSR* (New York: Viking, 1964).

23. Joseph Stalin, quoted in Milovan Djilas, *Conversations with Stalin*, trans. Michael B. Petrovich (New York: Harcourt, Brace & World, 1961): 114.

24. We distinguish between two overlapping phases of alliance formation during the Cold War. In the first phase, *alliances of position* were used to demarcate regions of vital

interest along the western and northeastern Eurasian strategic fronts. In the second, Washington and Moscow engaged in intense competition for new allies, wooing states from the periphery of the world system in an effort to outflank one another. Whereas the first phase tended to advance world order by providing prominent focal points for the tacit coordination of reciprocal expectations, the second was counterproductive, fostering overcommitment, confusion, and instability.

25. John A. Vasquez and Choong-Nam Kang, "How and Why the Cold War Became a Long Peace: Some Statistical Insights," *Cooperation and Conflict* 41, no. 1 (2012): 28–50.

26. See Aleksandr Fursenko and Timothy Naftali, *"One Hell of a Gamble:" Khrushchev, Castro, and Kennedy 1958–1964* (New York: W. W. Norton, 1997).

27. Alexis de Tocqueville, *Democracy in America* (New York: Doubleday, 1969).

28. Jack S. Levy, "Long Cycles, Hegemonic Transitions, and the Long Peace," in Charles W. Kegley Jr., ed., *The Long Postwar Peace* (New York: HarperCollins, 1991): 147.

29. For data on interstate crises and non-great-power wars, see Michael Brecher and Jonathan Wilkenfeld, "International Crises and Global Instability: The Myth of the 'Long Peace,'" in Charles W. Kegley Jr., ed., *The Long Postwar Peace* (New York: HarperCollins, 1991): 85–104; and J. David Singer, "Peace in the Global System: Displacement, Interregnum, or Transformation," in Charles W. Kegley Jr., ed., *The Long Postwar Peace* (New York: HarperCollins, 1991): 56–84. On the concept of the "long peace," see John Lewis Gaddis, *The Long Peace: Inquiries into the History of the Cold War* (New York: Oxford University Press, 1987). For an interpretation of the concurrence of peace among the great powers with interstate violence elsewhere in the world, see Max Singer and Aaron Wildasky, *The Real World Order: Zones of Peace/Zones of Turmoil* (Chatham, NJ: Chatham House, 1993).

30. Francis Fukuyama, *The End of History and the Last Man* (New York: Free Press, 1992).

31. See Charles W. Kegley Jr., "The Neoidealist Moment in International Relations? Realist Myths and the New International Realities," *International Studies Quarterly* 37, no. 1 (1993): 131–146.

32. See, for example, Robert Kagan, *The Return of History and the End of Dreams* (New York: Knopf, 2008); and John J. Mearsheimer, "Back to the Future: Instability in Europe After the Cold War," *International Security* 15, no. 1 (1990): 5–56.

33. Harry Truman, quoted in Charles W. Kegley Jr. and Eugene Wittkopf, *American Foreign Policy: Pattern and Process*, 3rd ed. (New York: St. Martin's Press, 1987): 52.

Chapter 5

1. George H. W. Bush, "Aggression in the Gulf," *Vital Speeches of the Day*, no. 1 (1990): 3.

2. George H. W. Bush, "America's Stand against Aggression," *Current Policy*, no. 1294 (Washington, DC: U.S. Department of State, Bureau of Public Affairs, 1990): 2.

3. *Time*, August 20, 1990: 11.

4. Lawrence Eagleburger, quoted in Michael R. Gordon and Bernard E. Trainor, *The Generals' War: The Inside Story of the Conflict in the Gulf* (Boston: Little, Brown, 1995): 172.

5. Gary Clyde Hufbauer, Jeffrey J. Schott, and Kimberly Ann Elliott, *Economic Sanctions Reconsidered*, 2nd ed. (Washington, DC: Institute for International Economics, 1990).

6. Colin Powell, quoted in *Triumph without Victory: The Unreported History of the Persian Gulf War* (New York: U.S. News & World Report, 1992): 172.

7. Francis Fukuyama, *The End of History and the Last Man* (New York: Free Press, 1992).

8. Interview with Secretary of State Madeleine Albright on ABC-TV's "Nightline" with Ted Koppel, February 20, 1998.

9. George W. Bush, quoted in Michael Hirsh, *At War with Ourselves: Why America Is Squandering Its Chance to Build a Better World* (New York: Oxford University Press, 2003): 17.

10. For a representative sample of the empirical studies that were published during this period, see Steve Chan, "Mirror, Mirror on the Wall . . . Are the Freer Countries More Pacific?" *Journal of Conflict Resolution* 28, no. 4 (1984): 617–648; William J. Dixon, "Democracy and the Management of International Conflict," *Journal of Conflict Resolution* 37, no. 1 (1993): 42–68; Joe D. Hagan "Domestic Political Systems and War Proneness," *Mershon International Studies Review* 38, no. 2 (1994): 183–204; Zeev Maoz and Nasrin Abdolali, "Regime Types and International Conflict," *Journal of Conflict Resolution* 33, no. 1 (1989): 3–35; Zeev Maoz and Bruce Russett, "Normative and Structural Causes of the Democratic Peace, 1946–1986," *American Political Science Review* 87, no. 3 (1993): 624–638; David W. Moore, "Foreign Policy and Empirical Democratic Theory," *American Political Science Review* 68, no. 3 (1974): 1192–1197; Clifton T. Morgan and Valerie L. Schwebach, "Take Two Democracies and Call Me in the Morning: A Prescription for Peace?" *International Interactions* 17, no. 4 (1992): 305–320; James Lee Ray, "War Between Democracies: Rare or Nonexistent?" *International Interactions* 18, no. 3 (1993): 251–276; and Erich Weede, "Democracy and War Involvement," *Journal of Conflict Resolution* 28, no. 4 (1984): 395–411.

11. Anthony Lake, quoted in Jack Hitt, ed., "Is There A Doctrine in the House? In Search of a Clinton Foreign Policy," *Harper's*, January 1994, 64.

12. *U.S. Foreign Relations: Hearing before the Foreign Relations Committee*, U.S. Senate, 103rd Congress, November 4, 1993 (testimony of Warren Christopher, U.S. Secretary of State). The declassified memorandum of conversation (MEMCON) from the October 22, 1993, meeting between Warren Christopher and Boris Yeltsin at the Russian president's dacha in Zavidovo sheds additional light on the different interpretations that each side gave to the Partnership for Peace (PfP) plan. See Svetlana Savranskaya and Tom Blanton, eds., NATO *Expansion: What Yeltsin Heard*, Briefing Book #621, National Security Archive (Washington, DC: Gelman Library, George Washington University, 2018).

13. George F. Kennan, "A Fateful Error," *New York Times*, February 5, 1997: A23.

14. Richard Holbrooke, quoted in Tim Judah, *Kosovo: War and Revenge* (New Haven, CT: Yale University Press, 2000): 227.

15. George Packer, "Elegy for the American Century," *Atlantic,* May 2019: 95.

16. The *Caroline* was an American ship that had been supplying Canadian rebels during an insurrection against the British in 1837. British forces attacked the vessel while it was docked in an American port on the Niagara River. The British claimed that their actions were justified by self-defense. Daniel Webster responded by arguing that preemptive self-defense must entail necessity and immediacy.

17. Ron Suskind, *The One Percent Doctrine: Deep Inside America's Pursuit of Its Enemies Since 9/11* (New York: Simon & Schuster, 2006): 62.

18. See Fareed Zakaria, *The Post-American World* (New York: Norton, 2009): 216–219.

19. Barack Obama, quoted in Jeffrey Goldberg, "The Obama Doctrine," *Atlantic*, April 2016: 77–78.
20. Hal Brands and Charles Edel, *The Lessons of Tragedy: Statecraft and World Order* (New Haven, CT: Yale University Press, 2019): 113.
21. Thomas E. Ricks, *The Gamble: General Petraeus and the American Military Adventure in Iraq, 2006-2008* (New York: Penguin, 2009): 315.
22. Bob Woodward, *Obama's Wars* (New York: Simon & Schuster): 106.
23. *Sustaining U.S. Global Leadership: Priorities for 21st Century Defense* (Washington, DC: U.S. Department of Defense, 2012): 3, 6. Italics removed.
24. Quoted in Ron Suskind, "Faith, Certainty and the Presidency of George W. Bush," *New York Times Magazine*, October 17, 2004.
25. M. Tayor Fravel, *Active Defense: China's Military Strategy Since 1949* (Princeton, NJ: Princeton University Press, 2019).
26. Letter from Barack Obama to Donald J. Trump, http://www.cnn.com/2017/09/03/politics/obama-trump-letter-inauguration-day/index.html

Chapter 6

1. *National Security Strategy of the United States of America* (Washington, DC: The White House, 1991): v.
2. Richard Wike et al., "Trump's International Ratings Remain Low, Especially Among Key Allies," Pew Research Center, October 1, 2018: 32.
3. Karen DeYoung, "In Trump, Some Fear the End of the World Order," *Washington Post*, June 8, 2018.
4. Lotta Themnér and Peter Wallensteen, "Armed Conflicts, 1946–2013," *Journal of Peace Research* 51, no. 4 (2014): 541–554.
5. Steven Pinker, *The Better Angels of Our Nature: Why Violence Has Declined* (New York: Viking, 2011): 30. For data on these trends, see Stockholm International Peace Research Institute, *SIPRI Yearbook* (New York: Oxford University Press, 2020); and Rachel Kleinfeld, *A Savage Order: How the World's Deadliest Countries Can Forge A Path to Security* (New York: Pantheon, 2018): 305n.
6. An example of the growing interest in Chinese models of world order can be seen in the popularity in China of *The Tianxia System: A Philosophy for the New World Institution*, which was published by Zhao Tingyang in 2005. According to one commentator, this best seller is a sign of a broader trend where imperial China's hierarchical mode of governance is updated and applied to twenty-first-century world politics. See William A. Callahan, "Chinese Visions of World Order: Post-Hegemonic or a New Hegemony?" *International Studies Review* 10, no. 4 (2008): 759.
7. Xi Jinping, quoted in Kurt M. Campbell and Ely Ratner, "The China Reckoning: How Beijing Defied American Expectations," *Foreign Affairs* 97, no. 2 (2018): 67.
8. Peter Baker and Maggie Haberman, "Trump, Defending His Mental Fitness, Says He's a 'Very Stable Genius,'" *New York Times*, January 6, 2018.
9. Donald J. Trump, *Great Again: How to Fix Our Crippled America* (New York: Simon & Schuster Threshold Editions, 2015): 46.
10. See Nadia Schadlow, "The Conservative Realism of the Trump Administration's Foreign Policy," Hudson Institute, and Henry Nau, "Freedom, Defense, and Sovereignty: A Conservative Internationalist Foreign Policy" in "Policy Roundtable: The Future of Conservative Foreign Policy," *Texas National Security*

Review, November 30, 2018, https://tnsr.org/roundtable/policy-roundtable-the-future-of-conservative-foreign-policy/-article.

11. See "Open Letter on Donald Trump from GOP National Security Leaders," March 2, 2016, https://waronthe rocks.com/2016/03/open-letter-on-donald-trump-from-gop-national-security-leaders. One signatory, in an evaluation of Trump's foreign policy following his election, groused that his "ham-handed" moves—bullying allies, launching trade wars, and vilifying multilateral institutions—have been "counterproductive," creating scars that will linger long after he is gone. Daniel W. Drezner, "This Time Is Different: Why U.S. Foreign Policy Will Never Recover," *Foreign Affairs* 98, no. 3 (2019): 16.

12. Charles Krauthammer, *The Point of It All*, ed. Daniel Krauthammer (New York: Crown Forum, 2018): 292.

13. See Robert J. Lieber, *Retreat and its Consequences: American Foreign Policy and the Problem of World Order* (New York: Cambridge University Press, 2016).

14. Donald Trump, quoted in Kristine Phillips, "Confronted with the Bloody Behavior of Autocrats, Trump, Instead, Blames the World," *Washington Post*, November 22, 2018.

15. H. R. McMaster and Gary D. Cohn, "America First Doesn't Mean America Alone," *Wall Street Journal*, May 30, 2017.

16. "Transcript: Donald Trump's Foreign Policy Speech," *New York Times*, April 27, 2016.

17. Robert D. Kaplan, *The Return of Marco Polo's World: War, Strategy, and American Interests in the Twenty-First Century* (New York: Random House, 2018): 215–216.

18. Hans J. Morgenthau, *The Purpose of American Politics* (New York: Alfred A. Knopf, 1960): 8.

19. Walter Russell Mead, *Special Providence: American Foreign Policy and How It Changed the World* (New York: Alfred A. Knopf, 2001), 243–259. While there are parallels between the Trumpian and Jacksonian creeds on foreign policy, differences exist on other issues. In stark contrast to Trump's code of personal conduct, honor is a core Jacksonian value. People achieve status through honest work, fulfilling commitments, and treating others with respect, not through inherited wealth, dodging accountability, and name-calling.

20. Micah Zenko and Rebecca Friedman Lissner, "Trump Is Going to Regret Not Having a Grand Strategy," *Foreign Policy*, January 13, 2017, http://foreignpolicy .com/2017/01/13/trump-is-going-to-regret-not-having-a-grand-strategy; Benjamin Carlson, "Why China Loves Trump," *Atlantic* 321, no. 2 (2018): 50.

21. Donald Trump, quoted in Ivo H. Daalder and James M. Lindsay, *The Empty Throne: America's Abdication of Global Leadership* (New York: PublicAffairs, 2018): 8.

22. Donald J. Trump, "Inaugural Address," January 20, 2017, https://www.whitehouse.gov/ briefings-statements/the-inaugural-address.

23. Daalder and Lindsay: 118–119.

24. For a compilation of Trump's compliments of Putin, see Callum Borchers, "Timeline of Trump's Praise for Putin while Trump Tower Moscow Was in the Works," *Washington Post*, August 28, 2017. Summarizing the results from his investigation into Russian interference in the 2016 U.S. presidential election, Special Counsel Robert S. Mueller III declared during his public remarks on May 29, 2019, "Russian intelligence officers who are part of the Russian military launched a concerted attack on our political system." Based on the evidence that his team of

investigators gathered, he asserted that the Russians "used sophisticated cybertechniques to hack into computers and networks used by the Clinton campaign. They stole private information and then released that information through fake online identities and through the organization WikiLeaks. The releases were designed and timed to interfere with our election and to damage a presidential candidate." In response to Mueller's charge, Trump tweeted on May 30, 2019, at 5:57 a.m.: "I had nothing to do with Russia helping me to get elected."

25. See, for example, Elliott Abrams, "The Struggle for Conservative Foreign Policy," *Texas National Security Review*, November 30, 2018, https://tnsr.org/roundtable/policy-roundtable-the-future-of-conservative-foreign-policy/-article.

26. Ronald Reagan, "Farewell Address to the Nation," January 11, 1989, https://www.reaganfoundation.org/media/128652/farewell.pdf. In contrast to Reagan, Trump's imagery tends to be foreboding. In his inaugural address, for example, he accentuated "American carnage," which included claims that the wealth of the middle class was being "ripped from their homes" and "rusted-out factories [were] scattered like tombstones across the landscape of our nation." Donald J. Trump, "Inaugural Address."

27. Anonymous, "The Quiet Resistance Inside the Trump Administration," *New York Times*, September 5, 2018.

28. Stephen M. Walt, *The Hell of Good Intentions: America's Foreign Policy Elite and the Decline of U.S. Primacy* (New York: Farrar, Straus and Giroux, 2018): 219.

29. According to data collected by the *Washington Post*, during Trump's first two years in office he made over 800 false or misleading claims on foreign policy issues. When all other topics are included, the total rises to 8,158. Retrieved at http://www.washingtonpost.com/news.fact-checker. Additionally, evidence collected by investigators working for Special Counsel Robert Mueller suggest that Trump has pressured aides to lie on his behalf. See Robert S. Mueller III, *Report on the Investigation into Russian Interference in the 2016 Presidential Election*, 2 vols. (Washington, DC: U.S. Department of Justice, 2019). For examples of conservative critiques of Trump's behavior, see Max Boot, *The Corrosion of Conservatism* (New York: Liveright, 2018); and David Frum, *Trumpocracy* (New York: Harper, 2018).

30. Bob Woodward, *Fear: Trump in the White House* (New York: Simon & Schuster, 2018): 175, 275.

31. See Michael V. Hayden, *The Assault on Intelligence: American National Security in an Age of Lies* (New York: Penguin, 2018); David Cay Johnston, *The Making of Donald Trump* (Brooklyn, NY: Melville House, 2016); Ronald Kessler, *The Trump White House: Changing the Rules of the Game* (New York: Crown, 2018); Brandy X. Lee, ed., *The Dangerous Case of Donald Trump* (New York: Thomas Dunne, 2017); Andrew G. McCabe, *The Threat: How the FBI Protects America in the Age of Terror and Trump* (New York: St. Martin's Press, 2019); John Walcott, "Willful Ignorance Inside President Trump's Troubled Intelligence Briefings," *Time*, February 15, 2019: 40–41; and Michael Wolff, *Fire and Fury: Inside the Trump White House* (New York: Henry Holt, 2018): 113–114, 184.

32. Tillerson's assessment was made in a May 21, 2019, meeting with Rep. Eliot Engel, D-NY, and Rep. Michael McCaul, R-TX, of the House Foreign Affairs Committee.

33. Donald Trump, quoted in *The Economist* 426, no. 9083 (March 17, 2018): 27.

34. John Kelly, quoted in Bob Woodward, *Fear: Trump in the White House* (New York: Simon & Schuster, 2018): 286.

35. James Mattis, quoted in Woodward: 219.

Chapter 7

1. Thomas L. Friedman, *Thank You for Being Late: An Optimist's Guide to Thriving in the Age of Accelerations* (New York: Farrar, Straus and Giroux, 2016): 93.

2. See David M. Edelstein, *Over the Horizon: Time, Uncertainty, and the Rise of Great Powers* (Ithaca, NY: Cornell University Press, 2017). Also see Chad E. Nelson, "Why the Great Powers Permitted the Creation of an American Hegemon," *Political Science Quarterly* 132, no. 4 (2017–2018): 710–718.

3. Quincy Wright, *A Study of War* (Chicago: University of Chicago Press, 1964): 132.

4. For statistical evidence, see Charles W. Kegley Jr. and Gregory A. Raymond, *When Trust Breaks Down: Alliance Norms and World Politics* (Columbia: University of South Carolina Press, 1990).

5. The leading example of this scenario is Martin Jacques, *When China Rules the World: The End of the Western World and the Birth of a New World Order*, 2nd ed. (New York: Penguin, 2012). Chinese commentators who hold similar visions are discussed in Randall L. Schweller and Xiaoyu Pu, "After Unipolarity: China's Visions of an International Order in an Era of U.S. Decline," *International Security* 36, no. 1 (2011): 59–62.

6. Wayne M. Morrison, *China's Economic Rise: History Trends, Challenges, and Implications for the United States* (Washington, DC: Congressional Research Service, 2018): 6–10.

7. Peter Frankopan, *The New Silk Roads: The Present and Future of the World* (New York: Alfred A. Knopf, 2019): 65.

8. Estimates of Chinese military spending vary. The statistics reported here are based on data collected by the Stockholm International Peace Research Institute, www.sipri.org/databases/milex.

9. *China Military Power: Modernizing a Force to Fight and Win* (Washington, DC: Defense Intelligence Agency, 2019): 9–10.

10. Ibid., 6.

11. Richard Maher, "Bipolarity and the Future of U.S.-China Relations," *Political Science Quarterly* 133, no. 3 (2018): 497–525.

12. Several scholars have made this argument. See Morton A. Kaplan, *System and Process in International Politics* (New York: John Wiley & Sons, 1957): 34; Roger D. Masters, "A Multi-Bloc Model of the International System," *American Political Science Review* 55, no. 4 (1961): 782; Joseph L. Nogee and John W. Spanier, "The Politics of Tripolarity," *World Affairs* 139, no. 4 (1977): 320–321; and Ronald J. Yalem, "Tripolarity and the International System," *Orbis* 15, no. 4 (1972): 1054–1055. For an analysis of tripolar politics in regional state systems, see Michael Haas, *International Conflict* (Indianapolis: Bobbs-Merrill, 1974): 337, 466.

13. Robert Gilpin, *War and Change in World Politics* (New York: Cambridge University Press, 1981): 91; Alvin M. Saperstein, "The 'Long Peace'—Result of a Bipolar Competitive World?" *Journal of Conflict Resolution* 35, no. 1 (1991): 68–79. For an alternative view of tripolarity, see Emerson M. S. Niou, Peter C. Ordeshook, and Gregory F. Rose, *The Balance of Power: Stability in International Systems* (New York: Cambridge University Press, 1989): 95.

14. For evidence, see Charles W. Kegley Jr. and Gregory A. Raymond, *A Multipolar Peace? Great-Power Politics in the Twenty-First Century* (New York: St. Martin's Press, 1994). Also see John A. Vasquez and Ashlea Rundlett, "Alliances as a Necessary Condition of Multiparty Wars," *Journal of Conflict Resolution* 60, no. 8 (2016): 1395–1418.

15. Richard N. Haas, "The Age of Nonpolarity: What Will Follow U.S. Dominance," *Foreign Affairs* 87, no. 3 (2008): 44–56; Ian Bremmer, *Every Nation for Itself: Winners and Losers in a G-Zero World* (New York: Portfolio, 2012).

16. George Modelski, *World Power Concentrations: Typology, Data, Explanatory Framework* (Morristown, NJ: General Learning Press, 1974): 2.

17. G. John Ikenberry, "Why the Liberal Order Will Survive," *Ethics & International Affairs* 32, special issue no. 1 (2018): 17–29.

18. Hans J. Morgenthau, *Politics Among Nations*, 6th ed. (New York: Alfred A. Knopf, 1985): 589.

19. Charles Krauthammer, "The Unipolar Moment Revisited," *National Interest*, December 1, 2002: 17.

20. Winston Churchill, *The Gathering Storm*, vol. 1 of *The Second World War* (Boston: Houghton Mifflin, 1948): 48. As portrayed by Churchill, balance-of-power politics entails a mixture of acting independently and acting in solidarity with other states. On the one hand, a balancer must have the freedom of maneuver to act according to the strategic needs of the moment and not be constrained by cultural, historical, or ideological affinities. On the other hand, maintaining the balance may require forming countervailing alliances with states holding different values, although such combinations tend to be short-term, aimed at addressing immediate threats.

21. For a discussion of offshore balancing, see Stephen M. Walt, *The Hell of Good Intentions: America's Foreign Policy Elite and the Decline of U.S. Primacy* (New York: Farrar, Straus and Giroux, 2018): 260–278.

22. F. S. Northedge, *Descent from Power: British Foreign Policy, 1945–1973* (London: Allen & Unwin): 171.

23. Miles Kahler, "Rumors of War: The 1914 Analogy," *Foreign Affairs* 57, no. 2 (1979–1980): 395.

24. Sir Edward Grey, quoted in James Joll, *The Origins of the First World* War (London: Longman, 1984): 45.

25. See John Gerard Ruggie, "Multilateralism: The Anatomy of an Institution," *International Organization* 44, no. 3 (1992): 561–598; and Robert O. Keohane, "Reciprocity in International Relations," *International Organization* 40, no. 1 (1986): 1–27.

26. T. V. Paul, *Restraining Great Powers: Soft Balancing from Empires to the Global Era* (New Haven, CT: Yale University Press, 2018); Robert Anthony Pape, "Soft Balancing Against the United States," *International Security* 30, no. 1 (2005): 7–45.

27. Jean-Jacques Rousseau, *The Social Contract* (New York: Hafner, 1947): 8.

28. Henry Kissinger, *World Order* (New York: Penguin, 2014): 9, 66, 367.

29. Quincy Wright, *A Study of War* (Chicago: The University of Chicago Press, 1964): 132–133.

Chapter 8

1. For evidence on how the practices of power politics increase the probability of war, see Paul D. Senese and John A. Vasquez, *The Steps to War: An Empirical Study* (Princeton: Princeton University Press, 2008).

2. Paul Kennedy, *The Rise and Fall of the Great Powers* (New York: Random House, 1987).

3. Robert D. Kaplan, *The Return of Marco Polo's World: War, Strategy, and American Interests in the Twenty-First Century* (New York: Random House, 2018): 45.

4. Henry Kissinger, *World Order* (New York: Penguin, 2014): 344–345.

5. P. W. Singer and Allan Friedman, *Cybersecurity and Cyberwar* (New York: Oxford University Press, 2014): 68–70, 145–147.

6. Adam Segal, *The Hacked World Order*, 2nd ed. (New York: PublicAffairs, 2017): 86–92, 234.

7. Albert Speer, *Inside the Third Reich* (New York: Galahad Books, 1970): 521.

8. Christian Brose, "The New Revolution in Military Affairs," *Foreign Affairs* 98, no. 3 (2019): 124, 130–132.

9. Henry L. Stimson, "The Nuremberg Trial: Landmark in Law," *Foreign Affairs* 25, no. 2 (1947): 189.

10. Donald Trump, quoted in conversation with Mika Brzezinski, www.reuters.com/article/us-usa-trump-nuclear-idUSKBN14B1zz.

11. Nina Tannenwald, "The Vanishing Nuclear Taboo?" *Foreign Affairs* 97, no. 6 (2018): 22.

12. A declassified version of the report is available at www.defense.gov/News?SpecialReports?2018NuclearPostureReview.aspx. For an analysis, see Michal Smetana, "A Nuclear Posture Review for the Third Nuclear Age," *Washington Quarterly* 42, no. 3 (2018): 137–157.

13. David Lektzian and Christopher Sprecher, "Sanctions, Signals, and Militarized Conflict," *American Journal of Political Science*, 51, no. 2 (2007): 415–431.

14. Trudy Rubin, "The View from China: Will Trump, Xi Avoid a Cold War?" trubin@phillynews.com.

15. There have been various occasions when individuals and firms have continued business dealings with their country's adversaries during wartime. See, for example, Charles Higham, *Trading with the Enemy: The Nazi-American Money Plot 1933–1949* (New York: Barnes & Noble, 1983).

16. *The Economist*, May 18, 2019: 9.

17. Donald J. Trump, quoted in Paul K. McDonald and Joseph M Parent, "The Road to Recovery: How Once Great Powers Became Great Again," *Washington Quarterly* 41, no. 3 (2018): 22; *The Economist*, October 30, 2018: 21.

18. India has also demonstrated an anti-satellite capability. In March 2019, it successfully destroyed a satellite with an interceptor missile.

19. Norman Cousins, address delivered to the faculty and students of the University of South Carolina, Gambrell Hall, February 8, 1979.

20. Michelle Nijhuis, "On the Trail of the Climate," *New York Review of Books*, February 21, 2019: 22.

21. Elaine Ganley, quoted in Shannon L. Blanton and Charles W. Kegley, *World Politics: Trend and Transformation* (Boston: Cengage Learning, 2017): 476.

22. Annual reports of the UN Intergovernmental Panel on Climate Change (IPCC).

23. Observations by David Lloyd George on March 25, 1919, www.nationalarchives.gov/uk/education/greatwar/transcript/g5cs1s2t.htm.

24. Dwight D. Eisenhower, "Special Message to the Congress on the Mutual Security Program," March 3, 1959, www.eisenhower.archives.gov/all_about_ike/quotes.html.

25. M. Taylor Fravel, *Active Defense: China's Military Strategy since 1949* (Princeton, NJ: Princeton University Press, 2019).

26. Xi Jinping, quoted in Evan Osnos, "Making China Great Again," *New Yorker*, January 8, 2018: 39.

27. "Geopolitics," *The Economist*, February 9, 2019: 71–72.
28. Adam Segal, "When China Rules the Web," *Foreign Affairs* 97, no. 5 (2018): 11.
29. Kevin Drum, "Tech World," *Foreign Affairs* 97, no. 4 (2018): 46.
30. Hans J. Morgenthau, *Politics Among Nations*, 6th ed. (New York: Knopf, 1985): 52.
31. François Delattre, "The World Grows More Dangerous by the Day," *New York Times*, June 13, 2019, https://www.nytimes.com/2019/06/13/opinion/france-united-states.html.
32. William J. Burns, *The Back Channel* (New York: Random House, 2019): 9.
33. John F. Kennedy, Commencement address delivered at American University, Washington, DC, June 10, 1963.

Index

Boxes, figures, maps, and tables are indicated by *b*, *f*, *m*, or *t*, respectively, following the page number.

Vietnam War, 82, 83*m*, 84
  see also World War I (1914–1918);
    World War II (1939–1945)
"War guilt" clause in Versailles Treaty,
    38, 41
War indemnities, 38–40, 39*b*, 41, 57*b*
Warsaw Treaty Organization, 78*t*, 88,
    89, 104, 120, 144
Wars of Louis XIV (1688–1713), 12*f*,
    145
Weaponry
    balance-of-power theory, 30
    China, 130*t*, 147, 171
    first world war, 27
    outer space programs, 78*t*, 175
    Turkey, 129*t*
    weapons of mass destruction,
        115–116
    see also Nuclear weapons
Webster, Daniel, 116
Weimar Republic, 41–42, 44, 49
West Germany, 61, 78*t*
Westphalian design for international or-
    der (1648), 3–6, 5*f*, 9–10, 106–108
WikiLeaks, 169
Wilhelm II (Kaiser), 22*t*, 25, 26, 28
Will, George, 138
William I (King of Germany), 25
Wilson, Woodrow
    Fourteen Points speech, 28, 34,
        37, 49
    liberal philosophy, 32–34, 93–94,
        104, 122
    Versailles settlement, 32–33, 36–37,
        45
Winthrop, John, 104
World Disarmament Conference (Ge-
    neva, 1932), 44–45
World Trade Center terrorist attacks,
    102*t*, 103, 115
World Trade Organization (WTO),
    120, 124, 132, 172
World War I (1914–1918)
    armistice and peace negotiations,
        28–29, 49
    collective security, 145

hegemonic wars, 12*f*
military fighting and morale, 27–29
origins and causal factors, 21–22,
    22–23*t*, 24–27
political alliances, 40*m*
psychological factors, 24–25
see also Versailles settlement
World War II (1939–1945)
    collective security, 145
    global impact, 63, 87
    hegemonic wars, 12*f*
    major Allied conferences and dec-
        larations, 54–56*t*, 63, 66
    military victories, 53–54
    origins and causal factors, 48–52, 50*t*
    post-war geostrategic landscape,
        59*m*
    post-war peace planning, 53–54,
        57–61, 63
    spheres of influence model, 64–66
Wright-Patterson Air Force Base (Day-
    ton, Ohio), 112

Xiaobai (Duke Huan of Qi), 65*f*
Xi Jinping, 124, 147, 173, 177, 178
Xinjiang region (China), 148

Yalta Conference (1945), 54, 56*t*, 57*b*,
    59, 66
Yeltsin, Boris, 93*b*, 105
Yemen, 129*t*
Yugoslavia
    boundary challenges, 109
    collapse and disintegration, 109,
        110*m*, 111
    ethnic composition, 109, 111
    political alliances, 43
    post-disintegration conflict,
        111–115
    spheres of influence implications,
        64
    Versailles settlement, 40, 41*m*

Zero-sum game, 45, 75
Zhdanov, Andrei, 77
Zhou dynasty, 152